The Legend Begins

THE LEGEND BEGINS

The Texas Rangers
1823-1845

by

Frederick Wilkins

STATE HOUSE PRESS
Austin, Texas
1996

Library of Congress Cataloging-in-Publication Data

Wilkins, Frederick, 1916-
The legend begins : the Texas Rangers, 1823-1845 / by
Frederick Wilkins. — 1st ed.
p.   cm.
Includes bibliographical references and index.
ISBN 1-880510-40-5 (alk. paper).
ISBN 1-880510-41-3 (pbk.: alk. paper).
ISBN 1-880510-42-1 (ltd.: alk. paper).
1. Texas Rangers—History. 2. Texas—History—To
1846. 3. Frontier and pioneer life—Texas. I. Title.

F390.W65   1996
976.4—dc20   96-8497

Printed in the United States of America

Cover design by David Timmons

STATE HOUSE PRESS
P.O. Box 15247
Austin, Texas 78761

For Freda Louise and BF

Acknowledgments

I wish to thank Donaly Brice and the staff of the Archives Division of the Texas State Library for their help in researching ranger documents of the Republic of Texas. Their on-site advice and photocopying speeded a lengthy task, and their willingness to satisfy mail and phone requests saved me many a trip to Austin.

Dora Guerra, in the Special Collection of the library of The University of Texas, San Antonio, generously shared her extensive knowledge of Texana and of the many works in that library. Personnel in the libraries of Trinity University, The Institute of Texan Cultures, and the Library of the Daughters of the Republic of Texas, all in San Antonio, aided in my research. Many thanks also for the help of Tom Burks and the staff at the Texas Ranger Hall of Fame in Waco, Texas.

Table Of Contents

Preface

This is a story of legends, and of real men who became legends. This is also history, insofar as any narrative of legendary men can be, but the recording of history includes the painstaking task of dealing with myth and fable to determine what passed for truth at the time. It happens, now and then, that history is not as kind as legend.

The Texas Rangers have always been a mixture of fact and fancy, with history and fable so blended it is difficult at times to separate. To most of us, the rangers were a small force of peace officers, in the latter half of the past century, which became famous in part for such fabled comments as "one mob, one Ranger;" but by the time this famous legend had developed the rangers were already an old force, tested in many a frontier skirmish, veterans of one war, and had converted from a military command to a civilian peace force.

The early rangers, a defense force predating the Texas Republic, have been mentioned in other histories, and individual accounts have given considerable detail about specific events and personalities, but it has been sixty years since Walter Prescott Webb's pioneer study, *The Texas Rangers*, was published. Webb attempted the impossible task of covering the entire history of the rangers in one volume, and he has been faulted for this or that omission. Despite some faults in his work, we all start with Webb, and his book is still in print. Fortunately, source material is better preserved now than in his day, and more accessible; many events accepted as fact in 1935 are now known to be fables. It is time to retell the ranger story. *The Legend Begins*, the first of four books to attempt that daunting mission, gathers into one volume all the material on the rangers prior to Texas' statehood. In doing so some old concepts and ideas must give way. For many years and for many writers, for example,

John C. Hays has been considered *the* ranger of early Texas, the original developer of the concept of a ranger force. Careful study does not support such a preeminent position for Hays. He was not the first but merely one of several prominent partisan commanders in the Texas Republic, and he did not originate the ranger system. He did, however, adapt a recognized concept and did much to develop the organization, using Colt five-shot revolvers as a major weapon.

I am *not* attempting revisionist history, but I have tried to gather together all the materials bearing on the early rangers and to make whatever judgments seem justified by a study of these facts. Because historical events must be judged in terms of the morality of the day, I have tried to avoid the prejudices of our later era. The first rangers lived and fought in a time when morality was more black and white than it is today, and an enemy was anyone who tried to hinder the development of the land the settlers considered their own.

The rangers were formed to meet a need, as seen at the time. They did not change until the times changed, generations later, after most of the legends about them had long since been accepted as fact. Questioning some of these sainted fables is not a sure road to popularity, but this is the tale as I see it.

—1—

Colonial Texas

It often comes as a surprise to Texans to learn their state was not always considered a place of awe and wonder, but the early Spanish explorers saw nothing of any real value in the vast, unknown lands above the Río Bravo del Norte. The first exploration of Texas was only accidental, when part of a large Spanish force was driven ashore on the Texas Gulf Coast in 1528. Cabeza de Vaca and three companions, survivors of this group, wandered over a large area in Central and West Texas until 1541 and eventually reached safety in western Mexico. The second group to visit what would become Texas was only part of another venture, Coronado's fabled effort to find the golden cities, and members of this expedition explored parts of the Panhandle. In 1542 Luis de Moscoso, who had taken command of the deceased De Soto's expedition searching for wealth in Florida, traveled through parts of Texas in an abortive attempt to return overland to Mexico.[1]

Nothing seen by any of these explorers offered enough promise to the officials in Mexico City, or distant Spain, to justify further exploration much less settlement. Not until late in the 1600s did Spain show any interest in Texas, and this only in response to a perceived threat from France after Rène Robert La Salle, a French explorer who thought he was in Louisiana, landed on the Texas coast in 1685. He built a log fort—the extent of his settlement—and was killed by his own men. His colony vanished, but rumors of his landing alarmed the Spanish and a force under Alonzo de León—the first *planned* Spanish exploration in Texas—was sent north in 1689 and again the next year to find and destroy any

French settlement. De León found and destroyed the abandoned French fort, laid out the first roads in Texas, and made the first deliberate observations of the country.[2]

In the following years, the Spanish sent several expeditions north of the Río Bravo, the modern Rio Grande, opened several roads, and obtained more detailed information about the interior. They found nothing to encourage any major settlement, but their continued fear of a possible French invasion led them to establish several missions in East Texas as a barrier to any movement from Louisiana. The site of what what would become San Antonio was visited late in the 1600s, and a mission was established in 1718, but it was not until 1731 that a few families were brought in from the Canary Islands to establish an official town.

There had been no permanent settlement before San Antonio; residents of northern Mexico saw no reason to move to a new and unfriendly land. Without precious metals to pay the cost of settlement, the Spanish government had little incentive to found towns. Despite official neglect, however, over the years a few of the missions grew into settlements. Goliad began as a mission in 1749. Nacogdoches, established as a mission in 1716, had a stone fort and trading post by 1779 and became the center of trade with Louisiana. Laredo was established on the Rio Grande in 1755. Some hardy souls settled on isolated land grants, but generally the Spanish followed the European custom and lived in towns and villages.

Efforts, some of them extensive, to expand settlements to the north and west of San Antonio were unsuccessful, largely due to Comanche raids. The Marquis de Rubí, inspecting the region in 1766, even suggested abandoning the country above the Rio Grande and giving it back to the Indians and nature.[3] A mission and presidio were established on the San Saba River near present-day Menard, but the Comanches destroyed the mission and forced the Spanish to abandon the stone presidio in 1769. Comanche raids into northern Mexico and New Mexico were common by the mid 1700s, but resistance in New Mexico, where a skilled governor fought them on their own terms, encouraged the Indians to concentrate on the helpless towns and villages in

Mexico. After 1790 the Comanches raided at will throughout northern Mexico. They had a well-defined war trail across their Plains hunting lands, and through the Texas Big Bend where the war trail split east and west into Mexico. For generations they pillaged, killed, took captives, horses and anything else they fancied. The Mexicans had no local defense forces, and in desperation the townspeople took to bribing the Comanches, hoping they would raid other settlements and leave them alone.[4]

The outbreak of the Mexican rebellion against Spanish rule in 1810 did nothing to halt the Comanche raids. The Spanish authorities, needing every soldier to combat the rising republican forces, could not spare troops to fight the Indians, who had no interest in Mexican politics. To some degree, the Indians' continued and unhindered raids for horses and plunder caused the Spanish to look with favor on American plans to settle in Texas.

A number of Americans had entered the Spanish province, mostly looking for adventure and a chance for profit. Some settled and married into Mexican families, and a number of them took part in the fight against the Spanish. When the Spanish were finally forced out in 1820, the sparsely populated province of Texas had suffered severe losses in people and property. San Antonio had almost as many graves as inhabitants, and Nacogdoches was deserted.[5]

In 1820, during the last year of Spain's control of Mexico and Texas, the Spanish granted Moses Austin permission to bring a number of American settlers to Texas, but he died before he was able to do more than visit Texas and identify possible colony locations.[6] His son Stephen, heir to his scheme to colonize Texas, was able to take advantage of the new Republican government's continued problems with Comanche raiders. Placing a buffer between the towns of northern Mexico and the Plains Indians still seemed a workable plan to the Mexican authorities.

Stephen F. Austin was a settler, not a speculator, and was patient, eager to learn Spanish, and willing to work within the Mexican system. Fortunately his father had made influential friends in Texas, and his son maintained these relationships. In 1821 he traveled over much of central Texas, evaluating its potential for settlement and becoming acquainted with the delays built into the Spanish-Mexican governmental system.

Aware that any real progress and final decisions would have to be made in Mexico City, Austin started for the Mexican capital, but his trip was interrupted when he and his party were captured by a Comanche raiding band. The Comanches at that time had no quarrel with Americans—in fact they semed to have had a very profitable trade with illegal immigrants in Texas—and the party was released.[7] Austin lived in Mexico City for over a year, learning Spanish and how to deal with the Mexican authorities, and acquired a grant to settle three hundred families in Mexican Texas.[8]

During Austin's long stay in Mexico there had been some settlement in Texas, though rumors of his death, bad crops and Indian trouble had slowed immigration. In 1822 Austin's first grant—the Old Three Hundred—settled in colonies along the Brazos River in present-day Washington County and along the Colorado River near Columbus. Fortunately they came with weapons and a tradition of local self defense, because they ran into Indian raiders as soon as they entered Texas. In a historical irony the Comanches, who had indirectly influenced the Spanish decision to allow Anglo-American settlement, did not bother the new arrivals. Comanche territory was north and west of Austin's colony, and the initial threats to the new colonists came from the Karankawas, a small tribe of reputed cannibals living on the Gulf Coast, from the Wacos along the Brazos, and from the Tehuacanies and the Tonkawas between the Brazos and the San Antonio rivers.

The settlers' earliest form of defense, or defensive unit, was little more than a civilian posse hastily formed to strike at an Indian raiding party. In the early fall of 1822 a band of Karankawas raided the settlements, severely wounding colonist Robert Brotherton, so Robert Kuykendall collected a dozen settlers and tracked the Karankawas on horseback, finally discovering them in a camp in a thicket. At daylight the dismounted settlers rushed the Indians and shot most of them.[9]

The first formal military organization in the settlements took place late in 1822 when the Mexican governor ordered the creation of two military districts, one to include the American settlers on the Colorado and another on the Brazos.[10] This same organization also provided for civilian leaders in the two militia districts, with *alcaldes* as the civilian leaders. Gibson Kuykendall mentions this first organization, formed in December 1822 for the Brazos settlement, and recalls that Josiah H. Bell was elected *alcalde*, Samuel Gates selected as captain, and himself selected as lieutenant.[11] By April 1823 the militia was developing on a more standard basis and included all males between eighteen and fifty-five. As more colonists came to Texas, the original military districts were divided, and by November 1824 there were six districts.[12] Organization of these military districts, some no more than militia companies, was an initial step in defending the settlers and identifying officers who could form militia units for campaigns or for defense against Indian raiders. Time was not to be lost in time-consuming elections to select commanders.

The militia filled a definite need and was the only formation possible at the time, providing a more-or-less organized body of armed men for campaigns against hostile Indians. It had limitations, however, as it was not a quick reaction force. Composed of all able-bodied males, when the militia took the field most civilian activities ceased and the settlements were left undefended. Austin's land grants were for men with families, as were later grants, and there were few single males available for special military duty. The settlers were mostly farmers with work animals, and it is doubtful if any large proportion of a militia unit could have been mounted on suitable horses. Over the years service became a burden, especially when there was no imminent threat of Indian attack, and Austin complained in 1829 that few men even bothered to vote for officers.[13]

Despite these limitations, militia companies saw extensive service on various campaigns, too numerous to discuss here and outside the scope of this volume, but the basic problem of coping with small raids still faced the colonists.

The only recourse for the settlers was to gather together

whatever men were available and chase after any Indians who raided. This posse-type of action was carried out in the summer of 1823 when John Tumlinson, *alcalde* of the Colorado settlement, was killed by Indians. When word spread that a band of thirteen Waco Indians camped about fifteen miles above present-day Columbus might have killed Tumlinson, one of his sons, John J. Tumlinson, collected all the men he could and started for the Indian camp. Many of the settlers in the posse were little more than boys; Joe Tumlinson, another son, was only twelve or thirteen but acted as scout. The posse caught the Indians by surprise and killed twelve of the thirteen.[14] This action illustrates the already recognized need for a more permanent force, something between the hastily formed posse and the slow-moving militia.

The colonists were willing to defend themselves, although they did want the Mexican government to pay any men who were serving on an extended basis. Ironically, John Tumlinson had been one of the proponents of a proposal to form just such a permanent unit. On January 7, 1823, several months before he was killed by Indians, Tumlinson and Robert Kuykendall had written Governor José Trespalacios asking permission to raise fifteen men to serve with ten regular soldiers from San Antonio. The men would build blockhouses and small boats and make a combined sea and land attack on Indians when the coastal marshes dried enough to use horses. Moses Morrison, the lieutenant of the militia district of the settlement on the Colorado, was to be the commander. Morrison managed to enlist ten men and the unit was finally mustered in on May 5, 1823. Through no fault of their own, these volunteers were unable to build any blockhouses and were able to do little to control Indian activities; they had to spend most of their time hunting to stay alive, and even hunting must have been difficult because they lacked gunpowder. When powder was sent to them, it was not suitable for their rifles. The detachment camped and explored the land near the mouth of the Colorado River, but in August Austin brought the men up to the Colorado settlement. Although there had been adequate provisions for pay and supplies, there is nothing to indicate any payment was ever made. Evidently the unit disbanded for lack of pay.[15]

During this period the Mexican government was not indifferent to the difficulties facing the colonists. Unfortunately there was neither enough troops to cover all threatened areas nor money to pay them. In May, when Morrison's detachment was formed, Trespalacios sent a sergeant and fourteen soldiers to the mouth of the Colorado River in an effort to control the Karankawas. For a time the soldiers were of value, but there was no suitable provision to pay the troops and the detachment probably just left.[16]

Austin, acting on his own authority, made an effort to provide protection. He offered employment to ten men, to be paid by himself, to serve as rangers attached to the command of Lieutenant Moses Morrison.[17] The exact date of Austin's offer, written on the back of a proclamation by the Baron de Bastrop dated August 4, 1823, is unknown. There is no formal record of the formation of this detachment, but it is nevertheless important because it is probably the first use of the term "ranger" in Texas. It is interesting to note that Austin, evidently making a distinction between rangers and the men already in service, specified these men would serve as rangers and would be attached to Morrison's detachment. Austin also wrote letters on August 11 and November 30 asking for a sergeant and ten additional men.[18] Nothing came of these requests.

The word "ranger" had long been familiar in the English colonies in America, predating even Rogers' Rangers who had earned a distinguished name in the French and Indian War. The term described a body of men who operated apart from the regular military establishment, irregulars, men who literally ranged the frontiers. Austin must have had this concept in mind when he tried to organize his detachment but, failing to form his ranging unit, Austin fell back on what was at hand, the militia.

In 1824 Austin led several expeditions against the Karankawas, finally signing a treaty of peace with them if they stayed west of the San Antonio River. This treaty marked the end of the trouble with this tribe—those not already killed by the Americans soon died from disease.[19]

American immigrants continued to enter Texas, many without official permission, and at the end of 1825 Austin applied for permission to bring in an additional three hundred families.[20] When Moses Austin had passed through Nacogdoches in 1820 it had contained only a few people; by 1825 an estimated sixteen hundred people lived in the area.

The increase in population is reflected by the size of the force Austin was able to collect for a campaign in May 1826 when the Wacos and Tehuacanies became troublesome. Austin set out on a long march with 190 armed men, but found no hostile Indians though several abandoned villages were located by his smaller advance party of scouts.[21] This large force, raised entirely from Austin's colony, required most of the men. To protect the colony from surprise while they were away, Austin ordered Kuykendall and eight men "to range" the country between the Colorado and the Brazos along the San Antonio Road, watching for any sign of Indian movement towards the settlements.

In August Austin called representatives of the six militia districts to meet with him to plan for the defense of the frontier, particularly for periods when the militia was campaigning and their homes and settlements were left undefended, and to establish protective measures until Mexican troops could reach the settlements. The ranging idea was still in Austin's mind, and the plan eventually adopted called for a ranger company of twenty to thirty men on patrol at all times. Each landowner, or a substitute, would be liable for service for a month for each half league of land he owned.[22] Evidently nothing came of this ambitious plan, but the proposal showed there was an understanding of the need for a permanent force to guard the frontier.

American settlement of Texas advanced at a rate that even Austin had not anticipated. At the same time, however, immigration from Mexico was almost at a halt. The Mexican government's vision of a horde of European immigrants to match the Americans never materialized, but when it was able to function between coups and counter-coups, the government became increasingly concerned at the expanding American population in Texas. Equally alarming was the growing fear that the United States would make some move to annex Texas. As early as 1826 one Mexican official warned "who knows that they will not try to separate from the state and unite all the territory that they occupy to their native country?"[23] The earlier American acquisition of Florida in 1819 continued to be viewed as an example of American expansionistic greed.

Mexican General Manuel de Mier y Terán spent much of 1828 in Nacogdoches on a boundary survey, objectively observing conditions in the province and becoming well acquainted with Austin, who had the ability to maintain friendly relations with Mexican officials while still working for his colonists. Terán wrote his president that conditions in Texas must be addressed and brought under control, noting that the colonists held the local Mexicans in contempt, and he discussed the growing population of slaves, illegal under Mexican law. A fair man, he also noted that the union of Texas with the Mexican state of Coahuila was unpopular with both Mexican and American settlers. He was not in favor of making Texas a federal territory and thought, rather, that a court of appeals and a sub-political chief in Texas would suffice. Terán's conclusions and recommendations were submitted to the Mexican government in 1830.[24]

The eventual result of Terán's study was a law that effectively cut off American immigration into Texas, and on April 6, 1830, the settlers were faced with a different set of rules. Even though numerous colonists continued to enter under one article of the new law that could be interpreted as allowing the completion of existing contracts, it was not enough to satisfy the thousands of others who wanted to enter. It also did nothing to allay the fears of those already in Texas, who saw the 1830 act as a betrayal by the Mexican government. Until then, it appears most colonists had been willing to continue the existing relationship with Mexico despite the religious and educational restrictions.[25]

Other provisions of the 1830 act created more serious problems. Terán had recommended vastly increased military garrisons in Texas, both to combat Indians and to control the rapidly growing American population, now far larger than the Mexican. The act's strict provisions for cutting off outside trade also caused widespread unrest. Despite a

definite change in attitudes after 1830, however, there was
no major confrontation, and Austin and Terán continued to
work together, with Austin still urging moderation and cooperation. He was listened to and respected by most of the
American colonists, but in 1832 there was further deterioration of relations as incompetent Mexican officials created
intense ill will. On June 26, 1832, a strong force of colonists
besieged and captured a heavily fortified post at Velasco,
inflicting considerable casualties on the Mexican garrison.[26]
This was the first actual armed conflict between the colonists
and the Mexican government, but the incident did not lead
to other actions and there was still no widespread desire for
a break with Mexico. Most of the Anglo Americans in Texas
did, however, want to be rid of their union with Coahuila, as
did many Mexicans. The growing Indian troubles and their
feeling that they had been abandoned and betrayed by the
central government led the Anglo-American settlers to call
for a convention to discuss Texas' problems.

The various settlements were each asked to send five
representatives to San Felipe de Austin. Fifty-eight delegates
arrived from sixteen settlements, but San Antonio, largely
Mexican, refused to send representatives, saying any such
convention was premature. A number of Mexican officials in
Texas later saw this convention as the beginning of a break
with Mexico.[27]

The convention took little action that could be considered
rebellious, at least by the settlers themselves. The delegates
worked to amend the tariff set up by the 1830 act, and they
organized militia forces in Austin's colony, forming a regiment of two battalions of six companies each. Well aware of
the necessity of mounted units to chase Indians, the delegates suggested forming a forty-man company to range the
frontiers of the Austin and DeWitt colonies, but there is no
record of this company's ever being formed.[28]

This rather tepid convention, whose resolutions were
never presented to Mexico, was followed by a second convention in 1833 as affairs continued to deteriorate. The
Mexican authorities arrested Austin after he had presented
this second convention's resolutions to Mexico City, and
Austin became increasingly convinced that Mexican General

Antonio López de Santa Anna was heading for a despotic rule of Mexico. Despite his belief, he was encouraged by the passage of a number of acts that either repealed restrictions on the settlers or granted them new freedoms: self government was granted to a number of new districts; English was allowed for official documents; and religious freedom was granted. These actions had a calming effect.[29]

During Austin's long twenty-eight-month absence, there was no popular call for rebellion in Texas; malaria and cholera epidemics gave the people too much to worry about to concern themselves with politics. In 1834 Colonel Juan N. Almonte was sent to Texas to inspect conditions in the province, to learn which men were leaders and how many were armed. A fair man and a keen observer, Almonte conducted a lengthy survey and eventually made recommendations essentially similar to what Austin had been suggesting to the Mexican authorities. On his extensive travels, Almonte found little sentiment for an outright break from Mexico.[30]

The establishment by Mexican authorities of custom houses with armed guards was resented by the settlers, but did not lead to any widespread feeling for rebellion even after June 29, 1835, when William Travis gathered a small band of men and a small cannon and forced the garrison at Anahuac to surrender and return to Mexico. To the contrary, citizens meeting in Columbia the day previous to the Anahuac incident condemned the acts of small groups that might lead to a conflict with the Mexican government. Those attending this meeting declared that separation from Mexico was "neither the wish nor the interest of the people," and other communities and settlements followed the lead of Columbia. In mid-July, sentiment among the settlers was for continued peace and cooperation—unless there was some extraordinary provocation.[31]

Provocations were soon provided. On October 2, 1835, the Mexican commander in San Antonio sent a small force to recover a cannon in Gonzales. There was a minor skirmish; the American colonists drove back the Mexican soldiers and kept their cannon. It was little more than a few rounds fired, but the action marked the beginning of the

Texas Revolution, and in the confusion General Martín Perfecto de Cós reached San Antonio undetected with a sizable force, heavily reinforcing the town garrison.

Volunteers began arriving in Gonzales, and an "army" of three hundred men was formed, a militia force with the men supplying their own weapons and equipment. There were few men with even basic military skills and experience, and Austin, who had received a hero's welcome when he returned from prison in Mexico, was tasked to assume command of the volunters. No professional soldier, Austin nevertheless was the most respected and best known man in the province, and he managed to bring some order out of the chaos. The few with any military background agreed it would be fool-hardy to attack a defended town like San Antonio without artillery or trained soldiers, and November began without further military action.[32]

While some of the settlers were engaged in forming a ragtag army at Gonzales, others were trying to establish some form of civil government at San Felipe de Austin. From early October 1835, delegates from the various settlements went through several stages of organization. The overall deliberations of this group are outside the scope of this study; what is of interest are the actions taken that bore on the formation of a ranger force.

On October 17 a resolution was proposed by Daniel Parker authorizing Silas M. Parker to employ and "superin-tend" twenty-five rangers between the Brazos and the Trin-ity. In addition to Parker, Garrison Greenwood was to form ten rangers for duty on the east side of the Trinity River, and D.B. Fryar was to organize thirty-five rangers for duty be-tween the Brazos and the Colorado. These designated "su-perintendents" were to be vigilant in carrying resolutions into effect and had authority to contract for ammunition and to request pay for their forces. It should be noted that a superintendent did not command the ranger unit—the com-panies would elect their own officers who would report to the superintendent. The exact duties of the superintendents were not spelled out in detail, but it appears they were to enlist the rangers for a detachment, or company, and oversee operations. Ranger companies would unite when considered necessary. They were not to interfere with friendly Indians on the borders.[33]

Additional rangers were authorized on November 1, with twenty-five volunteer rangers allocated for duty between the Colorado and the Brazos rivers, twenty-five between the Brazos and the Trinity, and thirty-five east of the Trinity. Each volunteer was promised one dollar and twenty-five cents a day.[34] From the locations assigned and the lack of any designated commanders, it can be assumed these rangers were a realignment of the forces authorized earlier.

On November 6 a resolution proposed to extend the ranger line from the Colorado to the Guadalupe, and by November 9 a line from the Colorado to the Nueces was being considered. It was decided to extend the line to the Cibolo, and a company of twenty rangers, under the superintendence of George Washington Davis was authorized and directed to rendezvous at the big spring or head of St. Mark's River. At the same time Silas M. Parker was authorized to add ten men to his company before going to the rendezvous. Both companies were authorized to draw arms and ammunition from John Lott at Washington, or any other place where public ammunition was stored.[35]

Obviously these resolutions did not consider the rangers as anything other than a frontier force to protect the settlements against Indian raids. A strong, more regular, military establishment was needed to fight the Mexican army, and a Regular Army of eleven hundred and twenty men, rank and file, was authorized, with a two-year enlistment period. Article 9 of this act provided for a corps of 150 rangers, divided into three or more detachments, commanded by a major. When this force was in the field under the commander-in-chief, it would be grouped together as a battalion.[36]

The formation and status of this ranger force was clarified on November 24, 1835, by the passage of an Ordinance and Decree to "establish and organize a Corps of Rangers" to be commanded by a major, with three companies of fifty-six men led by a captain, a lieutenant and a second lieutenant.

The men were to be enlisted for one year, rather than the

two years of the Regular Army, and would receive a dollar and twenty-five cents a day for themselves and their horses. Officers were to be paid the same as Dragoons in the United States Army, plus the pay of ranger privates.

Privates had to furnish a good horse, saddle, bridle and blanket, in addition to weapons and a hundred rounds of powder and shot. If these were not available, the company commander could purchase any item necessary and deduct the cost from the ranger's pay.[37] Nominations and election of officers for the new Ranger Corps were held on November 28 and Robert McAlpin Williamson was elected major while Isaac Burton, William A. Arrington and John J. Tumlinson became the three company commanders.[38]

Except for a few extant but sketchy references to the actions of the companies commanded by Tumlinson and Burton, the activities of this Ranger Corps is pure speculation, but it is obvious that the ranger concept had developed out of the settlers' familiarity with ranger-type service prior to 1835. Although there are only a few references of "ranging" in the reminiscences of Kuykendall, Austin's desire for ranger companies in 1826 and 1832 suggests familiarity, if not actual experience, with the concept. It seems unlikely that so much time and effort would have been spent authorizing ranger commands without prior experience with such units. Whatever the facts, the delegates of 1835 set the basic requirements for the rangers: paid volunteers who furnished their arms, equipment and mounts—good mounts—to defend the frontiers. These requirements would remain throughout the rest of the century.

Few records survive to show to what extent the proposed units were organized. There is a suggestion that Silas Parker had some men in service, because he requested that a surgeon be assigned to him. The request was refused; it was believed that the army surgeons could treat Parker's men.[39]

These early architects of what would be Texas, besides outlining the basic composition of the ranger forces, initiated one other tradition affecting the rangers: they authorized companies on an extensive scale with little or no means to pay or supply the units. The rangers would be hampered by lack of funding through the decades. In the fall and winter of 1835-1836, however, it is doubtful if many men gave much thought to where the money would be found, because they were already at war.

While members of the fledgling government were drafting ordinances and acts, a growing number of volunteers had been forming into a very rough command at Gonzales, with Austin as leader. On October 12, 1835, this Texas Army of roughly three hundred men started for San Antonio where Cós was secure in the barricaded town with seven hundred men and artillery. Not many in the little rebel army thought they could attack the town unless they also obtained cannon from somewhere. When Austin returned to San Felipe for duties as an envoy to the United States, the military command passed to Edward Burleson who laid a rough siege around San Antonio. A few hundred impatient men followed Ben Milam in a wild rush into town and engaged in a savage street fight until Cós surrendered what was left of his command on December 9, 1835. Although Milam was killed, the Texans had their first big victory in their war for independence, but the weaknesses of Texas' military power hardly suggested it would be able to maintain any degree of freedom from Mexico. In February 1836 there were disturbing rumors that Santa Anna, despite cold weather and the lack of roads, was advancing northward.

What the ranger companies were accomplishing in the early days of 1836 is unknown. At least one of the three companies authorized on November 24, 1835, was organized, although no muster rolls or official records remain, and was in service in the early days of 1836; John J. Tumlinson had his unit ready for duty and on the move to their station on the Colorado frontier. Considerable confusion has arisen over the dates of this ranger unit because some writers show John Tumlinson commanding a ranger company in the fighting in late 1835 in and around San Antonio. This company in 1835 was *not* a ranger command but, rather, a unit commanded by Captain John A. Coleman, who was sick during all the fighting at San Antonio. Tumlinson, a lieutenant in the unit, commanded the men during the fighting and was called captain by his men, bringing on the confusion in later years between his ranger command and the unit at San

Antonio.[40]

Tumlinson's ranger company must have been organized shortly after the surrender of San Antonio. From memoirs of a member of the unit, the Tumlinson rangers were sent to the Colorado frontier in January 1836.[41] During the Texas Revolution, most of the Indian tribes remained relatively quiet; in order to allow the colonist to concentrate on fighting Mexico, the new government was careful to sign treaties and keep the Indians from making raids. The treaties held during the war, especially with the eastern and more settled Indians. The dispatch of the Tumlinson rangers to the advanced position on the Colorado frontier, however, suggests the colonists were beginning to have trouble with the Comanches.

Noah Smithwick was one of the privates in Tumlinson's ranger company. A veteran of the early fighting around San Antonio, Smithwick thought the war was over when the Texans captured the city, and he enlisted in the ranger company to see some action on the frontier. He thus escaped the slaughter at the Alamo and lived to write one of the most interesting accounts of early Texas life.[42] Tumlinson's company was assigned the task of building a blockhouse on the headwaters of Brushy Creek, about thirty miles northwest of present-day Austin.[43] The rangers gathered up all the tools and materials they could find and started for their rendezvous point. While waiting to resume their march up the Colorado River, they learned of a woman who had just escaped from Indians.

Sarah Hibbons told the rangers a sad story. With her husband, brother and two children she had been traveling to their home on the Guadalupe when they were attacked by an Indian band. The two men were killed, and she and the children were taken prisoners. The youngest child, little more than a baby, cried constantly, and the irritated Indians eventually killed the infant. They tied the three-year-old boy to a mule and started out again. Mrs. Hibbons watched for her chance and slipped away from the Indians, who had become careless probably believing she would not abandon her boy, and followed the Colorado River until she saw some cows grazing. Afraid to call out for help, she hid all day, followed the cows home at night, and reached Hornsby's Station where Tumlinson's men were gathering before marching to their new post. She gave a description of the Indians to the rangers, who believed they were Comanches, and described the mule her son was riding. After eating supper, a ranger party started out to find the boy, with Reuben Hornsby as guide.

The rangers managed to find a trail but were afraid they might lose it in the growing dark and rested until daylight. The scouts soon found fresh tracks, and they followed a clear track until about ten o'clock when they sighted a Comanche camp. The Indians, not yet out of their blankets and robes, had probably been given a false sense of safety by the isolated countryside and the weather. When they saw the rangers galloping towards them, they scrambled for the shelter of some cedars.

Each warrior grabbed what weapons were at hand and abandoned everything else, running deeper into the cedars. Smithwick, riding a spirited horse, ran through the scattering Comanches and one Indian fired at him, missed, then vanished in the thick brush. Finding it hard to ride through the cedar, Smithwick dismounted and continued the chase on foot, knowing the Indian had an empty musket and wanting to catch the man before he could reload. He fired at the running Indian and saw the man fall but kept on, reloading as he shoved his way through the dense growth. When a limb knocked Smithwick's hat from his head, another ranger saw him and thought he was an Indian. Yet another ranger stopped the first from firing and saved Smithwick.

The fight passed over the supposedly dead Comanche, who was alive and waiting with a loaded musket. When Captain Tumlinson rode through the thicket, checking on his men, the Indian shot at him, killing his horse. Ranger Conrad Rohrer, going through the cedar on foot to check on any Indians overlooked by the horsemen, saw the Indian shoot at Tumlinson and ran over, wrenched the musket from the wounded Comanche, and clubbed him to death with the empty weapon.

The Hibbons' boy was saved, though more by luck than

plan. The Comanches had tied the sleepy boy to a mule before the rangers rushed the camp, and in the confusion the mule broke free and ran through the advancing Texans. One of the rangers thought the small figure in a huge buffalo robe was another Indian trying to escape and rode alongside and placed his rifle against the boy's back. The weapon misfired and the ranger pulled back, recocked, and was aiming again when another ranger recognized the boy and knocked the rifle into the air.

The Indians escaped in the cedar thickets, and the rangers gathered what booty they could find in the abandoned camp and started back to Hornsby's Station. They led the little boy and his mule, feeling proud that they had accomplished the main part of their mission. They had yet another trophy: Rohrer had gone back and scalped the dead Indian, insisting on awarding the grisly skin and hair to Smithwick because the wound inflicted by Smithwick would have eventually killed the Comanche.[44]

The brief, savage incident was just another two days' work to the rangers, who collected their supplies and equipment and marched up river to their new station and built what became known as the Tumlinson blockhouse. They had no way of knowing that their little skirmish was the opening round of a Ranger-Comanche war that would last almost forty years.

Tumlinson's rangers were cut off from the rest of the revolutionists and did not learn of the disasters at the Alamo and Goliad until considerably later. During this period, the only documented reference to the rangers is a message from Major Williamson, sent from Gonzales on February 25, 1836, forwarding information brought by courier from San Antonio that a Mexican army had arrived in the town and that the Americans had withdrawn into the Alamo. He signed the message: "R.M. Williamson, Comd'g the Rangers."[45]

Major Williamson had a title but little else. He was commander of a battalion of three ranger companies only if and when they were assembled as one unit. Without his ranger units, he was no more than another citizen-soldier, and it would be some weeks before he was again part of the ranger force in other than name.

The ranger concept was still alive, however, even though the Texas Army was in retreat. Despite the pressures of his position as commander in chief, Houston found time to write the following note in his camp west of the Brazos on April 6, 1836:

> Maj[—-]: I wish that a company of Spies would range as suggested by you. The army increases and the enemy do not advance as yet. Reinforcements are arriving from the East. The army is in good *spirits*, and the General *sober*.
> Sam Houston Com.in-Chief[46]

This letter is of importance as it was very likely written to Henry Wax Karnes, a stocky, red-headed Tennessean who came to Texas in 1835 just in time for the revolution. He had a natural ability as a scout, took part in the fighting around San Antonio and the capture of the town, and worked with the celebrated spy, Erastus Smith, scouting towards Harrisburg in search of the Mexican forces.[47] In March 1836 he raised a company at Goliad, evidently the company referred to by Houston.

The letter is one of the earliest records of Houston's concern with intelligence and security. During his time as commander and later as president he was almost obsessive about proper scouting and prompt reporting by spies. The sudden advance of Santa Anna and other Mexican commands, however, forced Houston on another hasty retreat, and the Texas farmers and townspeople in the hamlets and cities started a wild rush to get to safety in the east.

As Smithwick recalled events many years later, the rangers were ordered to abandon the blockhouse and march to Bastrop "about the first of March."[48] His memory in this instance was faulty, because the message was probably closer to the first of April. In any event the dispatch was received, ordering the rangers to cover the flight of civilians in the area and then join Houston. The loose discipline and organization of the rangers began to show—Tumlinson and Lieutenant Jo Rogers left to look after their families after turning over command of the company to Major William-son.[49] The remaining rangers started for Bastrop, where they met or were joined by Williamson. Smithwick and Jim Edmundson remained behind to watch for Indians, but after a few days Smithwick decided they would follow the others.

At Cedar Creek they found the first signs of what would be famous as the Runaway Scrape; the settlers had abandoned what they could not carry, and the two rangers found plenty of food. The following day they reached Bastrop, completely abandoned except for the ranger company. The unit was now down to twenty-two men because several more of the rangers had left to check on their families.[50]

The reduced company left Bastrop and marched ten miles downriver, where a courier caught up with them bringing orders for the rangers to move all the cattle they could find to the east of the Colorado. The rangers returned to Bastrop but, discovering there was no way they could move cattle across the high water, waited in the deserted town for a time while trying to decide what to do. They had no idea where Houston might be, or if he still had an army. They had no better idea about the location of the Mexican troops, though most felt certain none of the enemy would come in their direction, and the Texans were surprised when a large Mexican force appeared on the opposite bank of the river. The rangers left in great haste and less order.

Smithwick happened to remember the lone sentry whom Major Williamson had placed on the ford, and he rode up to the major and asked if they were going to leave "Uncle Jimmie."

"Good God! No; ride back and tell the old man to come on."

The ranger galloped back and found Jimmy Curtice sitting by a tree, a whiskey bottle beside him. He was quite happy, unconcerned about the large Mexican force a short distance away. Smithwick explained their danger, but the old man remained unmoved. Finally, Smithwick shouted they were alone, the company gone.

"The hell they are! 'Light and take a drink."

"The Mexicans may swim the river and be after us any moment."

"Let's drink to their confusion," suggested Jimmy, and the young ranger gave up and had a drink. They finally mounted and left the ford.

Later in the retreat "two old men," Jimmy Leach and Andy Dunn, somehow lost their mounts. The younger men took turns letting the two ride their horses, following the only road through the boggy countryside. Smithwick had no way of recalling days—it is doubtful if he knew the exact date at the time, much less years later—but sometime after this ride, Major Williamson, "being a little lame," decided to leave the company and ride ahead, hoping he could find the Texas army. He took two men and left.[51] It must have seemed the sensible choice then, and it cannot be greatly faulted today because he left Lieutenant George M. Petty in command and assumed the officer would keep the rangers on the move.

The rangers finally caught up with the bulk of the fleeing civilians, moving through a countryside of deserted farms and small settlements. The now small company passed herds of cattle, pigs, flocks of chickens, stray dogs and cats, all wandering loose. When the rangers reached Cole's Settlement—later Independence—they found a note left by Major Williamson telling the sad news of Fannin's command. It was one more gloomy note in a miserable retreat. Their lieutenant seemed afraid to make any positive moves, but what Smithwick thought cowardice at the time seems more like commendable caution in the reflection of later years. They knew that a large Mexican force was behind them—they had seen them—and Santa Anna was probably chasing Houston somewhere ahead. It was not an auspicious time for heroics.

The remnants of the ranger company, with two men on foot and others riding lame horses, must have been very edgy by now, tired, hungry, not as careful as they should have been. Company scouts were reconnoitering the road leading to Washington one night and saw what they believed to be a body of men. Surprised once before by the sudden appearance of Mexican troops, the scouts did not check closely enough to observe that what they believed to be enemy troops were actually cattle. They circled away from the road, crossed the Brazos over a ford, and met two groups of men who had been escorting families from their districts. Smith-

wick identified them as rangers commanded by a Colonel
Bain and Captain Bob Childress,[52] but it is unlikely the men
were rangers, certainly not officially. They could have been
militia; other than Smith's spy company, which was very
busy at this time, no other ranger-type units can be identified in this general period. Whatever they were, the men
believed their civilians were now safe and joined the Tumlinson rangers. None of the new men had any clear idea
where the Texas army might be, but it was likely close by.

The detour to avoid a supposed Mexican force took the
Tumlinson rangers off the Washington road and away from
the ferry at the town. Later they learned Major Williamson
had left the ferry behind so that they could cross the
Brazos.[53] Discussions among the rangers and the other men
at the ford must have taken some time, but finally the
combined group remounted and started out. For the first
time in Smithwick's narrative, a definite date can be placed
on events: the afternoon of April 22, 1836, when the rangers
were close enough to the San Jacinto battlefield to hear
distant rifle fire. Halting again, they were trying to decide
what to do when a courier galloped by, shouting the news of
the victory over Santa Anna.

The rangers and their new companions rode on, reaching
the littered and still-confused battlefield. Smithwick remembered he felt "mean and ashamed" to ride in, thinking they
ought to be drummed out of the army,[54] but the victors were
too excited and too tired to notice their arrival.

Smithwick makes no mention of it in his memoirs, but
there were a few ranger friends on the battlefield. Major
Williamson had been successful in his search for Houston's
army and fought in the battle as a private. Conrad Rohrer
left Tumlinson's company at an undetermined date and
became Houston's wagonmaster. Even though he had been
selected as commander of one of the three ranger companies,
Isaac Burton served as a private in Karnes' unit during the
campaign and battle.

The rangers were not the only late arrivals at San Jacinto. Individuals and detachments began arriving as soon as
the fighting was over, too late to share in the glory but eager
to hear about the battle. Santa Anna was taken prisoner the

next day, and a force of Texans several times the size of the battalion that had won at San Jacinto began following the now-retreating Mexican commands through a country ravaged by the marching and countermarching of several commands of the Mexican army. The rangers had the task of guarding the baggage trains, but in Victoria the Texans gave up the pursuit of the rapidly retreating Mexicans and went into camp, using whatever quarters could be found or building temporary shelters. While the army was trying to settle in, rumors of Indian troubles caused the Tumlinson rangers to be sent to a location near present-day Austin. Because their old blockhouse had been burned by the Comanches, they established a camp to act as a buffer against Indian raiders and served out the remainder of their time of service.[55]

Tumlinson's company is the only one of the three ranger companies authorized in 1835 that has any extensive history, thanks largely to Noah Smithwick. If Arrington's unit was ever formed, there is no record to show what they did. Isaac Burton served as a private soldier at San Jacinto, and his company was organized after the battle although the exact date is unknown. His unit must have been formed rather quickly, probably as a result of rumors of a Mexican invasion, and was sent to the coast to watch for any enemy landings. The first definite date of service for Burton's rangers was June 3, 1836.

On this early June day, a group of Burton's men were watching from a concealed position on Copano Bay, part of their patrol area. The Texans saw a suspicious vessel anchored not too far offshore and took a daring gamble, signaling the ship to send a boat ashore. The Mexicans apparently believed the men were there to receive supplies, and to the surprise and delight of the rangers a boat was lowered and the five Mexican sailors who rowed ashore were easily captured by the Texans. There was no shooting involved and nothing to alert the remainder of the ship's crew that anything unusual had happened. Acting boldly, the rangers decided to try again. They managed to load sixteen men in the boat, rowed out, and captured the *Watchman.*

The ship was loaded with supplies for Mexican troops, a

windfall for the always-short-of-everything Texans. Satisfied that boldness wins, the rangers overestimated their skill and decided to sail the ship to Velasco, the nearest Texas port. When the wind came up, they started out but found that sailing a ship was considerably more difficult than riding a horse. They were in some danger until the wind died down and becalmed the ship. In the confusion of trying to sail the ship, the rangers had not noticed that two other vessels had dropped anchor in the bay. Gambling again, the rangers coerced the captain of the *Watchman* to trick the other ship commanders into coming aboard. Suspecting nothing, the captains of the *Comanche* and the *Fanny Butler* were rowed over and taken prisoner, and their crews surrendered in short order. The three ships were eventually sailed to Velasco where their cargoes, worth an estimated twenty-five thousand dollars, were turned over to the Texas forces. Burton's men were dubbed "horse marines" for their successful operation, the only time the rangers were ever to serve on the open water.[56]

This action, six weeks after San Jacinto, was actually a continuation of the war for independence and marks the end of the colonial and revolutionary era in Texas. The prerepublic period of Texas' history saw the beginning of the ranger concept and force. Admittedly, the start was on a small scale, but the ranger force never would be large. Nor can their service to the independence effort be considered significant, and it was clear that any future successes would depend on proper leadership. By the time of Texas' independence, however, there was a demonstrated need for a force of mounted riflemen, apart from regular army troops, to range and defend the frontier. A beginning had been made to fill the need.

—2—

The Early Republic

Day to day life in the new Republic did not change significantly from what life had been prior to independence from Mexico; many homes and commercial buildings had been destroyed or damaged, but the people who had come to Texas were a hardy lot who did the best they could with what was at hand. Even though Mexican troops were no longer a danger, the settlers soon faced new Indian raids. Previous attacks by Comanche Indians against the settlements had been little more than curiosity forays, but as the Texans edged out onto the prairies they began to trespass into areas claimed by these Plains Indians. The first major attack took place on May 19, 1836, shortly after the Battle of San Jacinto, east of present-day Waco where the John Parker family had constructed a blockhouse surrounded by a log wall. Like other frontier forts, it served as a place of shelter for nearby families.

The Parkers had taken no part in the revolutionary fighting, and on the morning of May 19 the men were out working. A considerable party of Indians, mostly Comanche, rode to the fort and forced their way through the open gate, killing almost everyone inside. The Comanches rode off when they saw some of the men running in from the field, but they took with them two Parker children as captives. The girl, Cynthia Ann, grew up with them, married a war chief, and became the mother of Quanah Parker, the last great chief of the Comanche.[1]

There is nothing to suggest the attack was a premeditated initiation of systematic war on the Texans; the group, which probably included some Wacos, was more likely a war party out for loot and glory. The Parker attack does, however, provide an example of the deterioration of relations between the Texans and the Comanche tribes. Accustomed to demanding tribute from the other tribes they disdained, the Comanches did not understand that the Texas settlers were as little accustomed to paying for their safety as they were to tolerating raids against their property.

Initially, peaceful contact between the two races had not been uncommon, and Sam Houston made a special attempt to keep the peace with the Comanches. In early December 1836 he sent them a letter:

TO THE COMANCHE CHIEFS, DECEMBER 3, 1836

Comanche Chief—Brothers

You as well as the Americans have always been free and never conquered. Your enemies and ours are the same. I send you my friends to talk to you—to give presents and to make peace with you and your people.

You have many things to trade and swap with us. You need many things that we can let you have cheaper than you have ever been able to get them from the Mexicans. You can let us have horses, mules and buffalo robes in change for our paints, tobacco, blankets, and other things which will make you happy.

I wish to have a smoothe path, that shall lead from your camp to my house, that we can meet each other and that it shall never become bloody. I do not wish that your women and children should be scared or unhappy. You may believe the words that my friends may speak to you for me.

When the grass rises in the Spring, you must come with your Chiefs to see me and I will make you and them presents. I am the Chief who sent the silver medal to the Great Comanche Chief from San Antonio in 1833.

[Private Seal] Given under my hand and private Seal, at Columbia, this 3 day of December,

A.D.1836, and of the Independence of Texas the
First.

Sam Houston[2]

Houston's effort to make peace with the Comanches did
not stop other tribes from raiding after the Texas Republic
was established. As settlers returned to abandoned farms
and new arrivals began moving west and north, they encountered more Indian troubles. The last half of 1836 saw several
more major efforts by the Texans to control Indian trouble
by raising ranger or ranger-type units. In late summer,
Robert M. Coleman received the following message:

War Department
Velasco, Aug. 12th, 1836
To Coln R.M. Coleman

Sir
You are hereby ordered to raise for the term of
one year three companies of mounted men for the
Special purpose of protecting frontier inhabitants
of upper Brazos-Colorado-Little River-and Guadalupe; —you will make your headquarters at some
suitable point above the settlement and take such
other measures as you may deem best calculated
to protect the persons and the property of the
Citizens-Aforesaid. So soon as a Company shall be
Complete you will order an Election of officers the
result of which you will report to this office that
the persons elected may be Commissioned to the
Secretary of War—You will See that the necessary
provisions &c are furnished your men.
You will at all times bear in mind the purpose
for which you are detached, the complete protection of the inhabitants will not, it is hoped, be
disappointed.

By order of the President
F.A. Sawyer
Acting Sec at War[3]

This order does not specifically designate these men as rangers. Certain parts of the order, however, show they were considered as such; the two key phrases were the references to "mounted men" and to the "Special purpose of protecting frontier inhabitants. . . ."

Authorizing Coleman's three companies did not solve the problems of frontier defense. Later in the year, the Texas Congress passed several acts to create a military establishment and replace the revolutionary units and volunteers, many of whose term of service was expiring. It was clear some additional, authorized military force was necessary. One act, specifically designed to protect the frontier and signed by President Houston on December 5, 1836,[4] authorized the president to raise a battalion of 280 mounted riflemen to protect the frontier. This was a legislative action rather than a directive of the War Department, and it formalized the requirements for the ranger service. These men were intended for the ranging service; each man was enlisted for one year and had to furnish his weapons, equipment and horse. For the first time a rifle was specifically required, as well as a brace of pistols. Horse and weapons were to be inspected before the man was enlisted. Other legislation enacted by the Texas Congress authorized a Regular Army and militia units; the members of the battalion of mounted riflemen were to receive the same pay as these regular army and militia commands, plus an extra fifteen dollars a month for the upkeep of their horses and weapons.

These mounted riflemen were not designated by the term "ranger," but the requirements for their service followed the pattern set during the revolution: furnishing their own clothing, weapons, equipment and mounts, with the duty of defending the frontier areas. Another act signed into law just a few days later on December 10, 1836, clearly shows the intent of the congress. This act, defining the pay of mounted riflemen and covering all who had been in the ranging service since July 1835, provided that "every Mounted Rifleman who has entered the *ranging service* [italics added], . . is hereby entitled to twenty-five dollars per month as pay, and the same bounty of land as other volunteers in the field."[5]

Documentation concerning both the three companies of

mounted men which Coleman was directed to raise and of the battalion of mounted riflemen authorized by the act of December 5, 1836, is found mostly only in the recollections and memoirs of the men who served. These memoirs suggest Coleman formed at least two companies. Noah Smithwick stated that neither Tumlinson nor any of the other lieutenants of the Ranger Corps authorized in 1835 returned to their units after San Jacinto, but the enlisted rangers still had service time remaining and were sent to join Coleman's new command which had been instructed to build a post on Walnut Creek about six miles from present-day Austin. The fortification consisted of several log cabins surrounded by a stout palisade, and Smithwick recalled that their arrival checked Indian activity, at least for a time, and that the settlers could move out of the fortified posts where they had been staying and begin to farm again.[6]

Smithwick is often vague on dates. His arrival on Walnut Creek was probably early in the fall of 1836, because Coleman would have required some time to form his companies, move to the frontier and construct the fort. Whatever the exact date, Indian activity must have slackened as Smithwick claimed, because he was allowed to visit the settlements and work in his blacksmith trade from time to time. During one of these trips he met the woman he would later marry.[7] When Smithwick's enlistment was up "about the beginning of 1837," he agreed to continue in service as a substitute for another man who wanted to return to his family. The weather was cold and wet at the fort, and the rangers suffered from lack of clothing. Even though the men were required to provide their own equipment and clothing, the Texas government bought some old U.S. Army uniforms and distributed them to Coleman's men. Most of the uniforms were undersized, and considerable alteration was required before the pants and runabouts fitted.[8]

Smithwick recalled that Colonel Coleman was the commander at the fort, but whether he was in command of one of the companies or was using the fort as his general headquarters is not clear. It is clear, however, that Coleman was not popular with the settlers, however much they welcomed the rangers. Coleman was evidently a lax disciplinarian and allowed his men wide license in foraging.[9] One of his officers, a former U.S. Army soldier he had promoted to the rank of lieutenant and identified by Smithwick only as Lieutenant R., was abusive and hated by the men in the company. The lieutenant tied up a drunk ranger one evening, so that the man could sober up, but the ranger became entangled in his ropes during the night and choked to death. Frightened at the outcry caused by the death, the lieutenant deserted and left Coleman to face the angry civilians and friends of the dead ranger. Charges were preferred against Coleman, who was relieved of his command and ordered to report to the War Department at Columbia. The incident was never adjudicated by a court, and Coleman drowned a short time later in a hunting accident. He was replaced by an officer Smithwick called Captain Michael [Micah] Andrews.[10]

This ranger company had an Indian encounter in the early spring of 1837. The rangers were entertaining themselves one night shortly after dark, telling wild tales while some of the younger ones danced to Smithwick's fiddle, when a sudden flame atop one of the high knolls near the fort brought the festivities to an abrupt halt. No settler would risk a blazing fire in Indian country, and the rangers concluded that Indians, unaware of the ranger fort, had camped on the knoll for the night. The rangers' new commander, who Smithwick said was easygoing and hated to order out the boys in the night, suggested waiting until dawn and striking the Indians at the regular crossing on the Colorado.[11] Andrews instead agreed to Smithwick's suggestion for volunteers to attack right away, and almost every ranger in the fort stepped forward. Lieutenant Nicholas Wren selected fifteen men, who started out immediately to surprise the Indians with Wren, Smithwick and ranger Jo Weeks in the lead as scouts. During the night they stumbled on a large *caballado* of stolen horses and mules, and continued the search for the Indian camp after the startled animals quieted down. The Texans missed their chance to destroy the raiders when Wren, with half of the party, became confused in the dark and went beyond the camp. Smithwick and the other half of the men were unable to catch the Indians between the two ranger forces. Returning, Wren and his men made enough noise to awaken the Indians, who broke for better cover, firing as they ran. One Indian was hit, but managed to get away; the return fire of the Indians killed ranger Philip Martin. Recovering a large number of stolen animals and capturing all the Indian camp equipment was a poor exchange for a ranger life.[12]

The Comanches, shamed by the loss of the animals they had stolen, soon came back to recover them on a morning when the careless Texans did not have their horse guards mounted. The animals were grazing near a creek, close to some timber, when perhaps a dozen Comanches, on foot, ran from the timber, blowing whistles and screaming. One mounted Comanche galloped ahead of the scattered horses and led them up the creek, followed by the other Indians, but many of the horses, Smithwick's fine American mount among them, broke loose and returned to the fort. The Indians let them go, keeping as many as they could. Despite a three-day chase, the rangers never did catch up with them, losing the trail when wild mustangs obliterated all tracks. Houston relieved Lieutenant Wren for the unit's lapse in security, but the men in the company petitioned the president for reinstatement and Wren was returned to the company. Despite ranger precautions, the Comanches later ran off a few more horses, apparently satisfying Comanche honor, and there was a degree of peace in the region.[13]

Early in the summer of 1837, two Comanche chiefs and six warriors who wanted a peace treaty approached Coleman's Fort under a flag of truce. Smithwick, the ranger who best understood Spanish, went out to speak with them and, with understandable reservations, returned with them to their camp about thirty miles distant. He stayed with the Comanches for three months. When he returned, it was with the understanding that he would arrange for a trading post to be established to serve the Comanches, but for reasons beyond his control the post was never opened. To the Indians Smithwick became a man without honor, hated by the Comanches for breaking his word. While he had been away in the Indian camp, the highly regarded Captain Andrews had retired and there was a new company commander,

Captain William M. Eastland; additionally, Smithwick's enlistment had expired during his Indian sojurn, and he quit
the ranging service and opened a shop in Bastrop.[14] Considerable information on the Coleman rangers is found in
the memoirs of George Bernard Erath.[15] Born in Austria,
Erath came to Texas in 1833 and worked as a laborer and
on a survey crew. Like many other single men, he fitted in
with life on the frontier and in 1835 took part in an expedition, against Waco Indians, commanded by John H. Moore
who will appear again in this narrative. When the Texas
revolution began, Erath enlisted and fought at San Jacinto;[16] liking military life, he enlisted again after Texas
became a republic. For a few months Erath served in ranger-
type units and mentions he was attached to "Robertson's
(possibly Sterling C. Robertson) company against the Indians." In July 1836 he was transferred to the company of a
Captain Hill which operated between the Brazos and the
Colorado. While with Hill, he was in an Indian fight in
August.[17] Nothing is known about these units, probably
volunteer commands formed to protect the frontier following
the attack on Parker's Fort; however, Erath's mention of
"transferred" to explain his movements from unit to unit
suggests some control over the various companies.

Erath is not clear as to what constituted "enlisting," but
he states that he enlisted "again" on October 1, 1836, in the
corps of rangers commanded by Colonel Coleman and served
as a lieutenant in the company commanded by a Captain
Barron (Thomas H. Barron), stationed at the Falls of the
Brazos. These men were paid twenty-five dollars a month
and received a land bounty, as authorized later by the act of
December 10, 1836. In early November Erath, with two
sergeants and over twenty men from Barron's company, was
sent to establish a new fort on Little River. Colonel Coleman
and a few men, accompanying the rangers to their new post,
marked and cut out a new road from the Falls to the new
fort and then on to his own fort on Walnut Creek. With only
a little coffee, several axes and some other tools, a steel mill
for grinding corn, a wagon and two yoke of steers, Erath and
his men were on their own at their new fort.[18]

Erath has a graphic description of life in his new post:

An attempt to settle the surrounding country had been made the winter before, and here and there unfenced patches of corn, planted in the spring, had reached maturity in the unusually favorable season, and had not been eaten up by buffalo or other wild stock. By going or sending out I could procure a few bags of nubbins, and I issued my men an ear of corn apiece a day for bread, which they ground on a steel mill. Our meat was wild game which was plentiful. Honey had to be kept in rawhide or deerskin sacks with the hair outside, and at Christmas we had several hundred pounds of it about the Fort. A very little coffee was brought up with us, and used with great economy....Pots and other cooking utensils and useful household things were found around the evacuated country in or near deserted cabins where the settlers had hidden them in thickets or other favorable spots before running away [this reference is to the Runaway Scrape].

My memory for details on almost all subjects is good, but I am at a loss to account for the amount of work done that winter by men who had to guard, hunt, cook, dress deerskin, and make clothes of it, particularly moccasins, and in all ways provide everything, and yet in six weeks time, by Christmas, I had up seven or eight houses with wooden chimneys, well covered, and with buffalo hide carpets down.[19]

In what must be a reference to the act of December 5, 1836, Erath said that congress reorganized the ranger force and added new officers, retaining most of the old ones and promoting a few juniors. Around Cristmas 1836, a Lieutenant Curtis arrived at the new fort on the Little River with orders placing him in command. There were also orders for Erath to hold himself in readiness to proceed to Coleman's Fort on Walnut Creek as soon as special orders arrived for Colonel Coleman. The orders for Coleman arrived on January 4, 1837, just as word reached the rangers that Indian tracks of about a dozen Indians had been found about twelve miles away, heading "down the country".[20]

The rangers did not intend to allow the Indians to approach the settlements, but there was a night of discussion before an agreement was reached on how to proceed. Even though rangers were required by law to furnish their mounts, more than half of the detachment in the new post were still on foot. Lieutenant Curtis had a fine horse, but he decided not to lead the scout after the Indians and instead suggested that Erath command the patrol, taking dismounted rangers. Too experienced for such foolishness, Erath took what horses were available and, delayed by a heavy rain, eventually left with ten rangers and three civilian volunteers. Most of the rangers had rifles, but one was armed with a musket and another with a shotgun. Only three of the men also had pistols. Three of Erath's party were boys, two of them not yet fifteen, but despite their ages they were all good shots and experienced woodsmen with good rifles. Only four in the party, including Erath, had ever been in a fight.[21]

A few hours after starting out, the detachment discovered the Indian trail indicating a force nearer to a hundred warriors, all on foot. The rangers thought they could handle "wild" Indians, but if this party were Caddos or other settled Indians possessing muskets, they would "find our hands full." After following the Indians all day, the rangers lost the trail, found it again, tied up their horses and started out again on foot.

Just before daylight the rangers came on the Indians, who were starting their morning cook fires. Without being seen, from a position below a creek bed they observed that the Indians, in a small horseshoe bend in the creek, were well armed and numbered close to a hundred. A dog wandered over from the Indian fires and sniffed about on the bank above the hidden rangers and ambled back again.

Afraid they would be discovered in the increasing daylight, the rangers opened fire. Their surprise volley dropped several Indians, and the rest grabbed their weapons, scattered in the trees, and began firing to try to locate the rangers. After all the rangers had emptied their rifles—Erath noted that if they had all had a brace of pistols as prescribed, they could have charged the still disorganized Indians and probably kept them running—they had to drop down below the bank to reload, not a quick process with a rifle. The advantage switched to the Indians.

The braves, continuing to fire, began to move to flank the small ranger detachment. Two men on Erath's right, ranger David Clark, described by Erath as "an elderly man," and Frank Childers, one of the civilian volunteers, were mortally wounded, though still able to move. Ordering them to fall back, Erath divided his men into two groups and instructed them to take cover behind some trees while he reloaded, but the Indians began yelling and rushed forward. Erath killed one Indian, who fell almost at his feet, and the fire from the other rangers temporarily stopped the Indian charge.

Unable to climb the high bank, Erath was saved by two of his men who rushed back and stretched out on the level ground to reach down and haul him up the icy bank. Erath had one group of his men fall back while he stayed with the others and covered their withdrawal. The first squad then provided covering fire while Erath and his group retreated. They fell back several hundred yards in this manner, one group of men reloading its rifles, while the other continued firing at the now cautiously advancing Indians.

The Indians were too numerous to be put off for long, and in a sudden and concerted rush Erath and Sergeant McLochlan were cut off from the others and took shelter in a small ravine where they found David Clark, one of the seriously wounded men, hiding. The dying man offered the sergeant his rifle, knowing he would not have any need for it, but McLochlan refused and managed to run around the Indians to take cover with the other rangers. Erath stayed with the wounded man until, spotting a large group of Indians approaching, he managed to slip away and hide in some brush. Noticing a few rangers hiding in an elm thicket, he called out and joined them without being seen.

The Indian chase stopped, probably because some of them had found the dying Clark. Erath saw those near him turn back, and heard yelling as the Indians butchered the wounded man. Not hearing any further yells or cries, the rangers assumed the second wounded man had managed to hide. Shortly the Indians began a sad howling, a moaning cry which Erath thought indicated they were mourning their dead and preparing to leave. When he explained this to his men, they did not wait to see if he was right and immediately ran from the woods.

The rangers were fortunate to escape from the unequal fight with only two dead. The sergeant's gun lock had been smashed by a ball, another round had shattered his ram rod, a third had destroyed his powder horn, another had pierced his coat, and one had even cut the handkerchief he had about his head. The inexperienced rangers wanted no further fighting that day; they found their horses and rode back to the fort on the Little River that night, January 7, 1837.

The next morning Erath and four rangers started for Coleman's Fort on Walnut Creek, carring the special orders which had arrived at the post three days earlier. Erath does not further identify the packet, but it was undoubtedly the orders relieving Colonel Coleman. Erath laconically notes that President Houston "deposed" Colonel Coleman and appointed a Major Smith to take his place. The news of the attempted raid and the efforts to recover the bodies lost in the fight caused considerable activity among the several posts, but none of the subsequent scouting parties led to other engagements. Erath, who later heard the Indian had ten dead,[22] soon left the ranging service and returned to surveying.

From what scanty records remain, the rangers apparently saw little activity during the rest of 1837. Undocumented accounts say Captain Eastland remained in service at least until January 22, 1838, indicating that at least one of Coleman's original companies remained active during 1837. According to A.J. Sowell, Eastland took part in a joint Indian scout leaving Fort Prairie, some five miles below present-day Austin, in October 1837 with a Captain L. Lynch. Despite the name of Fort Prairie in Sowell's account and the discrepancy in miles from Smithwick's version, this had to be Coleman's Fort with Eastland still in command of one of the original companies. He and Lynch could not agree over who would command the expedition, and the two senior officers and most of their men returned to the fort. Two lieutenants and sixteen men continued on and engaged in a bitter fight with Indians, with ten rangers killed and three wounded.[23]

There is definite evidence that another ranging company, or detachment, led by Erastus "Deaf" Smith, was in service during early 1837. Smith, one of the legendary scouts of early Texas, was born in New York on April 19, 1787. He came to Texas in 1817 and stayed a short time, returning in 1821 in poor health. His health gradually improved though his hearing was gone, and for the rest of his life he was known as Deaf Smith. He married a Mexican in 1822 and had a number of children, staying in San Antonio when not out roaming in the wilderness.

Smith evidently had little political interest and was neutral when the revolution started. When Mexican troops refused to let him enter San Antonio to visit his family, however, he abruptly declared for the rebels and joined the Texas Army. An accomplished scout who became the stand-ard by which others would be judged, he fought in the battles around San Antonio and became Houston's chief scout. His most famous exploit was burning the bridge over Buffalo Bayou, cutting off any retreat by the Mexican army at San Jacinto.[24]

It is possible that Smith was leading a ranger-type unit during late 1836, probably one of the units authorized on December 5, 1836. He can definitely be located in March 1837 when he was operating out of a camp on the Medina River. Smith led his men down to Laredo and had a brisk fight with troops from the Mexican garrison there. About five miles from the post, Smith lured the dismounted Mexican cavalrymen through the brush and opened fire on them at close range. The ranger rifles inflicted considerable loss, although the Texans suffered two wounded, and the men also captured most of the Mexicans' horses. Smith, however, made no effort to enter or capture Laredo.[25]

Sam Houston was not in favor of Smith's expedition. On March 31, 1837, he wrote Henry Karnes, "Commanding Texian Cavalry," and gave him instructions for obtaining horses and defending the frontier. Additionally, he com-plained he had never ordered Smith to march on Laredo, "I am afraid our friend Deaf Smith and his men have acted badly...." He stressed Smith was not to draw on San Antonio merchants without Karnes' authority.[26] There are no additional documented accounts of Smith's being active in 1837. He must have done some scouting, however supplied, because a William Small did considerable blacksmith work for the company. Smith died on November 30, 1837, before he could certify Small's bill. As late as the end of 1839 Small was still trying to collect from Texas.

Smith's unit was certainly a ranger-type command, and he was the prototype scout, the best of his day. His service was the beginning of a shift to fighting in the regions west and south of San Antonio where the Comanches had not been overly active; despite the cultural clashes that almost started a war,[27] the treaty signed in San Antonio in the winter of 1837 held up for many months. As more Anglo Americans settled in San Antonio, however, trade increased with Laredo on the Rio Grande, and Mexican bandit raids upon these traders would soon bring the rangers into the region.

There was another effort to provide for defense of the northern frontier in the summer of 1837. On June 12, 1837, an act was approved to raise a three-divisional corps of six hundred mounted volunteers to serve for six months. Requirements for equipment and weapons followed earlier ranger proposals: a good, well-shod horse, equipment and provisions. Additionally each man had to have extra horseshoe nails, two hundred rounds of ammunition and a pack mule. The most interesting provision allowed each division to have, if practicable, a company of friendly Indians to act as spies. They were to be paid as might be agreed upon between them and the president.[28] Houston took a personal interest in passing this measure and even took a leave of absence to supervise organization, but the grand force never took the field.

In the summer of 1838 another ranger or ranger-type action took place west of San Antonio. The commander was another ex-scout, Henry Karnes, who had remained active in the military forces after the revolution. Sent to Matamoros to help in a prisoner exchange, he was captured by the

Mexicans but soon escaped and headed for the frontier, living with the Comanches for a time. He was first their prisoner, and the Indians were fascinated by his red hair which, believing it had been somehow dyed, they spent some time trying to wash out. Karnes undoubtedly learned a great deal about their tactics and fighting abilities during this period, which was fortunately before the Comanches became deadly enemies of the Texans.

On his return Karnes led some form of ranger unit, but the exact strength is unknown. Like Deaf Smith's command, exactly what authority was used to form Karnes' unit is speculation. During the summer of 1838 he was scouting with a detachment of twenty-two men west of the Medina River when they were attacked on the Arroyo Seco by a large Comanche war party. The subsequent fight shows the developing skill of some of the Texans in fighting mounted Indians.

Karnes kept his men under control as they ran to the shelter of the arroyo's banks, dismounted and secured their horses. The men fired in relays, one third shooting, another third reloading, the rest waiting to be next to fire, one relay always ready with loaded rifles. The system had obviously been rehearsed. The Comanches charged up to the ravine, yelling, keeping a shower of arrows in the air then breaking away to hide behind their horses. Remaining calm and taking careful aim, the Texans brought down twenty of the Indians and the rest retreated, unwilling to make a long fight of a losing cause. Karnes was the only ranger casualty; in his eagerness to direct the fire, he climbed atop the bank for a better view and was hit by an arrow[29] but recovered to fight another day. Karnes was one of the most skilled of the frontier fighters and undoubtedly worked out some of the tactics used by later commanders. He continued to serve through 1839.[30]

The difference made by good leadership and training in these early fights can best be demonstrated by looking at another battle a few months later. In the opening days of 1839 a considerable Indian force, mounted and afoot, attacked settlements along the east bank of the Brazos, near the Falls, killing a number of settlers. Driven off from one farm, the Indians regrouped and continued raiding.

A group of settlers rallied and decided they could either chase the Indians or abandon this section of the frontier. Forty-eight men decided to fight, elected Benjamin Bryant commander, and began trailing the raiders. From the tracks they followed, the settlers thought they were faced by sixty-four horsemen and a considerable number of Indians on foot. Despite the odds, they kept on the trail and caught up to the raiders on January 16, 1839, in an open meadow near a dry ravine. In the initial exchange of rifle fire, both Bryant and the Indian leader, José María, were wounded.

The Indians retreated to the shelter of the ravine and continued fighting. Bryant's wound was serious enough to take him out of the fight; although command of the settlers fell to Ethan Stroud, there was no longer a real leader. The charge that had driven the Indians to the ravine convinced the whites they had won the day, and each man began acting on his own with no attention paid to reloading or staying together. José María, despite his injury, kept control of his men, saw they reloaded, and at his yell had them suddenly charge the widely scattered settlers. Trying to exercise some control over his men, Stroud yelled for them to fall back and reload, but this was taken for a signal to run. In short order the settlers were scattered, shot down or stabbed; three had been slain near the ravine, and another ten were killed and five wounded in the rout that followed.

There were several acts of coolness and bravery in the rout. Eli Chandler had managed to get back to his horse when he saw a settler surrounded by Indians. Riding through the attackers, Chandler scattered them, lifted the man up behind him and galloped to safety. Three others repeated this act and prevented the death toll from being higher.

Bryant survived his wound but not the stigma attached to the settlers' loss, and "Bryant's Defeat" has come down as a classic example of poor leadership. It is also important because it was the first time Eli Chandler appears in an Indian fight, at least officially. He was a keen observer and would become a noted ranger commander.[31]

By 1838 it was clear that Mexico could not mount any

serious invasion of Texas. Internal conditions, bordering on civil war, tied up all the Mexican troops, but Mexico could use Indians to create chaos and perhaps even turn much of Texas back to a wilderness. Mexican incitement of the Indians became a growing concern among many Texans, and their fears became reality when Pedro Julian Miracle was killed, in unexplained circumstances, near the Red River in August 1838.

On Miracle's body was a journal showing his extensive travels throughout Texas and up into Arkansas. Listed were contacts with most of the settled tribes, and also accounts of the travels of Indian delegations to Matamoros where they had been warmly received by Mexican officials and given considerable quantities of powder and lead. The journal, which indicated Miracle was operating under the orders of Vicente Filisola, commander-in-chief of the Mexican Army, suggested the Mexicans were trying to embroil the Indians into a war with Texas. Important enough to be brought to the attention of the United States[32], the journal was the beginning of a break with the settled tribes, especially the Cherokees. Hostilities suited Mirabeau Bounaparte Lamar, the new president of Texas, who was convinced the Indian and the white man could never live together.

Politics began to play a role in ranger affairs, even if indirectly. Sam Houston, a firm believer in peaceful existence with all Indians, had made sincere efforts to live in peace with the various tribes, but in doing so he sometimes promised more than he could deliver. Treaties with the Comanches had pledged that the line of settlements would not advance, but neither Houston nor anyone else could slow the movement out onto the prairie. When the Comanches discovered surveying parties in their hunting range, they felt betrayed and acted accordingly.

Lamar, as opposed to peace and compromise as Houston had been in favor of harmony, was a talented man, an intellectual, a skilled politician, a veteran of San Jacinto and as patriotic as Houston. He also hated Houston with a passion that went beyond politics. When Lamar took office in 1838, there was a decided shift in military policy. Strategy against the Indians was no longer to be defensive, a mere reaction to Indian attack. Lamar was determined to drive the tribes out of Texas.

In the closing days of 1838 an act to provide for the protection of the northern and western frontiers was passed by the Texas Congress in an attempt to reestablish the Regular Army. A regiment of 840 rank and file, divided into fifteen companies of fifty-six men, was proposed. Service was to be for three years. The various companies of the proposed regiment were to be stationed in specific locations. Each unit would build a blockhouse and clear land around the fort. A military road would connect the various forts, stretching from the Red River to the Nueces. The regiment was to be an infantry force, but the president had the authority to convert any part of it to cavalry. The act was approved December 21, 1838.[33]

No significant military force resulted from this act. Most of the money provided to organize the regiment was used up before any significant number of troops was enlisted, but some posts or forts were possibly established. Attention was turning more towards the growing threat of the Plains Indians, the Comanches. On December 29, 1838, a few days after the proposal for the Regular Army, the Texas Congress passed another act to defend the frontier and authorized eight companies to serve for six months. The men were to receive the same pay as mounted riflemen in the ranging service, as stated in the act of December 10, 1836.[34] In addition to these eight companies, another unit of fifty-six men was provided for the protection of Gonzales County and five thousand dollars set aside to cover costs for three months' service. The commander was to be appointed by the president, with the approval of the senate, and would make his reports to the commander of the first brigade, a militia unit, and to the Secretary of War.[35]

The acts clearly show that the Texas Congress made a distinction between rangers—by whatever name—and the Regular Army. The most obvious difference was in the length of service. Also, ranger units were always mounted. The chain-of-command reporting requirements, however, sug- gests a subordinate role for the ranger commander, who reported to the first brigade commander, part of the militia when organized, as well as to the Secretary of War.

The militia had continued to be a part of Texas' military force during the days of the republic, though for the most part it was a paper army. Trying to document organizational details is even more difficult than tracking down ranger units. It is likely that the basic military structure which had developed during the revolution remained in force, with all the able-bodied men within a region part of the militia for that region. From reference to certain units, there were at least three brigades. Though of little use in swiftly meeting Indian raids, the militia constituted a force that could be assembled to counter an invasion. It had one special feature that appealed to Lamar—militiamen were paid only when on active service, unlike the Regulars who were paid whether or not actively fighting.

On January 23, 1839, Congress passed another act to raise three more companies to defend Bastrop, Robertson and Milam Counties. These men were to be paid according to the act of December 10, 1836, but without any land bounty. Someone had been checking the treasury, because the act specified the men would be paid, at the end of their service, from any monies on hand not already appropriated.[36] It is difficult to sort out men and units formed under these acts, or even to know how many companies were really organized. It is generally believed that in 1839 Henry Karnes led a company formed under this authority.

Lamar was determined to fight Indians, despite the miserable condition of the Texas treasury. On January 24, 1839, an act was passed requiring the president to discharge all soldiers on active duty, or furlough them, except the regiment protecting the north and west and the Ordnance Department.[37] This left only the ranger-type companies in operation.

Three days later, now worried about conditions to the south, another act was passed by congress authorizing two companies to form a corps of rangers to defend San Patricio, Goliad and Refugio. The act makes no reference to the 1836 act, but states the men would receive twenty-five dollars a month and would furnish their own mounts, weapons and equipment. Service was to be for six months. The Secretary of the Treasury was to issue fifteen thousand dollars in promissory notes to pay the men.[38] These various acts provided for a considerable ranger force, at least on paper.

The company authorized for Gonzales County ran afoul of Texas politics when, in some unknown manner, Mathew Caldwell was designated captain. Caldwell, born in Kentucky around 1798, evidently had some reputation as a scout by 1839 but had not attracted official attention until selected as captain of this ranger company. A redhead with patches of prematurely grey hair, Caldwell was known as "Old Paint." He seemed well qualified to head a company, but Lamar vetoed the bill authorizing him to raise the fifty-six man unit. He explained he had no personal objection to Caldwell, but his selection violated the Texas Constitution under which only the president could appoint military officers. Lamar was determined to exercise his duty under the law.[39] Caldwell must have had friends who spoke in his behalf, because Lamar soon designated him as commander of the ranger company. On February 24, 1839, James W. Robinson wrote the president:

> Dr Sir,
> Capt. Mathew Caldwell of this place accepts
> the appointment you were pleased to extend to
> [him] as Captain for the term of 3 months to range
> on the frontiers of Gonzalez county & will proceed
> to raise the company as soon as possible....I do
> think him the best Capt. of Spies in Texas, even
> superior in many respects to the old veteran Deaf
> Smith. He caught a mustang stallion the other day
> & held him until his fellow hunter shot an other,
> & skinned a larriette to tie him, & they have him
> here now, an exploit not surpassed by Gen. Put-
> nam's wolf story.[40]

In late February 1839 Lamar issued a call for each county to raise a company for its protection, and most of the defense of the republic fell to these ranger-type units.[41] Some of the counties had already filled their obligation by raising units under earlier acts; others didn't bother, especially the eastern counties. Erath came back into service and was elected captain of the Milam County Rangers in March 1839. He remembered 1839 as a bad year for Indian troubles.[42]

The counties along the frontier raised companies, either by congressional authorization or other authority. Those raised under specific acts were listed by "J. Snively, Pay-master-Gen," with their estimated costs:

Field and Staff, ...	$2,450
Capt. Emberson's 6 months, Red River .	9,500
Capt. Smith and Box's, Nacodgoches and Houston	7,000
Capt. Erath's, Milam	4,430
Capt. J.D. Mathew's, R County	4,500
Capt. M. Andrew's, Lagrange	2,825
Capt. Eastland's, ...	2,400
Capt. S. Adam's, H. County	7,820
Capt. M. Caldwell's, Gonzales	4,572
Capt. N. Doyle's, R. County	4,500
Capt. Bird's, Fort Bend, ...	2,964
Capt. Smithwick's, Bastrop, ...	<u>2,225</u>
. . . .	$55,186.00

This is not a complete list of ranger commands; Snively printed a second pay estimate for ranger companies serving on the Red River frontier in 1838-1839, and none of the above units is on this second list.[43] It is also certain that Henry Karnes commanded a company operating out of San Antonio at this time, though it does not show on either of the pay estimates submitted by Snively. The funds listed are estimated sums, and it is extremely unlikely they actually received anything close to the printed amounts.

At this time, there was evidently still no generally accepted definition of a ranger company. Any volunteer unit that furnished its own weapons, clothing, equipment and horses, or paid for these items out of the members' pay, was considered a ranger company. It was partially a matter of furnishing all equipment and partially a matter of the type of service: ranging the frontier, scouting, spying. At times mounted rifle units were part of regular or militia commands, with the specific assignment of acting as scouts, such as the detachment commanded by Captain Antonio Menchaca. Part of Colonel Juan Seguin's regiment, Menchaca's unit served from October 1836 until mustered out of service when most of the army was disbanded in March 1837. The nineteen-man unit was organized from Mexican-born citizens of the municipality of San Antonio.[44]

In addition to the conventional ranger companies, there were several Indian ranger units. The act of June 1837, discussed earlier, authorized the formation of such companies from the Choctaw, Cherokee, Delaware and Shawnee tribes. One such unit was in service in 1838; the muster roll for "Capt. Panthers Comp'y of Shawney Indians" can be found among the Ranger Papers in the Texas State Archives. This company was attached to one of the militia brigades, with the brigade commander's certifying the muster roll and swearing that all of the men had horses. It is a decidedly informal document, listing thirty rangers with such names as Spy Ruck, Little Spy Ruck, Little John, Fox, Thompson, PoCoeash and Pachilla. The company commander, named Panther, became Captain Panther.[45] There is no record of this company's being in action.

Another Indian company led by Chief Castro, in service and in combat in 1839, was composed of Lipans, a small tribe that was in constant battle with the powerful Comanches. Authority for the organization of the unit is unknown; since it was not formed from the four "friendly" tribes, it could not have been from the 1837 authorization. Very likely the unsettled conditions that led to the formation of ranger units in 1839 led also to the establishment of this Lipan company, which was official enough to have a muster roll.[46]

One predominantly Hispanic ranger unit was in service during the summer of 1839. Captain Lewis Sanches' company was part of the third militia brigade, formed for duty in the Cherokee campaign. While most of the names on the muster roll are Spanish, there are several Anglo-American listings.[47] Sanches' men served over a month during the drive against the Cherokess and received $840 in payment.[48]

While many of these ranger companies undoubtedly saw service during 1838-1839, few have documented records. In January 1839 John Henry Moore took the newly formed LaGrange and Bastrop companies on a strike against the Comanches. Moore was the most prominent figure in the Bastrop area, the founder of LaGrange, and was well known and respected. He had seen service at Gonzales, and his election to command the two ranger companies was not an empty honor. Moore had been on Indian expeditions in the 1820s and in 1834 and 1835; unfortunately, he had never fought Comanches. Noah Smithwick, back in service and leading the Bastrop unit, recalled that Lipan scouts had located the Comanche encampment. Too few to risk a fight, the scouts had hurried back to the settlements to report their find and ask for help.[49]

In his report of the campaign, Moore mentioned he was forwarding the muster rolls of the three companies formed by an act of Congress for the protection of the frontier, the units' being activated January 25 and placed under his command;[50] however, every record of the march and fight lists only two ranger companies, those of Smithwick and William M. Eastland, plus Lipan scouts led by Castro. It is quite possible Moore's third company was the Lipan spy unit commanded by Castro.

The small force of sixty-three Americans and sixteen Lipan scouts left LaGrange the morning of January 26, 1839, and marched up the banks of the Colorado River. It was very cold and the men, departing with only salt, coffee and some bacon, had made no real provisions for a winter campaign. A trader sold them beef, at a cheap price because they were going to fight Indians.[51] Bad luck would dodge the expedition. They were forced to take shelter at the head of the Lampasas River while a severe norther passed. One of the Lipans in the camp knocked over a rifle, accidently firing the weapon and wounding one of the rangers. Moore sent the injured man back with two other rangers, but he died on the way and was buried on the banks of the Colorado.

The column marched through terrible weather, following a spy detachment of two rangers and two Lipans who kept well ahead trying to find the Comanche camp. The main body was near the San Saba River on February 13 when the spies returned and told Moore they had found the camp. The combined force started out the following day, moving through the trees in the Colorado bottoms, traveling northwest towards the junction with the San Saba. Although he was the senior commander, Moore was not the most experienced man in the group and was careless with the horses when he had his men hide their packs in a sheltered location. No guards were left to watch the animals. The Indian horses were picketed some distance from the camp, and after sunset eight Lipans led by Juan, one of Castro's men, managed to cut out a considerable number without attracting attention. The Comanches evidently considered their camp far enough from the settlements to be safe from attack and had little security either for their horses or for their main camp. The valuable horses secured, the Lipans started them back to their own camp, as ordered, leaving the others to fight the battle. Moore divided his companies—Eastland and the LaGrange men on the right, Smithwick's Bastrop boys in the center, Castro and the remaining scouts on the left.

It was difficult to make a thorough reconnaissance in the dark, and the spies who had located the camp had not made a thorough check of the terrain nor estimated how many braves might be in the area. Moore, doing the best he could in the circumstances, decided to drive the Indians away from the shelter of the woods and out onto the open prairie, keeping the woods to his back. Eastland opened the attack, marching down between the woods and the camp at first light, then Moore gave the order for everyone to charge. The entire force rushed the camp, taking most of the Comanches by surprise. The rangers broke into the tepees, shooting many Indians in their sleeping robes. Although the rangers and Lipans had achieved an initial surprise, they were in turn themselves surprised by the large number of Indians in the camp area. In their eagerness the rangers had all fired at much the same time, and the entire command thus had to reload at the same time. Surprised, many unhurt Comanches momentarily rushed into the open, but a meandering creek provided a shelter where the Comanches rallied to form a defense line.

At this point Moore's report and the recollections of some of the rangers begin to differ. Moore stated that there had been good light when they first attacked, but soon the powder smoke covered the camp area and he ordered a retreat to reload and regroup. Smithwick stated flatly that Moore ordered a retreat for no good reason at a critical moment when everyone was busy recharging their rifles.[52] Castro was so disgusted he walked away, taking his Lipans with him. Falling back in some confusion, the Texans managed to reload and began firing at the Comanches, who had started a charge of their own. Close fighting continued until about ten o'clock in the morning when the Comanches suddenly drew back, firing from a considerable distance. The fortunate break in contact was probably due to the loss of the Comanche chief; loss of an Indian leader usually halted their combat until a new leader could be selected.

At 11:30 Moore ordered another retreat. Some of the rangers had been scouting during the lull in the fighting and had estimated that there were five hundred Comanches in the area. Although undoubtedly high, this estimate was enough to keep the Texans moving. The Texas wounded were hauled back on make-shift litters to where the horses had been tied; Moore's report does not mention that they found almost all their horses had been stolen by Comanches!

While the rangers were checking on the few remaining mounts, a Comanche party approached with a white flag and a parley took place, obviously an attempt by the Indians to discover how many Texans were still alive and whether they had taken any prisoners. The Lipans had captured several Comanches in the initial attack, but soon killed them. Evidently the Comanche party had been badly mauled in the fighting; when they saw the rangers had no prisoners and seemed about to leave, the Indians simply broke off the parley and departed.

The Texans were willing to call it quits and started on the long march home, taking turns carrying the six wounded men on litters. Although Moore did not mention he had any horses stolen, he did note they lost a "considerable number in all, including those that had died from various causes, forty-six." He did report that the Lipans managed to run off ninety-six Comanche horses, but they turned in only forty-six at LaGrange.

Moore graciously commended several officers of his command, including Eastland and a Lieutenant Dawson of the LaGrange company. He cited Lieutenant Bain of the Bastrop unit and his adjutant and praised all the other officers and men for their bravery and subordination and good conduct. Moore estimated, he thought conservatively, that they had killed thirty to forty Comanches and wounded fifty to sixty.[53] It was a victory of sorts, though the loss of nearly all their horses embarrassed many of the rangers, who still had much to learn about fighting Comanches. Moore was a brave man, but the Plains Indians were a formidable foe. To his credit, he learned fast.

Continuing Indian raids, or threats of raids, caused settlers on the upper Brazos, Trinity and Colorado rivers to petition congress for help. A small company commanded by Lieutenant W.G. Evans was formed in Houston, and John Bird formed a fifty-nine man company from the vicinity of what would be Austin. These units met at Fort Milam, an army post about two miles from present-day Marlin. Bird assumed command of the combined units after his arrival on May 6, and on May 20 he left the fort with fifty men, marching to Fort Smith on the Little River. They encountered no Indians on the march. Bird seriously reduced his available forces when he had trouble with deserters and sent back a strong detachment guarding five men accused of deserting, with orders to report to Colonel Edward Burleson, who was apparently the nearest army commander.

On a Sunday afternoon, May 26, Bird left his temporary camp with thirty-five men to search for Indians. Ranger scouts eventually located a trail. About five miles out on the prairie the unit saw a small group of Indians and chased them for several miles, but the Indians managed to keep out of range and Captain Bird finally called his men to a halt. The rangers regrouped and were walking their tired horses back along their trail when they were suddenly rushed by as many as forty Comanches, yelling, circling and firing their arrows. The rangers broke through the circling braves and gained the shelter of a small ravine some six hundred yards away. The Comanches moved out of range atop a slight rise about three hundred yards from the rangers, and in a short time a large force of as many as two hundred warriors joined the first band.

After much yelling and shaking of lances and shields, the Comanches attacked the men in the ravine from several directions, but the rangers took their time, firing in relay, always with loaded rifles for any individual or group that came too close. Their steady rifle fire broke two charges, and the Indians retreated with some of their dead and wounded but left many dead and wounded horses. The fighting died down, but each force held its position, the rangers in the ravine and the Indians on the hill until dusk when the Indians split into two groups and rode off. Bird had been killed early in the fight and Nathan Brookshire, who had assumed command, had their four dead rangers buried in the ravine banks. The other rangers, carrying two wounded, started back to Fort Smith and arrived about two in the morning.

Bird's unit had achieved a rather more decisive victory than had Moore's; Brookshire estimated they had killed thirty or forty and wounded about the same number. The Indians had been mostly Comanche, but there had apparently been some Caddo and Kickapoo warriors with them, judging by the number of firearms used against the rangers.[54]

However dearly won, this fight reveals the growing experience of the rangers and the continuing use of a tactical system utilizing terrain for shelter and firing in relays. Bird may have had advance knowledge of the Comanche trick of using a few decoys to lure unwary pursuit into an ambush, or he may have just been cautious when he halted the initial chase of the small group of Indians.

Bird's fight with a large Comanche war party was one of several Indian engagements in early 1839. Burleson had a fight, in late February near Bastrop, against a combined

band of Caddos, Wacos and Keechies, inflicting some casualties[55] and raising a troubling question: what would happen if some or all of the interior tribes joined with the distant
Comanches? Worse, what would result if the Indians joined
with Mexican forces? The Texans could count on Lipan
loyalty, and the so-called settled tribes had seldom caused
trouble, but now, suddenly, it seemed possible that all the
tribes might join the Mexicans to attack the republic.

Suspicions raised by incidents in the Miracle journal
were found to be well-justified causes for alarm. In May 1839
the activities of another spy party of Mexicans disclosed
further plans to start a full-scale Indian war. On May 14
between San Antonio and Seguin, a combined group of
Indians and Mexicans came upon a man named Ballenger
and three Mexican helpers who were away from their main
party, probably on a surveying job. There was no reason to
risk disclosure by showing themselves, but the Mexican and
Indian spies murdered all four men. The sound of firing
alerted the rest of the party, who rode to the spot, found the
four bodies, and immediately rode to San Antonio to spread
the alarm.

An express reached Burleson on May 17, and the following morning he rode out with about two hundred men to try
to locate the trail of what they supposed was an Indian war
party. The Mexicans, evidently believing the four men they
had killed had been alone, made no attempt to hide, scatter,
or even increase their pace across the unsettled country, and
were slowed by their pack train of over a hundred animals
bearing a large load of powder and lead. By sheer chance
Captain Micah Andrews, out with his rangers on a routine
scout, cut their trail on the Colorado River about ten miles
west of Austin.[56]

Andrews was a large man and his horse had begun to
slow just as they crossed the maze of prints, so he sent
Lieutenant James O. Rice and seventeen men of his company to follow the fresh trail of the invaders. The ranger
detachment rode at full speed, catching up with the Indian-
Mexican escort and the pack train on the banks of the San
Gabriel about twenty-five miles from Austin. Even though
they estimated the opposing force at twenty to thirty Mexi-

cans and Indians, Rice and his seventeen men charged and killed the leader, Manuel Flores, and two other men in the first rush. Though they outnumbered the rangers, the remaining members of the party abandoned their pack animals and scattered in every direction, some towards the Brazos Falls. The rangers gathered up the pack animals and considerable quantities of equipment and supplies.

The most valuable finds were several incriminating papers found on Flores, including a letter from another Mexican agent, known as Cordova, who regretted he could not accompany Flores on this trip but who would continue to be part of the plan to incite Indians in Texas.[57] These papers were part of a series of documents that seemed to indicate that the Cherokees and other East Texas tribes had been plotting with Mexican officials to fight the Texans. The Mexicans were inciting the Indians in hopes of forming a buffer between the United States and Texas, but how far the Cherokees and other tribes really intended to cooperate is still disputed. They certainly listened. They had delegations in Matamoros at least once, and they definitely accepted powder and lead and weapons from the Mexicans, but whether or not they agreed to help, other than talk, will never be known.

On April 10, 1839, Albert Sidney Johnston had written Cherokee Chief Bowles a friendly but cautionary letter warning against engaging in any Mexican alliance. Johnston told Bowles he knew of earlier comunications and meetings with Cordova, but Texas would keep the peace as long as the Cherokees refrained from aggressive actions or any alliance with unfriendly Indians.[58]

Other than providing interesting speculation for later historians, peace overtures during this period did not really matter—Lamar had already decided on a policy of driving the Indians from Texas. The East Texas tribes had entered Texas about the same time as the first American settlers and had occupied fertile and desirable lands. They had farmed with considerable success, and Anglo-American land speculators wanted their land. For the most part, these Indians had lived in peace with their neighbors, although after the revolution there had been some talk of raiding. The 1839 report of the Secretary of War listed several serious breaches of the peace in the preceding year. In one incident a family of eighteen people, men, women and children, had been massacred, supposedly by Plains Indians. Later, it was discovered the Cherokees had been responsible.[59]

President Lamar began to move to rid the country of Indians, and nothing would be done to stop the march toward a fighting conclusion. Martin Lacy was appointed commissioner to the Cherokees and other tribes and sent with instructions to preserve the peace until the condition of the Indians could be brought to the consideration of congress.

At this time, a Major Walters was authorized to raise two companies for six months to occupy the "Saline of the Neches," where his men could prevent traffic between the Cherokees and the Comanches. Walters, able to form only one company, marched to the Saline where Bowles told him through the commissioner, that any attempt to establish a post would be repelled by force.[60] Unable to fight the entire Cherokee nation, the volunteers retreated to the west bank of the Neches and established a post.

Colonel Burleson, forming a command on the Colorado in preparation for a strike at the Brazos and Trinity Indians, was instructed to change his plans and proceed to Cherokee country. Shortly after this change in plans, Burleson intercepted letters from General Canalizo, the Mexican commander in Matamoros, containing more plans and instructions inciting the Cherokees to engage in war with the Texans.[61] As a result, Burleson was directed to increase his command to four hundred men and to march against the Cherokees, but Burleson was not able to recruit this many men nor to begin his march at the time directed. He started with what he had on July 14, 1839, and was joined by militia troops from Shelby, Sabine, Harrison and San Augustine commanded by Colonel Willis H. Landrum. The Nacogdoches militia regiment was already in the field, awaiting orders. All of the various units were placed under the command of Brigadier General Kelsey H. Douglass.

The campaign to drive the Cherokees out of Texas began on July 15, 1839, when the entire Texas force moved to attack the main Cherokee settlement on the Neches. Colonel Landrum's troops crossed to the west bank of the Neches and moved up the river. Burleson's men and the Nacogdoches regiment under Colonel Thomas J. Rusk marched directly on the main camp, but the Indians had retreated to a strong position near a Delaware village about six miles distant. Captain James Carter's spy company, joined by twenty-five men from Captain Jackson Todd's company of mounted volunteers, located the retreating Indians. A brisk fight developed, and the mounted troops were soon joined by the main body of Texas infantry, which formed a line and charged, firing as it came. It was almost sundown when the firing began, and the Cherokees managed to slip away during the night, but the Texans captured considerable baggage and supplies, including five kegs of powder and 250 pounds of lead. They found many horses and cattle and stores of corn in the village.[62]

About ten o'clock the next morning General Kelsey H. Douglass started in pursuit of the Indians, led by Carter's spy company, and again they encountered the Indians. Fighting began immediately and the Cherokees put up a stubborn and well-conducted defense before they were finally driven back. It was not a cheap victory for the Texans, but Chief Bowles had been killed and the Cherokees had lost their villages and lands, animals and supplies. The Texans destroyed everything of value—villages, corn fields, abandoned equipment and supplies—as they pursued the Indians. Scouts and spies, working on a wide front well in advance of the main column, decided on July 25 that there was no organized Indian force remaining in the region and further pursuit was useless.[63] It was the end of the Cherokee Nation in Texas.

The remnants of the Cherokee tribes fled to Arkansas and other parts of the United States. The Shawnees signed a treaty with Texas and were paid for their lands and escorted out of the country. The other tribes lost everything and scattered into the United States or Mexico. The defeat and expulsion of the East Texas tribes left only the Indians on the Brazos and the Trinity rivers in close proximity to the Texas settlements, and it seemed that a considerable potential for trouble had been removed. In the process, a sizable amount of desirable farm land had become available for Texans to settle on.

Troops in this campaign were mainly militia units, with some companies that could be considered ranger-type commands. In his report, General Douglass mentions the spy company led by Captain Carter. This certainly indicates a ranger unit, but lists of the companies and units taking part in the campaign do not include a company by that name.[64] Douglass mentions that companies led by Captains Todd and Tipps were sent to the aid of the spy company, and these two companies do show on the payment list for the fighting. Muster rolls in the archives indicate these two companies were mounted volunteer commands.[65]

There were two other ranging units in the campaign, led by Captains James Lewis and Mark B. Ownsby. These units performed ably in the fighting and are mentioned by Douglass in his report, but they are not on any pay records because the men were volunteers, a technicality that may have kept other deserving companies from leaving any written records. As mentioned earlier, another ranger-type company was led by Captain Sanches, receiving some pay and official notice.

The complete listing of ranger, spy, mounted volunteers, mounted riflemen and other units in the ranging service in these early days of the Texas Republic will never be known. Records were not always maintained and many documents have been lost over the years, but a number of pay or muster rolls remain for detachments or companies which qualify as ranger-type commands:

> A detachment of Fannin County Mounted Gunmen, a sixteen-man unit led by a lieutenant, served as part of the 2nd Regiment of the 4th Brigade from December 1, 1838, to January 14, 1839.
>
> Captain James W. Sims' Company of Volunteer Mounted Riflemen was active from August 2, 1839, to November 2, 1839. There is a notation on his muster roll "that each Member of the Company

Mounted and equipped him Self as the Law directs for Mounted Riflemen." Another notation shows a horse was lost in service, valued at $100.00.

Captain James Smith had a company of spies and signed his roll, "Capt of Spies." This company served from March-September 1839 as part of the 2nd Regiment of the 3rd Brigade.[66]

This is a random sampling of many company rolls that remain in the Ranger Archives. Other units were officially designated as ranger commands during 1839. John Emberson's company, listed earlier, saw much service on the northeastern frontier along the Red River. Emberson's activities and his opinions on Indians were important enough for forwarding to the United States for information.[67] Working with Emberson was a company in Fannin County. Supply estimates for six months of service show them requesting beef, corn, salt and coffee. They also needed—or requested—five kegs of powder and five hundred pounds of lead. The requisitions of a thousand gun flints and two dozen percussion caps reveal the still-widespread use of flintlock weapons by the rangers.[68] Other documented ranger units are listed in an appropriation bill for the Gonzales Rangers for 1839 and for "Captain Wortham's co of rangers" from September 30,1838 to September 30, 1839.[69]

A number of individuals were beginning to emerge as local commanders, ready to "range" the land after Indians, such as Ben McCulloch and his brother Henry. Both men had fought at San Jacinto and then settled in the area around Seguin and Gonzales. Early in 1839 Ben planned a winter campaign, using some Tonkawa guides, but a massive snow and sleet storm, rare for the area, completely blocked any travel. Trees were so laden with ice most of the limbs broke off; brush and undergrowth turned into an icy barrier. The ice and snow were so unusual that most of the men in the area refused to leave home, even when the weather cleared somewhat. The McCulloch brothers finally found three men willing to hunt Indians, and the five men started out across the snow with some Tonkawa scouts. Surprisingly they cut a trail of some foot Indians heading towards Gonzales, probably Comanches out to steal horses.

The small party caught up with thirteen Indians, who saw them and hid in the icy brush. McCulloch placed the Tonkawas in a line to cut off retreat, while he and the other settlers opened fire into the tangle of twigs and ice. The rifle balls tore through the concealment, which offered no protection, killing four of the Indians. The others fled, easily bypassing the Tonkawa scouts.[70]

As the decade ended, the ranger tradition was firmly established in Texas. A considerable part of the day-to-day defense had been provided by the rangers, spies, mounted riflemen or other ranger-type companies. A growing number of experienced frontiersmen with Indian-fighting experience were becoming known as leaders, or potential leaders ready to organize and lead ranger companies.

—3—

Tools of the Trade

At least some of the success the Texans had achieved in their battles had been due to their widespread use of rifles far superior to the muskets and other, less technologically advanced weapons used by the Mexicans and Indians. The Anglo-American settlers in Texas brought along the weapons and tools they had used in the United States. For the most part, these early colonists came from the southern states and the then-frontier states of Kentucky and Tennessee, where they used a weapon which modern collectors call a "Kentucky Rifle."

This weapon was actually developed by colonial gunsmiths in Pennsylvania who modified earlier German rifles to suit frontier conditions. By the time of the American Revolution, this had become a somewhat standard weapon, ideally suited to hunting and fighting in the woods. The rifles became so popular in the wild Kentucky country that they became known as "Kentuckies." A typical Kentucky rifle was roughly shoulder high, with an octagonal barrel forty-four to forty-six inches long. The caliber, ranging from .36 to .45, was small in comparison to the .69 caliber of the military muskets still in use.

A distinctive feature of the Kentucky-Pennsylvania rifle was the pronounced drop in the stock, which was generally made of polished maple or cherry. Fittings were of brass, often ornamented. All of the weapons were flintlock with gun locks of iron. Many were works of art.[1]

A rifle had a distinct advantage in accuracy and range over a smoothbore musket. Legendary tales of rifle accuracy abound in story books, but controlled tests with old weapons or replicas verify the fabled accuracy; a good marksman with a Kentucky could hit a target at a hundred yards with the accuracy of a modern weapon. Even though body hits at two hundred yards were not difficult, and the killing range stretched as far as three hundred yards, the Kentucky's lighter ball was subject to wind drift at increased ranges, decreasing velocity and killing power at ranges over a hundred yards. Still, when compared to the standard musket of the 1800s, inaccurate beyond fifty yards, the rifle was in a special class.

The drawback of the rifle was the time required to load and reload. Like the musket, the Kentucky rifle was a muzzle loader. The ball had to be rammed down the muzzle, using a greased patch to grip the raised rifling to compensate for the difference between the size of the rifled bore and the projectile. Properly centering and ramming the patched ball took time and skill. Loaded cartridges could not be used in these rifles; in this respect the musket was superior. Even though both rifle and musket required the same time to charge the pan, it was a more simple matter to load a smoothbore weapon, even if with loose powder and ball. Most military muskets, however, employed paper cartridges containing both powder and shot which could be placed in the bore and rammed home in one thrust of the ramrod. While a rifleman was firing one round, the soldier with a musket could fire several.

Because of the time required to reload, the rifle played little part in eighteenth and early nineteenth century warfare. Although riflemen could inflict casualties at ranges far beyond the reach of the infantry musket, well-disciplined troops with muskets could take these losses and return greater firepower at closer ranges. Despite fond legends to the contrary, rifles played little role in winning the American Revolution, and the men who came to Texas were hunters and farmers, not soldiers. In the early 1820s they settled in Texas' wooded country, much like their old homes, and the Kentucky rifle was their ideal weapon.

By the early 1800s the southern mountain people had started developing a rifle that became known as the Tennessee or "mountain" rifle. It was easier to handle and had a heavier bullet; the barrel was cut back to thirty-eight inches and the size of the bore increased to allow a projectile that could bring down bigger game. Walnut began to replace maple and cherry because the heavier barrels required stocks stronger and more in line with the barrels than were the old, dropped-curve stocks. Brass fittings gave way to iron.

The new rifle was just as accurate as before and was more suited for use on horseback. Along with the earlier, longer-barreled rifles, Texas settlers arrived with many weapons with these newer modifications which they found more suited to the frontier conditions as they advanced out onto more open country inhabited by buffalo and other large game not easily brought down with the older and lighter Kentuckies. They also found the heavy balls were better able to penetrate the padded leather shields of the Comanches.

The Tennessee, or mountain, rifle was joined in the late 1830s by another variant, now known as the Plains rifle, as frontiersmen and traders began encountering large game such as buffalo that could not be stopped by the smaller caliber Kentucky and Tennessee rifles. Gunsmiths, especially those in St. Louis, brought the Plains rifle to full development around 1840, and it remained the premier rifle until the development of cartridge weapons.

The Plains rifles were usually better constructed than were the earlier rifles, many of which did not have buttplates. The St. Louis gunsmiths were fine craftsmen and manufactured excellent weapons, but they did not go in for the fancy work that distinguished the earlier Kentucky long rifles. Stocks were almost never carved, and the fittings were of plain iron which did not reflect the sun. These advanced rifles, initially designed for the hunters and trappers on the northern plains and in the Rocky Mountains, soon found their way to Texas, which had developed a significant amount of trade with St. Louis. Soon the numerous smiths in New Orleans were also exporting these weapons to Texas.[2]

A few smiths became famous in the weapons industry. Frontiersmen coveted the Henry or Hawken rifles, and a number of superb rifles made by Eastern gunsmiths found their way to Texas.[3] There are no records of any smiths in Texas making rifles, but numerous pay vouchers and receipts indicate that there was a considerable number of smiths who could modify and repair all types of weapons.

All of these rifles were flintlocks, and this ignition form continued in use through the Texas Republic era. Introduction in the 1820s of the percussion cap to fire the powder charge was a marked improvement, the first new feature in firearms in centuries, but was an innovation not immediately adopted everywhere. Because of the cost of percussion caps and an uncertain supply source, requisitions in the archives show flint continued to be the ignition form of choice for many years even after caps were available. As the cost decreased and supplies became more certain, caps began to replace flint by the 1840s, but the old ignition form remained in use well through the Mexican War.

Fortunately for rifle owners, the adaptation from flint to percussion did not require a new rifle. The old lock was unscrewed, the hammer and pan and frizzen removed, a new hammer placed on the old fittings, and a special plug threaded into the old torch hole to hold the cap. The entire procedure was relatively inexpensive, using parts mass produced in one of the big gunsmith plants in New Orleans, St. Louis or Pennsylvania. With these parts, Texas gunsmiths and blacksmiths were easily capable of converting old rifles into percussion arms.

Popular belief would have it that every settler entering Texas carried a rifle. This is obviously not true. Cost of a smoothbore musket, as opposed to the far more expensive rifle, had much to do with the number or arms of each type in use in early Texas. Certainly not every settler used a rifle, and some early rangers undoubtedly used muskets. After December 1836 a rifle was specifically required for rangers, as described in the previous chapter, but rifles were probably in extensive use before this date. Noah Smithwick, for example, mentions using a rifle in the scout to find Mrs. Hibbons.[4] As improvements and modifications made the rifle more suited to mounted combat, it came into wider use by the rangers.

There is little documentation that sheds any light on how widespread was the use of rifles throughout Texas. The only record is a report by Mexican General Adrian Woll covering his expedition into Texas in 1842 [this invasion and Woll's report are covered in detail in Chapter Six]. Woll has two lists showing arms and equipment he claims his force captured from the Texans. His figures are possibly inaccurate, and there is no way of knowing who owned the arms, but the numbers are of some interest. Woll reported he captured 165 rifles and only sixty-five muskets, as well as twelve double-barreled muskets which were probably shotguns.[5] It should be noted that rangers used shotguns from time to time, as requisitions for buckshot indicate. In a close fight, a double load of buckshot was a deadly ally!

The rifle, in whatever form, was the basic weapon for the rangers, but another weapon was needed for fighting at close quarters or to fall back on when the rifle was empty.

The early rangers carried at least one pistol, when they could afford one, and several if possible. Pistols were a necessity in combating Comanches, whose battle tactics included close combat with their long lances after showering the rangers with longer-range arrows. The average pistol of the day was a very inaccurate weapon, suitable for use only at close range and when fighting Indians on foot.

Although the rifle had become somewhat standardized by the 1840s, pistols were of every size, caliber and design. Little is known about specific makers of the pistols used by the early rangers. James Nichols, a ranger of the republic period, told how he fired his rifle, slipped the empty weapon into a holder attached to the saddle horn, then drew "a larg Deringer." Nichols possessed a pair of English, brass-mounted holster pistols as well as his Deringer belt pistol.[6] The rangers often carried pistols in holsters on either side of the saddle horn, their "holster pistols;" additional "belt" pistols were stuck through the belt. Another settler, John C. Duval, also mentions Deringer pistols as being used during the late 1830s and early 1840s.[7] Henry Deringer became famous for manufacturing a single shot pistol that became a gambler's favorite and was the weapon used to kill Abraham Lincoln. Deringer also made larger pistols which were popular in Texas, and he is one of the few pistol makers identified by name in early ranger annals. Most of these early pistols, like the rifles, were flintlocks, but by the late 1830s pistols began to be modified for percussion caps. Woll's report supports the extensive use of pistols by 1842; he claimed that one hundred pistols and fifty-eight pairs of pocket pistols were taken in the fighting around San Antonio.[8]

A major advance in firearms during the mid-1830s was the introduction of a true revolving firearm. The idea, like most developments in firearms, was old, almost as old as gunpowder, but the early concept was limited by the lack of technology until a young inventor, Samuel Colt, took advantage of both the developing technological advances and his own inventive genius to patent the first practical repeating firearm in 1836.

Part of his success was due to the invention of the percussion cap. Even though double-barreled weapons were possible and had been in use for years, a true revolver was impossible using a flintlock. The technology of the industrial revolution provided Colt with something approaching a crude assembly line to mass produce his new weapons. The young inventor's most important innovation was in devising a system that revolved a chamber holding the powder and shot, locked the chamber in line with the barrel, and fired the charge when the trigger was pulled. Cocking the hammer revolved the chamber and aligned another charge for firing. Before Colt, repeating weapons had been multiple-barreled arms requiring each barrel to be revolved by hand prior to being fired.

The new Colt revolver held five charges in the cylinder, firing through a single, fixed, rifled barrel. Although these early weapons used a ball, the rifling gave considerable velocity and accuracy far superior to smoothbore pistols and muskets.[9] Colt made a number of improvements to his initial 1836 patent, the most important the addition of a loading lever in 1839 so that the cylinder could be reloaded without disassembling the revolver.

With his business partner, John Ehlers, Colt established a factory in Paterson, New Jersey, The Patent Arms Manufacturing Company, and began producing revolvers, carbines and rifles. During the time he was in production—1836 to 1842—his weapons were known as Patent Arms and were generally so listed in documents and contracts involving the Texas Republic. This has led to some confusion among recent writers, because the term "Colt Patent Arms" was also used in some of Colt's early advertisements in 1838.

Firing five shots almost as fast as a man could get off a single round with other pistols of the day, the Colt should have been an instant favorite. Despite accuracy and firepower, however, the new weapons did not catch on with the general public. Much of the failure to sell was simply a matter of money; the Colts were costly. The earlier single-shot pistols were clumsy but nevertheless hardy weapons, suitable for firing or clubbing, while the Colt was a relatively fragile weapon. The cylinder had to be removed for reloading in early models, and the frame and barrel were held together by a wedge. If this wedge was not properly fixed, the weapon could fall apart in firing. Even after the addition of the loading lever, simplifying recharging, a careless or hasty replacement of the wedge could cause the revolver to malfunction.

There were few potential customers in the relatively peaceful East. Colt's only chance for a commercial success was to sell his new weapons to the United States government. Military boards for the evaluation of weapons were extremely conservative; army and navy officials tested his weapons at length but eventually refused to make any major buys. Colt tried civilian markets in New York and advertised in New Orleans in 1838.[10] He personally took his weapons to the troops fighting the Seminoles in Florida in 1839 and obtained some highly favorable indorsements from individual officers, but no orders.[11] In 1841 he was advertising in St. Louis.

The first substantial sales he made were to the Texas government, when the Texas navy bought over a hundred Patent Arms. On April 29, 1839, Texas' Secretary of the Navy authorized Captain Edwin W. Moore, Commander of the Navy, to purchase 180 carbines and a like number of pistols, with loading levers and necessary accessorics.[12] The navy could not pay for the new weapons without getting a loan, but the government allowed ten percent interest per annum until the sum could be raised. Such documentation that has survived suggests they actually purchased 130 arms of each type. The Secretary of the Navy noted in his report for the year 1839 that the weapons had been received.[13]

There was some opposition to the new weapons. Ordnance officers in Texas were just as conservative as their counterparts in the United States—willing to test the Colts but seeing little place for them in warfare. In 1839 the Texas Chief of Ordnance, Colonel George W. Hockley, supervised Texas' purchase of flintlock muskets from the Tyson firm in Philadelphia. One of the reasons cited was cost—a musket cost twelve dollars and the Colt rifle was fifty-five dollars. In a report to the Secretary of War, Hockley mentioned he had rejected the Colt rifle.[14]

During the late 1830s and 1840s, evidently the Texas navy, army and ordnance departments each had authority to purchase weapons. To most historians, the first navy contract accounted for the bulk of the Colts, or Patent Arms sold in Texas, a belief supported by the only printed account, the Secretary of the Navy's report. In the report the Secretary also mentioned that an initial purchase of Patent Arms for the army had been refused by the Secretary of War, but there is no explanation for this rejection. Just who ordered the arms is not known, nor how many, nor why they were turned back. Nor is there any explanation of why and how the army *did* reorder Patent Arms a few months later.

Recently discovered documentation shows that Texas' army, on August 3, 1839, did order fifty Colt carbines with bullet molds, other accessories and equipment, at a unit cost of fifty-five dollars. It also contracted for fifty belt pistols, with loading levers, bullet molds and equipment, at a unit cost of thirty-five dollars. With an eye to unsafe conditions in the Republic, the army allowed an extra $281.25 to guarantee safe delivery. Fifty rifles were later added to this order.[15] On October 5, 1839, an additional forty belt pistols, thirty carbines and fifty rifles, with all accessories and equipment, plus the insurance, were ordered. On January 9, 1840, an additional 160 belt pistols, with all equipment and accessories, were ordered.[16]

There is no way to ever know if all these arms were received in Texas, but from scattered documentation it is clear that a considerable number of the Colt arms reached the republic and were issued to various units. An Ordnance Department memo, dated March 24, 1840, lists five cases of Patent Arms, in good order, in Galveston awaiting shipment to Austin. There is a notation of sixteen Patent Arms' being sent to one of the mounted infantry companies raised by the War Department in February 1840.[17] The 1st Infantry Regiment had thirty Patent Arms in the spring of 1840.[18] Vouchers for payment due on repair work show the weapons were in field use,[19] so these weapons had considerable wear and tear, if little or no combat use. Another indication that the weapons received were issued to the troops is the 1843 inventory of Texas armories, which does not list a single Patent Arms weapon in storage, although there were quantities of other small arms, especially the Tyson muskets.[20] There are several other interesting documents bearing on Colt weapons: the Treasury Department notified the Ordnance Department that a certain Lieutenant William A. Tennison was charged with the loss of one Colt pistol worth $37.50, a minor matter considering that a Lieutanant I.P. Lansing, deceased, was charged with the loss of thirty Colt pistols![21] Woll's report of equipment supposedly captured by the Mexicans in 1842 lists two rifles with five-shot cylinders, clearly Colts. He also mentions five weapons with seven-shot cylinders, probably the eight-shot variety of Colt's rifle. There is nothing to indicate that he captured any Colt revolvers.[22]

Despite the Texas sales, Colt did not have wide commercial success, and his firm went bankrupt in 1842. Some of his troubles were due to not being able to collect full payment for the sales to the Republic of Texas. Although Colt retained his patents, his partner, John Ehlers, obtained the business, such as it was, including a large supply of parts, and began assembling weapons. He was advertising Colt weapons in New York in 1843.[23] As late as December 1844, Ehlers was still trying to collect on the Texas debt, which amounted to slightly over $10,000. His memorandum requesting payment outlined *all* the orders by Texas, not just the initial navy contract [see footnote #15].

The new revolvers were available throughout most of the United States, and some undoubtedly reached Texas through commercial and business channels as well as through the military channels. There are a few accounts of Colt revolvers' being used in fights and duels in Texas in the 1840s. A few members of the Santa Fe Expedition in 1842 owned Patent Arms. Since the abortive expedition was basically a civilian enterprise, these arms must have been purchased commercially.[24] However, because newspapers and early writers frequently mentioned any use of weapons other than the older rifles and single-shot pistols most commonly used, it is safe to assume that Colts were not in wide use in the civilian community.

Colt had considerable competition in the revolving arms business. One repeater, the Allen, a multi-barrel pistol, clumsy and barrel-heavy but which cost only eighteen dollars, less than half the cost of the superior Colt, far outsold Colt's revolver. There is one mention of combat use of an Allen in Texas in 1840.[25]

John W. Cochran invented a repeating rifle, using the idea of a revolving cylinder firing through a single barrel. Unlike Colt, he used a flat, round turret to hold the multiple charges. These rifles were eight or nine-shot arms, and there are several documented uses of them in combat in Texas.[26] Ordnance records show repairs on nine-shot weapons, which had to be Cochran rifles.

Every ranger used a knife both as a secondary weapon and as a basic camp tool. In later years the designation "Bowie knife" became famous and was applied to every form of large knife. As is often the case, the legends about knives make better reading than dull, historic fact.

Contemporary accounts of the time frequently describe men fighting with butcher knives, a term used so often that it must have been a rather standard piece of equipment. One muster roll shows three men being issued butcher knives at a unit cost of one dollar each.[27] The butcher knife was large enough and had a stiff enough blade to be used both as a combat weapon and for preparing food in camp.

Noah Smithwick, who has figured in this narrative before, was a blacksmith by trade and left a specific account of the so-called Bowie knife which Bowie had used in a celebrated knife fight to disembowel two opponents. According to Smithwick, the knife was nothing special, other than for the blade, and had a plain wooden handle. Because the knife had saved his life, Bowie had the blade polished and remounted in an ivory, silver-decorated handle. Not wishing to ruin the now-celebrated weapon, he asked Smithwick to duplicate the knife with plain mountings. Smithwick's duplicate had a ten-inch blade, two inches broad at the widest part. Smithwick said he made a considerable number of copies, selling them for five to twenty dollars depending on the finish.[28] As is the case with much of the ranger story, other men later recalled that it was they or relatives who had made the knife for Bowie, but Smithwick is the only one with specific details and a plausible story.

It is quite possible that Smithwick's long, heavy blade became known as a Bowie knife. Lists of weapons supposedly captured by General Woll in the 1842 invasion show Bowie knives and "ordinary knives"[29] without further identification. Smithwick's ten-inch knife was sufficiently different to be considered a special weapon. In addition, the Texans used imported English knives from the factories in Sheffield and Birmingham.

As the population increased and more and more single men came to Texas, there was a larger group of non-family young men to fill the ranger units, men for whom an Indian chase or turning back a Mexican raid was more exciting than farming. These were the natural fighters, but they were a relatively small part of the population. It would take considerable time to recount the chases that never started because the settlers had to stop and mold bullets. No writer has ever assembled the names of the early settlers along the frontier who neglected to take a weapon with them when they went outside to perform some farm chore and fell easy prey to

Indian raiders. Although there are countless examples of families fighting to the death to protect their homes, many driving off larger numbers of Indians, defending a house was not the same as being able to ride for days, track signs across endless prairies, then fight and survive.

If the developing skills and the technologically advanced weapons of the individual rangers were critical to success, the growing confidence and ability of the company captains became the feature that enabled the rangers to fight generally superior numbers with such success. By the end of the republic period, there was a pool of what can be classed as well-armed, professional rangers.

—4—

Comanches

It is doubtful if people in Texas saw any great promise for improvement as 1840 began. Finances in the republic were not good, and there was always the possibility of a Mexican invasion. The Comanches were quiet, but the threat of raids was always present. In the towns and in the settled farm communities along the exposed frontiers, people were too busy trying to make a living and stay alive to worry much about the future. It was just as well there was no gift of foresight—1840 would be a troubled year.

One bright spot in the year was the appointment of John Coffee Hays as a ranger captain. In a few years Hays would become the premier ranger leader, but when he received his first command in 1840 he was relatively unknown. Hays was born in Tennessee on January 28, 1817. His father had served with Andrew Jackson at New Orleans and with Sam Houston in the Creek Wars. He was named John Coffee Hays, after General John Coffee, one of Jackson's commanders. His name and his father's connections would be of some help to the young man in later years. Hays' father died when he was fifteen, and the children were sent to live with various relatives. Hays and a younger brother and sister went to Mississippi to live with an uncle, Robert Cage. His uncle thought young Hays had a future as a store clerk, but the boy wanted no part of such a tame existence. Evidently with no hard feelings on either side, Hays went to work as a chainboy on a survey crew and, for the next two years, worked on various surveys, learning the trade and heading his own crew. He saved enough money to study at Davison Academy in Nashville but became ill during a bad winter and dropped out of school. [1]

Just when the young man decided to go to Texas is unknown, but by late 1837 Hays and William, his older brother, were preparing to seek their fortune in the new country. They left with a letter of introduction to Sam Houston, President of Texas, from Harry Cage, another uncle.[2] Cage's letter reminded Houston of his acquaintance with the older Hays and praised his nephews as young men of good habits and surveying skills, industrious and willing to work. He very politely asked Houston's help in finding employment for his nephews. Based on the date of this letter, November 19, 1837, Hays did not reach Texas as early as mid-1836, as some writers have stated, but more likely in late 1837 or early 1838. The letter, discovered in the papers of Houston's son, Andrew Jackson Houston, was presented to Houston, but Hays cannot be traced with any certainty for some months after reaching Texas. He and William followed different paths; Hays is definitely located in Texas in May 1838, and thereafter his brother is not mentioned. As might be expected, Hays put his surveying experience to good use, was working as a deputy surveyor in the San Antonio area in May, and began recording surveys in June of that year.[3] Mrs. Sam Maverick and her husband became well acquainted with Hays after his arrival in San Antonio, and she mentioned him frequently in her memoirs. She thought Hays was about nineteen when he came to San Antonio, which would have had him in town towards the end of 1836 and is probably too early a date. Mrs. Maverick wrote that Hays was a leader from his first days in San Antonio, and she remembered he became a deputy surveyor and had several brushes with Indians.[4]

A letter recommending Hays for the job of surveying the northern boundary of Travis County in February 1840 states Hays had been doing survey work for the preceding two years, as well as scouting.[5] Hays was on a survey that left San Antonio on September 21, 1838, and was in the Leon River area for a month without encountering any Indians.[6]

Hays also took part in scouting parties looking for Indians. Mrs. Maverick mentions one such expedition in June 1839 when Hays and her husband, Sam Maverick, and other Texans in San Antonio joined forces with Juan Seguín to destroy an Indian encampment in the Canyon de Uvalde. In a puzzling continuation of her story, Mrs. Maverick noted Seguín rode back into San Antonio ten days later and reported the woods full of Indians and the men likely to be killed. She was naturally extremely worried about her husband, but the group returned safely.[7]

Mirabeau Buonaparte Lamar, in his several important roles in the Texas Republic, collected a mass of papers and documents of every description, hoping to write a history of the country. In the Lamar collection is an account by Hays of his early days in the republic, including his participation in an expedition led by Henry Karnes in the fall of 1839. The sizable force—forty-five men from San Antonio and sixty men from Galvez (Galveston) under a Captain Wilson—was traveling up to the Pedernales River when the Mexican spies became alarmed and left, "whereupon Capt. Hays was dispatched with 3 men as spies with orders not to return until the enemy had been ferreted out." Hays' account is interesting because he already refers to himself as "captain," a rank he was not awarded until early 1840.

Hays and his three men located the Comanche encampment, approaching within eighty yards before they realized their danger and hastily retreated with the news. Karnes' Texans surrounded the camp and were in a position to surprise the sleeping Indians when a horse on the Comanche picket line broke free and alarmed them. Some of the Comanches made little attempt at resistance, breaking for the trees and brush, but others fought ferociously and left twelve bodies on the ground. One chief was thought to have been killed, his apparently lifeless body remaining on the battlefield for several days before the Comanches returned to seek out their dead. The wounded chief recovered and later recounted his amazing adventure in San Antonio.[8]

These activities, reported by Hays or Mrs. Maverick, and his surveying activities recorded in the General Land Office, fill some of the gaps between Hays' arrival in Texas and his nomination for a surveyor post in early 1840. If Hays was selected for the surveying job, he had no time to fill the post immediately because the threat of Indian raids prompted the formation of two ranger companies in February 1840 to protect the southwestern frontier. Young Hays was selected to lead the unit based in San Antonio; John T. Price was picked to command the company based in Victoria.[9]

The auspices under which these two companies were organized is unknown; authorization was not by an official congressional act. There were other companies in the field at this time under sometimes equally hazy authority; documentary records list nine other ranger companies in the period September 16, 1839, to June 1840, several formed under the authority of the War Department, one by the president, and another authorized by a militia general.[10] The list of these companies does not include the units commanded by Hays and Price, suggesting these two ranger companies were probably in a different category.

Little is known of the accomplishments of any of these units, but all of them seemed to have had problems getting paid. Captain Thomas N.B. Greer and his Boggy and Trinity Rangers served their three-months' term, leaving no record of their actions but also not receiving reimbursement; two years later Greer was still trying to obtain payment for his men's service. Sam Houston, again president and keeping his usual eye on disbursements, returned the bill without action.[11]

A company commanded by Donald R. Jackson is known only by Ordnance Department receipts showing he was in service operating in Fannin County during April-June 1840. The company was on duty as late as June 13 when forty rations were issued for a "detached party of Capt. Jackson's Rangers while on duty." The company had earlier drawn several thousand quarts of corn for horses, powder, lead, flints and caps and even three coffee makers.[12]

Militia General Felix Huston formed a spy company on July 14, 1840, and petitioned to have them paid later in the year. Organizing a ranger company was evidently not too difficult, but it was another matter to convince congress and the president to pay them. Huston stressed the service of his company, reporting they had served well and had discovered a major Indian trail, above a Waco village, leading far into the mountains. The trail, he believed, probably led to the main Comanche villages and would be of great value in future campaigns.[13] There is nothing to suggest these men were ever paid, even though Huston's petition shows that much of value was achieved by these units regardless of whether or not they actually engaged in battle. Just being in the field was a deterrent to Indian raids.

During this period in early 1840, Hays continued to be active, though not against Indians. In May thirteen men of his company, scouting along the Rio Grande near Laredo, were discovered near the town. When the Mexican authorities sent forty-two regular cavalrymen after the Texans, Hays and his men retreated to more suitable ground and prepared for a fight. Satisfied with the location, he and one other ranger rode back to the Mexicans for a parley and were met by the Laredo *alcalde* who told Hays that, since the cavalrymen were only the advance guard of a much larger force, the only hope for the Texans would be immediate surrender.

Hays must have developed an instinct for border fighting in this era and area where there were no rules other than those for survival. Not believing the Mexican for a moment, he told the ranger with him to fire. The Mexican was shot out of his saddle and his cavalrymen charged the Texans until the ranger rifles broke their attack and they fell back. As they retreated the Texans rushed forward. Inconclusive and inaccurate firing by both parties continued for some time, with the Mexicans continuing to fall back slowly, until Hays suddenly changed tactics. Instead of dismounting to load, then remounting, firing and again dismounting to reload, the rangers fired but did not wait to reload. Rushing forward on foot while the Mexicans were hastily reloading, they began firing their pistols at close range. Caught by surprise with empty weapons, the Mexican horsemen fled, leaving their mounts.

The Texans collected as many of the enemy horses as they could ride and galloped after the running cavalrymen, who were doing poorly as infantry. Most surrendered; they had lost eight men killed and others were wounded while only a few of the rangers had been wounded. Hays assured his captives they would be released, and as the two sides bargained, some of the Mexican cavalrymen expressed curiosity about the guns the rangers had used. A ranger demonstration of their rifles explained to the Mexicans' satisfaction why they had lost. [14]

His raid made Hays' a familiar and notorious name in Laredo, and the Mexicans decided to eliminate his spy company. General Rafael Vásquez with four hundred men marched north, crossed the Leon and camped about eighty miles from San Antonio. Not knowing the ranger strength in town and afraid to advance closer, the general decided to trick Hays into leaving the town.

Vásquez sent one of his spies, a convincing actor, into San Antonio with a plausible story of wanting to trade near the Rio Grande but afraid to because of the brigand Agatone, the current troublemaker in the Nueces country. Hays, who now had about forty men, began making plans to search for Agatone near the border. One of the San Antonio citizens became suspicious of the new arrival and advised Hays not to trust the supposed trader. Hays was not convinced and continued preparations for a major scout. On his own, the young man sought out the spy and told him in strict confidence to go ahead with his plans to leave for Mexico; he would be perfectly safe because Hays was being joined by a hundred men from Gonzales and all the Texans would join forces and escort the trader to the Rio Grande.

This was considerably more help than the Mexican spy wanted, so he slipped out of town but was followed at a distance by the forty rangers. Hays came on Vásquez sooner than expected, having pushed his now-jaded horses, and decided on an immediate attack before Vásquez could prepare his defenses. The forty rangers galloped through the enemy camp, firing as they charged. Vásquez had heard his spy's report, based upon the fabricated story of the young man in San Antonio. Assuming forty men would not charge into ten times their number unless they were the advance guard of a larger force, the disorganized enemy camp broke up as the soldiers began a rush to escape. Hays, cautious, followed the rapidly retreating force all the way to the Rio Grande. Vásquez later learned the truth about his withdrawal before a Texas force one-tenth in size. Thoroughly humiliated, he bitterly resented any mention, even if jocular, of his retreat. [15]

There had been concern for the safety of San Antonio after Hays left, but his safe return was cause for celebration. It was the last service of his first company, and both his and Captain Price's companies were disbanded. Hays noted that Price had been out several times without seeing action.[16] Hays turned again to surveying; Bexar County survey records for 1840 show him locating over eighty claims, some of them up on the Pedernales River.[17]

There are no muster or pay rolls for the 1840 units of Hays and Price, and other than Hays' brief notes, nothing reliable is known about them although legends abound. In later years William "Big Foot" Wallace recalled that he was living out on the Medina River in 1840 and returned to San Antonio when he heard about a ranger unit's being formed. In his recollections, many decades after the fact, Wallace remembered that Chapman Woolfork, Joe Tivey, Mark Rapier, Kit Acklin, Jim Galbreth, Tom Buchanan, Coho Jones, Peter Poe, Mike Chevallie and R.A. Gillespie were in the new company with him. Chevallie can definitely be placed in San Antonio during this time. Several others mentioned served with Hays in other companies, but a number of them do not appear on any surviving rolls and Wallace's name appears on only one roll of a Hays ranger company—in 1845.

Wallace also wrote that San Antonio was full of criminals, with horse thieves most prominent, and that the rangers captured a number of these criminals in 1840-1841, including a noted brigand named Antonio Corao whom Hays detailed Sam Walker, Wallace, Chapman Woolfork and William Powell to shoot. They took the man to the headwaters of the San Antonio River, north of town, and executed him. Wallace's account is not completely accurate, because Sam Walker did not come to Texas until 1842 and could not have taken part in an execution in 1840 or 1841.[18] Although Wallace did take part in several fights in 1840, as will be noted, there is some doubt about his claims to have been with Hays as an official member of this early company. In later years, when Hays had become a legend, more than a few men boasted of their service with him.

In March 1840 some of the Comanche chiefs sent word to Henry Karnes that they wished to make peace and exchange prisoners, welcome news because the Indians were known to hold a number of Mexican and Anglo-American captives. The Indians knew the red-headed Karnes, once a prisoner of theirs and a man who knew their customs. His skill as a foe made him all the more suitable as a representative in drawing up a treaty. Karnes, however, was to play no part in the events which followed the initial feelers for a truce. President Lamar appointed a special commissioner and a translator to conduct the negotiations with the Comanches. On March 19, 1840, twelve chiefs and a large party of warriors, women and children reached San Antonio.[19]

Although the preliminary negotiations had stressed bringing in all prisoners, the Comanches rode into San Antonio with only one, Matilda Lockhart, who had been captured in 1838 and almost retaken by Moore in 1839. When the twelve chiefs were asked in the council house why no more prisoners had been brought to town, their spokesman replied that the Lockhart child was the only captive they held; others had been traded. The Lockhart girl said this was untrue.

Because of the Indians' arrogance and lies, orders were quietly given for Captain George T. Howard's infantry company to surround the council house. The Comanches were told they were all prisoners and would be held until all the white captives had been brought in. When the Texans rose to leave, one of the chiefs rushed to the door and stabbed the sentry stationed there with a knife. In the melee which followed, Captain Howard was wounded but his company was close by and opened fire, killing all twelve Comanches.

In the streets other Indians, wandering about town while their leaders were in the council house, heard the shooting and began a desperate fight. A second infantry company forced the Comanches back towards the river bank and away from the streets.

Thirty-two warriors, all of the Comanche men who had entered the town, were killed. A Mexican renegade living with the Comanches managed to hide and escape. In the confused fighting three Indian women and two children were shot, the children probably accidently. As many as twenty-seven women and children were captured in the Council House Fight. Seven Texans were killed and eight wounded; most of these were civilian bystanders.

During the early stages of the fight, before most people knew the negotiations had degenerated into combat, Colonel Lysander Wells and several friends rode unknowingly into the area and were attacked by Comanche braves. Most of the party were not armed; Wells had one of the new Colt revolvers, but he obviously had not been well instructed in the operation of the weapon. The wedge was improperly placed, and when the startled Wells tried to shoot one of the Comanches, the Colt would not fire and the Indian grabbed the barrel, jerking it loose! Nearby soldiers ran up and saved the colonel, who sat back in his saddle and cursed Comanches and Sam Colt in equal measure.[20]

The Council House Fight was not a ranger affair. Mathew Caldwell, out of the rangers after accepting an appointment in the Regular Army, was visiting in San Antonio and took part in the fighting in a private capacity—unarmed and not expecting trouble, he defended himself by throwing rocks! Hays and his rangers were not in San Antonio and missed the action. A soon-to-be ranger, Mike Chevallie, was an army lieutenant and managed to get Mrs. Maverick to safety as the fighting began.[21]

Many earlier historians have stressed that the Texans made a serious blunder in killing the Comanche chiefs in San Antonio, assuming the Indians brooded over this loss, finally made a great raid to avenge their lost leaders, and brought on a war that was to last for generations. These assumptions fail to consider that the Texans and the Comanches were fated to be enemies. Either the Texans had to stop advancing onto the prairie, or the Comanches had to draw back and vanish into the unknown plains, courses of action which neither side was willing to consider. Nor did the Comanches hide and brood.

Shortly after the loss of the twelve chiefs in the council house, a war party of at least two hundred rode down to San Antonio and a new chief brazenly rode into town and dared anyone to fight him. None of the citizens had any wish to fight the chief and suggested he go along the river and fight the soldiers still in the area who had garrisoned one of the old Spanish missions south of town. Surprisingly, he took his warriors, rode south, stood outside the walls of the mission compound, and dared any of the soldiers to accept his challenge. The acting commander in the compound told the chief there was a truce for twelve days, which was true, but that they would be happy to accommodate him after that time. The disgusted Indians rode away.

Other than this bloodless incident, the frontier was quiet for a time in a lull which may have caused the Texans to believe the Comanche spirit had been broken. The loss of Comanche chiefs, however, was only a temporary setback for the Plains Indians; none of their leaders held hereditary war powers, and a chief on one raid could easily become a follower on later raids. The Comanches were regrouping, and the Texans were unaware they were being agitated and organized by Mexican agents.

Although there were no major raids or fights, the Comanches made several small raids into the settlements for horses, and volunteer units were formed to combat these forays. Most accounts of these scouts have been lost, but one volunteer expedition commanded by a Captain Clendenning is well documented. While scouting along the Frio River, part of his command broke away on July 4, 1840, to search for Comanche raiders.

Captain J.R. Cunningham led nineteen men, including a Tonkawa spy identified only as Antonio, in the scout. About an hour after leaving the main party, they rediscovered a trail which they had earlier found and lost. After five or six miles, Antonio found an abandoned camp. From the tracks they saw that six more warriors had joined the group and, with Antonio in the lead, they followed the trail to the west bank of the Frio, bearing towards the Leona and out onto the open prairie. Believing they would spot the Indians at any moment, Cunningham neglected to stop for water, riding out onto open country until it was too late to return to water the horses. They continued for nine hours in the summer heat, rider and mount suffering from lack of water.

Late in the afternoon the Tonkawa scout rode back to report the Indians, numbering about twenty, were ahead, and Cunningham crept forward to scout their camp. Antonio and four men were ordered to stampede the Comanche horses while the rest of the men were to charge the camp, Cunningham carefully explaining in both languages the necessity for silence. There would be no firing until he signaled the charge. He and his men crawled through the bushes and scrub trees to within twenty paces of the Indians, occupied in saddling their riding horses for a night march. At this close range, someone became nervous and fired at the Indians, who dispersed and fell back, trying to recover their wounded. Both sides were soon scattered all through the undergrowth. Cunningham rallied his volunteers and returned to the abandoned camp where there was water and food as well as weapons, saddles and camp gear. Antonio and his detail had captured the Comanche *caballado*; the victors divided the horses and mules and the camp trophies among themselves. In the horse herd was a mule identified as belonging to Vicente de la Garza, captured by the Indians while loaded with newly minted 1840 silver eagles. Several hundred dollars worth of these coins, discovered among the baggage in the Comanche camp, was "appropriated" by the men.

Cunningham found some of the new eagles in the possession of a man named Davis, who had disappeared when the fighting began. When the detachment returned to San Antonio on July 7, they entered the town with a shirtless Davis riding backwards, on a no-tail mule, his face and arms stained and a red cap atop his head. Silently the little procession marched through the main streets of the town and the two plazas. Cunningham wrote: "He left by the light of the moon."[22]

In early August a Comanche war party, the largest ever formed, started down the river valleys of the hill country towards the Texas settlements. The large force, estimated at from four hundred to a thousand and probably at least six hundred, was able to pass undetected and penetrate deep into the settled areas of the republic. Part of the tactical surprise they were able to obtain was pure luck, part geography, and there were no ranger units in service, either official or volunteer, to give the alarm. The Comanches had no trouble passing between the widely separated towns and reaching Victoria, near the Gulf Coast, without being seen.

On the afternoon of August 6, 1840, the Comanches reached Victoria. The unsuspecting town could have been destroyed, but the Comanches did not like to fight in streets or attack walls. There was resistance from the town, with some losses, and the Indians remained on the outskirts. The Indians rounded up an immense herd of hundreds of the horses and mules in outlying corrals and stables, and then made camp a few miles away. The following day they made another foray towards the town, killing two people, but the raiders made no organized attack before starting south towards the Gulf with the largest herd of animals in their memory.

None of the inhabitants of Victoria had been able to escape the town to raise the alarm, but the Indians had nevertheless been discovered. On the afternoon of August 6, a Comanche scouting party had caught Tucker Foley and Reverend Joel Ponton traveling cross-country to Gonzales. They killed Foley, but Ponton managed to hide and reached Gonzales the next day where Adam Zumwalt raised thirty-six volunteers and started out, believing he was chasing twenty Indians.[23]

Some idea of the true size of the raiding band was given by Z.N. Morrell, a Baptist minister and farmer who discovered an unusually wide trail suggesting hundreds of mounted riders. Despite driving an ox-pulled wagon, Morrell managed to drive thirty miles in twelve hours and spread the alarm in Bastrop. While he was describing the huge size of the war party, a courier arrived from Ben McCulloch telling of the raid and asking for help.[24]

Encouraged by the easy acquisition of the horse herd at Victoria, the Comanches moved south to the coast and attacked the tiny settlement of Linnville, a tactic which must have been suggested by Mexican agents because the Comanches had no way of knowing of the existence of the town, a port of entry with extensive storage for clothing, food stuffs and tobacco. As at Victoria, surprise was total. Unlike the larger town, there were no defensible buildings in Linnville; the citizens ran for the few boats to navigate far enough out in the bay to be beyond reach of the Comanche arrows.

To this point the Comanches had enjoyed great success, killing over twenty people,[25] obtaining huge quantities of clothing and trade goods, and acquiring a horse and mule herd that could have been in excess of a thousand animals. It must have been a jubilant war party that turned north, wearing white man's clothing, their horses bedecked with cloth streamers, but matters began to go sour for them on August 9 when John J. Tumlinson caught up with the column and had a brief fight, losing one of his men. Too few in number to challenge the Comanche force, Tumlinson fell back and shadowed the march north. Ben McCulloch, Adam Zumwalt and Clark Owen quickly raised volunteer companies to take up the chase with Tumlinson. If not officially rangers, these commanders and their men were rangers in both experience and spirit and followed the Comanches north, remaining unseen.

Up north in the Bastrop area Ed Burleson, gathering men to block the return of the Comanches, dispatched Morrell to Austin for reinforcements. Reasonably certain the Indians would try to escape into the hills, the Texans planned to intercept them along Plum Creek below Austin, hoping to stop the Indians before they reached the hill country. Placido and thirteen Tonkawa braves volunteered, joined Burleson's men, and ran along beside the Texans for thirty miles! Mathew Caldwell, already near Plum Creek with eighty-seven rifles waiting for reinforcements but ready to fight by themselves if necessary, was joined by Captain James Bird with about thirty men from Gonzales. On August 12 General Felix Huston of the militia assumed command of the forces at Plum Creek, later reporting he was requested to take command by the assembled volunteers, and formed the men into three companies commanded by Caldwell, Bird, and Lafayette Ward who had brought twenty-two men from the Lavaca settlements.[26] Resting a little during the night of August 11, the companies from the south circled and joined the units with Huston. Around daylight on August 12, scouts spotted the head of the war party riding leisurely towards their position.

Huston formed his combined forces into two lines, holding Ward's company in reserve, while the Comanches were riding in loose order towards the north, talking, whistling, and seemingly unaware of the Texans blocking their path. A party of Texas scouts caught up with the Comanche rear guard and shot several out of their saddles, alerting the main body to their danger.[27]

Huston had brought up his troops in good order but seemed uncertain about what to do once the battle started, holding his men in line under Comanche fire while the main body of the Indians slowly moved out of range. McCulloch rode up to Huston and admonished the general: "That was not the way to fight Indians!"[28] Huston made no mention of McCulloch's remark in his reports, but he did order Burleson to move around a point of woods and Caldwell to charge into the trees. The sudden charge by the Texans broke through the Comanche lines, and the Indians' withdrawal became a wild rout. Pursuit across the open prairies extended for miles and only slowed when the Texas horses began to tire. Burleson chased one band almost to the San Marcos River.

By any standard the battle was a considerable victory and revealed the growing ability of the Texans to meet mounted Indians in an open fight. Experience previously gained by many of the volunteers in their ranger companies was beginning to have major impact.

Some weeks later Huston submitted a supplemental report, based on more recent information and correcting some of the statements in his hurried original account. For the first time he noted there were reports that the entire idea of the great raid had originated in Matamoros and was planned to consist of six hundred Comanches and forty Mexicans. A considerable number of Mexican blankets and other trade goods were found on the field, supporting the idea of Mexican involvement.[29] The closing paragraphs of Huston's report are of interest.

There is one fact I wish particularly to remark—It has generally been supposed that the Comanche horses are fleeter and more durable than ours;—such, however is not the case. As the chase [sic], the Indian horses gave out, and they sought refuge in the thickets; and at its termination, there were not more than thirty Indians ahead of us, and they were compelled to abandon the prairies.

From long observation and experience, I am fully convinced that our corn-fed horses are superior to any grass-fed horses, in a long pursuit.[30]

Huston's is the first official mention of the need for superior mounts and corn feeding. He understandably exaggerated his "long observation and experience"—he had very little Indian-fighting experience—and Plum Creek would have been a different story without McCulloch, Burleson, Caldwell and other leaders. Many individuals in the fight had far more experience than Huston; Hays and Big Foot Wallace fought in the ranks that day, as did Mike Chevallie, though none of the accounts of the fight singles them out and just how they arrived at the fight is unknown.[31] Huston cited four men, "all of whom rendered essential service", but the fact that these four were his aides somewhat diminishes their glory. He mentioned Burleson and Caldwell and three others by name and said that the captains commanding companies acted with the utmost courage and firmness. Most of the Texans, a mixed group including three Baptist preachers, lawyers, merchants, farmers and frontiersmen, could have been cited.[32]

Another August event would have an impact on ranger history; Henry Karnes died on August 16, not in combat but from yellow fever. His stubborn nature and determination kept him from allowing time to recover properly, and he suffered a relapse and died. He was not quite thirty-eight. Texas lost a skilled fighter and talented commander, and it is interesting to speculate what might have happened had he lived.

The Comanche raid brought a counterstroke from the Texans. Although they could not mount anything on the scale of the Indian attack, several leaders in LaGrange decided to organize a Fayette County Corps to raid northwest into the heart of Comanche country. The men were to serve for three months and be ready to leave by September 12, 1840.[33] Despite his less-than-successful earlier effort, John Moore was designated to lead the expedition and collected ninety willing volunteers, including Castro and a number of his Lipans.

On October 4, Moore's party marched from LaGrange to the north of Austin and up to the headwaters of the San Gabriel River, keeping north of the hills. They then cut through the hills and reached the San Saba River, by now in Indian country, and trekked to the Concho and the Red Fork of the Colorado, remarking on the richness and beauty of the land. After rediscovering the old Spanish presidio on the San Saba River and carving his name into one of the door frames, Moore and his expedition began to see extensive Indian signs, including pictographs and painted rocks and markers. When pecan shells and other Indian signs alerted them to the nearness of Indians, Moore, now a wiser commander, halted his command in a sheltered location near a commanding hill. Castro sent out two Lipan scouts to reconnoiter the country to the north.

The Texans waited for two days, worried, certain the scouts had been caught, but when they finally rode back into camp it was with the news that there was a Comanche camp to the north. After eating supper, at about five in the afternoon the Texans traveled ten miles north to the Colorado River, then along the river where they found some cattle hidden in a thicket. Spies, sent forward to check on the Comanche village, returned at about three in the morning, reporting the camp was nearby on the south bank of the river and estimating there were sixty families with over a hundred warriors.

At daybreak on October 14, Moore had his pack mules hidden and guarded before his main body moved towards the sleeping Indians while a twenty-five man detachment circled to get to the rear of the camp. It was still early and the Texans crept to within two hundred yards before an alarm was given. Yelling, the Texans charged.

The surprised Comanches fought briefly then broke for the safety of the water and the river bank. Those who made it across the water to the open prairie had to face the Texans waiting there. The fight in and near the village was over in thirty minutes or less, but the chase across the open country stretched out for four miles before the Texans quit. Captain Andrews made good use of a new Colt rifle, praising its ability to fire ten shots while his men were loading and firing two.[34]

The battle was a complete and total victory for the Texans. Forty-eight Comanches were shot in the village, another eighty in the river; thirty-four women and children were captured. In the camp the Texans, who had only two men wounded although one man had died of natural causes on the march out and been buried, found much of the booty from Linnville. They started back with a few prisoners and over five hundred captured horses.

Even though they had been surprised and badly defeated, some of the Indian survivors, possibly joined by other Comanches, began trailing the Texas column to try to recapture the horses. On the Pedernales a small party managed to slip through the guards and stole four animals, including a saddle mule belonging to Moore.

The citizens of Austin had a celebration for the returning Texans. While most of the victorious volunteers were attending the ball, leaving the horse herd in a supposedly safe area, the stealthy Comanches took down the rails and led out thirty to forty horses without being seen or heard.[35]

Moore and his men divided the remaining animals between them, but it was all they received for the campaign. In January 1842 they were still trying to get a bill for redress through the Texas Congress, but Houston returned the bill unsigned, noting they had been more than compensated by keeping the captured animals.[36] Official rangers were at least promised pay, at a definite daily rate; the ranger-type units that fought at Plum Creek and in Moore's second expedition volunteered for a certain period and received whatever booty they captured as compensation.

Plum Creek and Moore's campaign brought cries for more strikes against the Comanches, and the newspapers carried a number of stories containing plans for hitting the

Indians far out on the prairie. Major George T. Howard and what army troops and volunteeers he could raise around San Antonio were ordered to move west to the Canyon de Uvalde and then north to the headwaters of the Colorado. Huston was authorized to raise sixteen hundred militia for an Indian campaign,[37] an impossible task, but Howard managed to round up about two hundred men in early December and scouted out to Las Moras Springs, near present-day Brackettville, where he discovered a large Indian camp. Most of the band's warriors were on a raid in Mexico, but the Texans killed a few Indian braves in the vicinity and captured a large herd of wild mustangs the Comanches had not yet broken. The unruly animals, extremely difficult to herd, were more of a liability than an asset, and a small band of Indians was able to recapture most of them.[38]

Regardless of their impoverished condition and lack of manpower on the frontier, the Texans continued to make grandiose plans for fighting the Indians. On December 11, 1840, a large group of Tonkawa and Lipan warriors gathered in Austin to accompany Burleson on an expedition to drive the Comanches from the San Saba area and build block-houses and secure the frontier,[39] but this expedition was never formed.

The *Telegraph and Texas Register* noted in an editorial in early December that the country was becoming dissatis-fied with the army and should rely instead on the militia, suggesting Texas could even do away with a regular army, and bringing up the old plan for a series of blockhouses from the Red River to the Nueces. Even though they had achieved two major victories over the Comanches, no one seriously believed this hardy foe had been beaten back. Despite tactical victories, the strategic outlook was still gloomy; the Secretary of War even solicited proposals for the defense of the frontiers. Friendly natives advised their friends in San Antonio that there was a good chance of a Mexican inva-sion.[40] Major Howard, now commanding the post at San Antonio, wrote the Secretary of War urgently requesting ammunition, saying he had only a single keg of musket powder. Howard regretted he could not comply with orders, possibly something to do with the trade between San Antonio and the Rio Grande, because his horses were in such poor condition. The major suggested all trade be discontinued because he believed most of the traders were Centralists and unfriendly to Texas.

Howard further reported that a courier had arrived in San Antonio a few days earlier, and he believed the man brought commissions in the Centralist Army for Colonel Juan Seguín, a Captain Oreola [sic] and Antonio Pérez. His request for funds to buy four good American horses for his spies, available for a hundred and fifty to two hundred dollars in par money,[41] reveals the wide use of spies, even in regular commands, and the need for the best horses for these special scouts.

The sad state of Texas' finances is demonstrated by the War Department's action on Howard's letter, which Secretary Archer forwarded to the president with a brief note.

> I regret to inform your Excellency, that this Department has not one dollar at its command; and cannot therefore extend to the troops, at Bexar, the munitions of dear necessity for their defense.
> The powder and lead are here, but we have no means of transporting either.[42]

Despite the impossible financial condition, Secretary Archer continued to make plans to defend his country. On Christmas Day 1840 one of his advisors sent him a comprehensive proposal for protection against Mexican invasion or Indian raids. The plan contained some old ideas, such as the blockhouse barrier along the frontier, but also had several new ideas for making use of a balanced force of militia and volunteer troops. It proposed having the more populated eastern counties share the defense burden, and for the first time suggested a draft system so that all men and all classes would have a role in protecting Texas. The plan considered the agricultural basis of the Texas economy and the need for calling up farmers at times least likely to cripple planting and harvesting crops.[43]

This proposal was too advanced and revolutionary for serious consideration, much less adoption. Given what they

had, or thought they could raise, the Texas Congress authorized the president to appoint and commission three persons
to raise fifteen men each to act as spies on the western and
northwestern frontiers for the space of four months, or less
if the president thought their services could be dispensed
with in a shorter time. The resolution, for it was no more
than that, was approved December 26, 1840.[44] It was the
last action of the year bearing on ranger or military matters.

—5—

Hays Makes a Name - 1841

The earliest fighting in 1841 involved Ranger George Erath, who served as the commander of a spy unit in an expedition against eastern Indians in January. This was a considerable force, including one hundred and twenty-five whites and almost as many Tonkawa and Lipan scouts. Erath commanded all the Indians and about twenty Texans who were members of his special spy company. The expedition's march up the Brazos River to Comanche Peak and to the Trinity and back again found nothing, and Erath's men were the only ones to see any action, killing two hostile Indians.[1] In his *Memoirs* Erath labeled the expedition a mistake, brought on by the misconceptions of newcomers to frontier warfare. He noted that the rangers had learned the Eastern Indians remained in their camps and villages only during the summer, when they could plant corn and other foodstuffs. During the harsh winters, they scattered to hunt, living on bear and buffalo.[2]

Formal ranger units were soon back in service in early 1841. In the notes he made for Lamar, Hays wrote that Indian troubles were the cause for congressional authorization of three ranger detachments in the closing days of the preceding year, mentioning that he was given command of one of the detachments.[3] While Houston, his sponsor, was no longer in office, young Hays must have made enough of an impression—or had enough friends—to be appointed to command one of the fifteen-man detachments. John Price was again selected to command another of the detachments, and there is little doubt that Antonio Pérez was appointed the third captain. The dates and sizes of the units listed in the only ranger records for the period which have survived, records for three units,[4] indicate these are the three detachments raised under the congressional resolution of December 1840. Placing two of the units in San Antonio was an indication of the growing awareness of the Comanche danger and the fear of a possible Mexican invasion.

There is some conflict between official records and recollections of contemporary writers regarding the formation of Hays' company. In his *Memoirs* John Salmon Ford described how, after merchants were robbed near Laredo, some of the San Antonio merchants decided to put a stop to the marauders and sent a delegation to Austin demanding a ranger company be formed to halt the robberies. According to Ford, the president formed a company, on his own authority, which a number of men joined and subsequently elected Hays captain. Ford said Pérez joined and was elected second in command.[5] Although Ford is usually a reliable source, his version of this company, including the list of members, is not accurate.

Fortunately, muster rolls for the three companies organized in January 1841 have survived, and Hays' roll lists only three of the men mentioned by Ford.[6] The captains of these three companies authorized by congress were not elected; they were appointed and subsequently enlisted the men for their units. Lamar, in his historical notes, specifically states Hays was appointed to command one of the fifteen-man units. The discrepancies are not of critical importance but do again illustrate the often-conflicting stories in early ranger history. Hays contributed to some of the confusion by stating he raised fifteen men who were soon called into service;[7] the three designated commanders were *authorized* to form fifteen-man detachments, but the organizational dates varied as personnel became available.

Pérez' muster roll show he was able to form his fifteen-man detachment without any problems, although not until January 20.[8] The Spanish surnames on his list indicate he drew fourteen of his men from among San Antonio natives; the fifteenth man was John O. Truehart whose brother joined Hays' detachment. Despite his report, Hays was not so successful in enlisting men and did not have even thirteen men until mid-March. Despite enlisting fewer men, however, his and Price's units were organized earlier than Pérez' and started scouting immediately. Both commanders rode south to the Nueces River, in a search for Mexican invaders, and met on January 9, 1841.[9]

Price left Hays and turned east towards Corpus Christi. Hays evidently rode south towards the Rio Grande, as evidenced by a dispatch on January 10 from San Antonio by 1st Infantry Captain Alexander T. Gillam, who mentioned that Hays was going to the Nueces and on to the Rio Grande but was expected back daily.[10] This dispatch and Price's report indicate Hays began operations before his detachment was officially organized on January 10, 1841. There are no other mentions of this scouting expedition.

Price's movements are better documented; he continued to the trading post and ranch of Henry Lawrence Kinney who had opened a business in 1839. From several people whom he contacted, Price formed an unsatisfactory opinion of Kinney, fearing he was siding with the Mexicans. Price reported that the trader had been promised no harm would come to him in the event of a Mexican invasion, and that Kinney had purchased the land he occupied from an officer in the Mexican army.

The ranger captain was worried about an iron cannon at Kinney's, part of a store of weapons and ammunition left at the ranch by the brigand Canales, and wanted it removed. Price also reported some very gloomy and greatly exaggerated estimates of the number of men being raised by the Mexican authorities for an invasion of Texas. In his report, written after returning to Victoria to rest his horses, Price stated that the ranger detachment had been operating during rainy weather and the deep mud was tiring on the mounts. He requested three or four good horses, because he had enrolled his men in haste and they had not had time to obtain suitable horses. He also asked for details on their time of service and means of communication, and reported that they would head west after staying in Victoria several days.[11]

Portions of Price's information had been reported earlier by Philip Dimitt, who lived near Kinney's and who had sent a letter to the government reporting on Kinney's purchase of the ranch property, which had been in a title dispute. Dimitt's letter also mentioned the rumors of an invasion, but his estimates on numbers were not as large as those reported by Price.[12]

This was the beginning of a number of incidents that would cast doubt on Kinney's motives in Texas, and he would have both detractors and defenders for his commercial endeavors. His ranch and trading post was the first settlement north of Matamoros, on the Gulf Coast, where ships could land supplies as well as receive goods overland from Mexico. He was also isolated, open to Indian raids and attacks by Mexican or American bandits, and he attempted to remain on good terms with groups on both sides of the border.

Kinney had good reason to be concerned. How completely undefended the south and southwest border regions were at the time is indicated in other sections of Captain Benjamin T. Gillam's report of January 10. He mentioned that a band of forty Mexican outlaws had been raiding at will south of San Antonio, attacking Seguín's *rancho* and other isolated places and stealing one or two hundred head of cattle. In an effort to catch the bandits, Major Howard had taken what men could be spared from the small San Antonio garrison, plus some civilian volunteers including Colonel Seguín, and started scouting for the Mexicans.[13]

It is possible that bad weather limited operations during the worst of the winter of 1841, because there are no records of further ranger activity until early spring when Hays again appears. He reported that Indian activity around Bexar caused him to follow a trail with thirteen men, all he had. This chase had to have been sometime in mid-March, at the earliest, because he did not have thirteen men in his command until March 10, 1841, when P.S. Buquor and M.H. Chevallie enlisted.[14] The small detachment trailed an Indian band for seventy miles, keeping well back because they were heavily outnumbered. Hays hid his men in a safe location and went forward with a Mexican scout to within good sight of the main Comanche encampment. They observed a dozen braves leave, heading back towards San Antonio, and trailed them until the Comanches stopped to prepare venison.

Twelve was a more reasonable number to tackle, and Hays and his scout went back to return with the other rangers, surrounding the warriors without being seen. The Indians were smoking meat out in the open when the rangers attacked them, but managed to get into a dense clump of brush where the tangle was too thick for horses to enter. Hays placed his men around the edges of the thicket, then he and two men forced their way into the brush and began isolating the Indians, killing them one at a time. Another ranger managed to force his way through the brush and the deadly game continued. Unable to use their bows successfully in the thicket, which the ranger rifles could penetrate, the Comanches fought hand to hand. Hays and two of his men were wounded, but they managed to find and kill ten of the Comanches braves and wound another who surrendered—the only time Hays ever saw this happen. The last Comanche turned out to be an Indian woman. Placing his wounded on litters, Hays led his men back to San Antonio without arousing the main encampment. [15]

The size of the Comanche camp, from which small parties could break off at any time and raid for horses and supplies all along the southwestern frontier, must have worried Hays, because when he was fit to travel he raised enough volunteers to bring his command to fifty men. He was joined by Flacco, who would in time become something of a legend in his own right, and ten Lipan scouts.

With his combined force, Hays marched back and found the camp had moved, leaving a broad track which Hays followed up into the hill country, crossing new territory. In the hills the Texans were spotted by Indian hunters, who turned and fled. Hays, aware the hunters would alarm the main camp, selected twenty-five men with the best horses and started on a forced march to locate the camp before it could be moved. The rangers were closer than they thought; after only an eight-mile run they saw the camp in which the women and children had already struck the tepees and were loading everything on horses. At least one hundred warriors rode back and tried to drive the approaching Texans away from the women and children.

The Texans maintained their fire against the Indians but

tried to have some of their rifles always loaded in case the Indians made an all out charge. At one point Hays and Flacco galloped up to near the Comanche line, intending to fire their rifles when they were at close range, but Hays' startled horse took the bit and ran through the Indian line. Flacco, not to be shamed, galloped behind Hays, but both men managed to break back through the Comanche line and ride back to the other rangers. After the fight, Flacco made his oft quoted remark, "Hays was bravo too much!"

The fighting chase of the retreating Indians lasted an hour and a half and began to wear down the Texas horses, already tired from the long ride from San Antonio. The Comanches, even with their slowly moving camp animals, began to pull away, and the rangers finally watched them vanish into unknown country to the north. It was no victory—the rangers never knew how much damage they had done because the Comanches had ample time and plenty of warriors to carry off their dead and wounded—but a potentially dangerous enemy had been forced to retreat away from the settlements. The rangers had suffered a number of wounded, and Hays took some time getting his men back to San Antonio, subsisting on the meat from their broken down horses.[16]

There is little information about the ranger detachment commanded by Antonio Pérez, although Hays reported that the two units cooperated at least once. In early April, acting on orders from the War Department, the two detachments started south to search for bandits preying on the San Antonio-Laredo merchants, particularly the two outlaw bands of Agatone with thirty men, and Ignacio García with about twenty-five. Hays and Pérez left San Antonio in a hurry, hoping to catch some recent attackers before they could get south of the Rio Grande, but local spies for the outlaws galloped around the rangers and warned the bandits, who had just reached Laredo.[17]

Just outside Laredo the two ranger detachments—only twenty-five men in all—were challenged by Ignacio García and his twenty-five bandits, reinforced by fifteen Mexican cavalrymen. To the blasts of a bugle, the Mexicans charged the Texans, firing and yelling that they had a large force behind them and demanding surrender. Hays had both units dismount and secure their horses while maintaining a defensive fire, killing one Mexican and wounding another and halting the Mexican charge. The Mexicans spread out and circled the rangers, but Hays slipped two scouts through the line to a nearby hill where they could see towards Laredo.

As Hays suspected, there were no reinforcements coming from the town. The rangers remounted their horses and walked them towards the high ground where the Mexicans had dismounted, awaiting attack. At two hundred yards, beyond the range of the Mexican smoothbores, they dismounted and charged. The Mexicans fled on their horses, but Hays had his horses brought up and chased after them. The fleeing force soon halted, dismounted and prepared to receive another charge. Much like his first fight outside Laredo, Hays had his men dismount, fire, then rush forward on foot to discharge their pistols at close range. Expecting a lull while the Texans reloaded, the Mexicans were caught by surprise and driven away from their horses.

Garcia and three of his men were close to their mounts and managed to escape, but the rest began fleeing on foot and were soon chased down by the Texans, now riding captured Mexican ponies. Twenty-five prisoners were captured with their arms, ammunition, equipment and twenty-eight horses. There were three Mexican dead and three wounded on the field—several others had been wounded early in the fight and been carried away by their companions—but there were no ranger losses.

This action, which effectively destroyed Garcia's band although Agatone continued to be a threat for some time, was described in the *Telegraph and Texas Register*, which some days later on June 16 printed additional information on the two ranger detachments. Noting that the term of authorized service for both detachments had expired, the writer said each ranger organization had volunteered to stay in service without pay for one more try at Agatone. Some of the town merchants made contributions to defray costs of the expedition, and several volunteers joined the chase after the bandit gang.[18] When the edition was printed, the rangers had already been out for six days with no word from them, and evidently no contact was made. When Hays and Pérez returned their detachments were disbanded, Hays' on May 10 and Pérez' on May 20.

The three ranger companies commanded by Hays, Price and Pérez were listed as "Spies" or "Spy Companies." This designation, and the limit of fifteen men to a unit, suggests they were never intended to do more than scout for major Indian or Mexican raids. From what meager information is available, they did an excellent job. Not even three *large* companies, however, could have covered the extensive southern and southwestern border regions much less cope with increasing Comanche raids from the north and the still-dangerous eastern Indians.

Several additional ranger-type units, by whatever name, were formed in the spring of 1841. George M. Dolson became captain of the Travis County Minute Men on March 28, 1841, and the next day had a lieutenant and two men scouting along Brushy Creek where they found an Indian trail leading towards Austin. Part of the new company and some volunteers from Austin set out in unsuccessful pursuit, but they did discover the trail of another group, that had stolen horses a few nights earlier, and followed it to a spot several miles above the Pedernales River. Dolson halted his command, resting the horses which had covered sixty miles in twenty-four hours, and sent out spies on the best horses in the command to locate the Indian camp. They were gone some time, returning with several Comanche horses and news of fresh sign in the Colorado bottoms.

The small detachment moved out about midnight, hoping to locate and attack the enemy encampment at daylight, but it was difficult trying to follow the tracks quietly in the dark. They halted frequently but eventually came onto the Comanche horse herd, early in the morning, and saw the camp ahead. There was no surprise; the Comanches actually opened the fight with a brisk discharge of firearms. The rangers and volunteers returned the fire and galloped through the camp area.

The Texans' attack on their camp caused many of the Indians to break away, but their chief rallied them for another stand before they broke again. Dolson was wounded in the first volley of fire, then was hit again but managed to keep the charge going until he became too weak and exhausted to ride. One of the volunteers, a man named Daniels, assumed command and kept the pressure on the Comanches. The chief steadied his braves for a second rally until he himself was killed. As was often the case, his death broke the will of his men and the Comanches scattered in the brush, carrying off their wounded but leaving behind eight dead. Other than Dolson, there were no Texan casualties. The abandoned camp gear and supplies were burned and the twelve rangers and six civilian volunteers returned to Austin with a number of the horses captured from the fleeing Indians. It had been a commendable victory over about thirty-five Comanches.[19]

About the same time Dolson was organizing his company, Eli Chandler was forming a ranger company in Robertson County. His command was officially in service on March 28 and saw its first action on April 1 when twenty-five men started out on a forced march after some Indians who had killed Stephen Rogers, Jr., and stolen eight horses on the east side of the Navasota River. They chased two Indians herding the stolen horses for seven miles before the Indians broke away and escaped. The rangers recaptured the horses and returned home. Chandler was sorry they had not managed to catch the Indians but was very pleased with the way his new company had performed.[20]

By 1841 there was a considerable number of experienced fighters in the frontier settlements, men looked to for leadership in an emergency. Ben McCulloch was the commander in the Gonzales area, a ranger in spirit and deed if not by official appointment. In April or early May a Comanche raiding party stole a number of horses from Gonzales and slipped away in the night. The next day McCulloch gathered a party of sixteen, all eager to regain their animals but aware they had no chance to overtake the Indians in their first wild dash to get away from the settlements. McCulloch, allowing the marauders plenty of time to believe they were safe from pursuit, followed the trail at a sensible pace.

The Texans found fresh tracks on the Johnson Fork of the Llano River, and McCulloch went forward on foot to scout the Comanche camp—one of the earliest of the scouts that would become his trademark. He then brought his men forward in a wild rush, catching the Comanches resting in the belief they were beyond reach. They killed five Indians in the first charge and wounded others. Scattering, the Indians abandoned everything but their weapons. Some even left their moccasins. The volunteers recovered the stolen horses, along with blankets, saddles and camp equipment.[21]

Eli Chandler was also active during May, with spies out for considerable distances from his bases in Robertson County. On May 16 his scouts encountered messengers from a surveying party who had seen Indians on Pecan Creek, a tributary of the Trinity River. Although the sighting was roughly one hundred miles from Chandler's main base, he took forty of his rangers and thirteen volunteers and started out.

On the morning of May 20, having spent the previous night riding, Chandler believed they were close to where the Indian camp should be located. Scouts found an abandoned village site with signs showing it had been visited recently. The scouts returned to the main body too late for it to move out, but early the next morning the combined ranger-volunteer party began a cautious advance. After about five miles they ran onto several Indians, who fled into the dense woods.

Chandler did not waste time chasing them and instead turned back to the old camp site where a thorough search turned up a trail which they followed. These tracks soon joined those made by the Indians who had vanished into the woods. They soon saw another village, but the Indians had been given the alarm and men, women and children were scattering in all directions, fleeing for the safety of the woods. Unable to make a mounted charge through the trees, although they were able to kill three Indians and wound others, Chandler dismounted his men and had a guard placed over the horses while the Texans spread out and made their way through the dense forest. They did not come upon any Indians but found much equipment and many supplies. One ranger was wounded in the hand.

After such a long march it seemed a small victory, but the rangers brought back twenty-three horses, quantities of powder and lead, axes, furs and camp equipment. They burned everything else, including many tepee covers and poles, a considerable loss to the Indians.[22]

Chandler's foes were eastern Indians, largely Waco bands, but other units were searching out Comanche camps to the south and southwest. Just how these other ranger-volunteer mounted gunmen commands were formed is unknown, but a company of considerable size was operating from Austin, scouting along the Nueces. Mark B. Lewis, again commanding a volunteer ranging company, reported to Secretary Archer that he was undecided about whether to keep his men in one group to block the passes above the headwaters of the San Saba, or to divide his company and chase smaller bands of Indians. He was inclining to the latter plan; the increasing number of smoke signals in the hills and the discovery of new trails by his scouts suggested the Comanches had stopped gathering in large camps. They were either breaking into small parties to hunt, or attempting to confuse his spies.

When Lipan scouts discovered fresh tracks, Lewis sent out a twenty-man group, followed by a ten-man detachment. The larger group killed three Comanches and scattered a raiding party. The smaller group ran onto another Comanche band and chased them until the Indians dismounted, killed their horses and vanished into the dense cedar brakes. Lewis sent out a third group of men which chased some Indians into the valley of the Nueces without inflicting any serious loss. Having scattered the Comanches in the area, Lewis and his volunteers turned back towards San Antonio on May 21, but his Lipans discovered another trail, this one a broad track made by several hundred horses. Following this path, the Texans discovered it was made by a large party of Cherokee men, women and children with much camp equipment. The volunteers began to get ready for a major battle, thinking the Indians had come down to raid the settlements, but the Lipan scouts soon determined the Cherokees were steadily moving south, heading for refuge in Mexico. They were left alone.

Back in town, Lewis learned that a considerable Comanche band had struck near San Antonio on May 21, killing a native and stealing some horses. Part of Lewis' group, led by Major Howard and joined by more volunteers from San Antonio, started in pursuit. They failed to catch the Comanches, but they followed so closely that the Indians again killed their horses and escaped on foot into the brush. These actions, while resulting in no real battles, forced the Comanches to abandon their major village bases and seriously limited their ability to raid the settlements.

In a lengthy report to Archer,[23] Lewis made no mention of Hays or Pérez, and the timing of his report suggests the ranger captains were either south on their Rio Grande scout after Agatone or, more likely, had already returned and disbanded their units. When the three detachments authorized in December 1840 were disbanded at the end of their service, only one was reorganized; Hays was allowed to form a new unit, officially activated on June 1, 1841. For a time he was the only member of the company, but he signed up five men on June 12 and another nine on June 23.[24]

Hays, trying to form a new detachment in San Antonio, had a difficult time recruiting men, partly because of the lack of suitable men in town but also because there was competition for volunteers. For some time President Lamar had proposed sending a trading expedition to Santa Fe. Lamar had several objectives to his plan, including the possibility that the Mexicans of Santa Fe might join Texas, but the primary reason for daring the long trip through largely unfamiliar and hostile country was the extensive trade between Santa Fe and the United States. For a number of reasons, Lamar never acquired congressional approval for an official expedition and decided to act on his own, using a volunteer force.

In early June, just as Hays was trying to recruit volunteers for his new ranger detachment, Lamar came to San Antonio looking to recruit expedition volunteers, to obtain merchant sponsors, and to create good will for his project. The Anglo-American citizens of San Antonio, delighted to have such a distinguished guest, held several balls in Lamar's honor. At one dance she attended, Mrs. Maverick noticed that Hays, Chevallie and Howard were only dancing every third dance; she finally observed that the three men were sharing a single coat, taking turns dancing.[25]

Lamar's time was well spent; he received considerable support in San Antonio. On June 19 a large force, basically a trading expedition, left Kenney's Fort on Brushy Creek, about twenty miles north of Austin, with twenty-one ox-drawn wagons containing $200,000 in supplies and goods. A considerable number or armed men went along, divided into five mounted infantry companies and one artillery company with one cannon. A few horsemen were employed as spies. Including the numerous drivers and soldiers, the expedition numbered 321 and was commanded by Hugh McLeod with George T. Howard, discharged from the army, as second-in-command. Mathew Caldwell was among the riders on this doomed quest. A noted journalist, George Wilkins Kendall, joined the expedition as an observer and was later to write the first of his accounts of action with Texas troops.[26]

The disastrous events of the long march towards Santa Fe are not a part of the ranger story, even though several of the men in the expedition later returned to fight as rangers. Unfamiliar with the territory to the northwest, the expedition was often lost and finally split to send the better-mounted riders out to locate Santa Fe. Mexican authorities learned of the march and deployed troops to intercept the Texans. For whatever reasons, one of the expedition members, William G. Lewis, managed to contact senior Mexican officials and arranged to surrender the expedition. Few of the Texans were disposed to fight, especially when Lewis and the Mexican officials promised they would soon be released, but they were instead treated as prisoners of war and marched on foot into Mexican captivity. Good men died along the way. When the surviviors were finally released in April 1842, the men who returned to Texas were bitter. There was rumors, never substantiated, that Juan Seguín had sent couriers to alert Santa Fe authorities about the expedition. Although never proved, the rumors intensified the growing hostilites between the Anglo Americans and the Hispanics in San Antonio.[27]

For the time being, however, Hays continued to cooperate with the native San Antonians; his ability to work with them and with friendly Indian allies in the struggle against the Comanches and Mexican brigands was a strong feature of his leadership. On June 27 he left San Antonio with sixteen Anglo Americans and twenty native volunteers under a Captain Flores. They moved at a rapid pace in an attempt to catch up with the Indians who had stolen cattle near town, but they instead encountered another Comanche party coming out of Uvalde Canyon, about two miles below the canyon entrance. In his report of the fight, Hays mentioned that the ten Comanches had broken off from the main camp, probably to raid San Antonio. His volunteers killed eight of the Comanches and captured the other two.

Hays' report is brief, giving no details of the skirmish other than mentioning that one man was wounded: "Mr. Miller, and he not severely." His pay roll for this period shows a Joseph Miller, but the wound must not have been serious enough to list on the roll. Hays said they could have continued to the main camp, which they knew was near, but instead went back to recruit more men and to rest their horses. He would return and find the main camp.[28]

Between July 1, when he wrote his report, and July 12 when he departed for Uvalde Canyon, Hays was busy recruiting, evidently with the authority to enlarge his detachment. He enlisted one man on July 4 and another the next day, but it took him until the following month before he could almost double the size of his unit. With about twenty-five of "our citizens," a volunteer band from Gonzales, plus ten to fifteen Lipan and Tonkawa scouts led by Flacco, he started out again with almost fifty men to find the Comanche base camp. They marched to the Frio, near where they had recently defeated the Comanche party, and found an abandoned camp, deserted after the Comanches had learned of the defeat of the raiding party. The departing Indians had paused only long enough to kill their prisoners, probably Mexican nationals or members of enemy Indian tribes because Hays would have mentioned the death of Texans.

At the time the Frio River was considered to have two forks, the east leading into Uvalde Canyon and today known as the Sabinal River which flows—infrequently—into the Frio a little south of the canyon. Hays said they took the west fork, the Frio proper, and followed it upstream through the passes at the head of the river. The only easy trails were along the streams that had cut canyons through the limestone hills.

The entire area had been burned by the Comanches, eliminating grass for the horses and making travel slow and difficult. After the headwaters of the Frio had been passed, they continued through the hills as best they could until they entered onto the prairie. At the beginning of the Llano River they began to find trails in all directions, indicating a camp was close. The Lipan scouts must have been worried by such abundant tracks indicating large numbers of Comanches, because they led the party off on a side trail to try to get away from the area. Early one morning the Texans were discoverd by a small Comanche hunting party which immediately scattered to warn their camp.

Whenever the Comanches thought they were facing a major war party, they tried to get their camp to safety; warriors would attempt to delay and confuse, giving time for the women and children to move the camp and for other braves to move the horse herd. About fifty warriors galloped back to meet the rangers and volunteers, striking them about a mile away from the camp.

The long march across rough country had tired horses and riders, but Hays gathered the men with the best mounts and started in pursuit of the slowly retreating Comanches. The superior Indian force, riding fresh horses, managed to delay the Texans long enough to allow the main camp to escape. The rangers and volunteers killed a number of the warriors, but the rest easily carried off all their casualties. Back at the deserted camp site, the Texans found a Mexican prisoner hanging by his heels, shot and lanced to death.

In his report, Hays estimated there were two hundred Indians with six hundred horses. There appeared to be another camp at the head of the San Saba, and yet another on the headwaters of the Guadalupe. The entire region had been burned, and Hays theorized this might be to provide fresh grass for a major campaign against the settlements.

His forces returned to San Antonio on August 4 after an absence of three weeks. Hays concluded his report:

> I cannot close this communication without men-
> tioning the service and bravery of Demacio (a
> Mexican) and Flacco (a Lipan) I truly regret that I
> cannot give a more favorable account of a Cam-
> paign which cost us much fatigue and depriva-
> tion.[29]

Flacco is well known. Demacio is probably Demacio Galvan, who appears on various muster and pay rolls for 1841.

The muster roll for this augmented company lists forty-five names, three times the size of the fifteen-man ranger detachments previously authorized. This impressive total lists men who served between June and August 31 when the company was disbanded. At mustering out, the company was only eighteen strong. Thirteen men served for twenty-two days, while twenty-four had fifty-seven days of service. The entry for John Flin shows ten days, with pay collected for only five days and a cryptic "killed" after his name with a date in July that is blurred and unclear. An interesting aspect of this company is the large number of men with Spanish surnames who enlisted on August 12. Antonio Coy, a former member of Antonio Pérez' company, had been with Hays since June 12, but this was the first time a large number of his compatriots had served as company members.

Although his force was mustered out, there was no break in service for young Hays who formed another company on September 1 to serve for a month. This unit, a mixed band of experienced rangers and new recruits, consisted of nineteen privates with Hays as captain. Peter Fohr and J.O. Truehart were back, as was Joseph Miller, his wound evidently healed. Antonio Coy and Damacio Galván reenlisted.[30] This company served thirty-one days but was paid for only fifteen. The pay roll reveals no explanation for the shortage in pay, likely due to the chronic lack of funds in the Texas treasury. There are no accounts of actions by this unit.

— ✪ —

While primary attention was given to the western frontier and the southwest, considerable activity was taking place along the Gulf Coast near Kinney's settlement at Corpus Christi. Most of the trade south went through San Antonio, but there was enough between Kinney's trading post and Matamoros to attract the attention of border outlaws. In early July Price reported he had raised forty men, following a requisition by the sheriff, and had marched to the Nueces to arrest a marauding band. They reached the river on June 23 and learned from a Mexican that three hundred Mexican soldiers under a Colonel Verial were hunting bandits who had surprised a group of eleven Mexicans and killed ten of them about thirty-five miles from Kinney's. Price found their bodies and thought they might have been part of a bandit group, led by a man named Yearby who had lived in Austin, which had earlier robbed some traders.

Price and his volunteers ran into a Mexican trader from Camargo and learned that another bandit named Owensby had been surrounded by several hundred Mexican soldiers who had killed eight or nine men and taken Owensby and five of his men prisoners. The trader told Price that Verial had returned south of the Rio Grande. Verial's activities convinced Price the Mexican government had a fixed purpose of retaining control of the area between the Rio Grande and the Nueces River. Price also reported the Mexican even had a weekly mail run between Matamoros and Kinney's ranch.[31]

Price and his men left the Corpus Christi area and returned to Victoria a few days too early to intercept a Mexican raiding party that came to the trading post of Philip Dimitt and James Gourlay and took Dimitt and three other prisoners. The raiders waited about, trying to find Gourlay, but he was away on business so the Mexicans looted the trading post and finally left. Later, Gourlay and James W. Byrne bitterly complained about the raid, asking for protection and pointing out that the nearby Kinney establishment had not been touched by the Mexicans.

Price's version of events near Corpus Christi was later supplemented by notes Kinney sent to Lamar. Two bandits, Ormesby and Yerbey (Price's Owensby and Yearby), had worked together during 1840 and 1841, robbing Mexicans and Texans alike; the bodies found by Price were actually a group of Mexican traders they had murdered. Another group of brigands, led by a man named Hull, was equally callous. One group of Texans even claimed to be rangers and operated for a time as a thinly disguised vigilante band led by a self-styled "Captain" Miles.

Kinney complained that men trying to trade with him were often robbed by Yerbey and his thirty-man gang of thieves and murderers, and claimed he tried to stop them, without success.[32] This was probably true, as Kinney had everything to lose if the bandits—Texan or Mexican—robbed and killed his traders. When the Mexicans learned of the slaughter of their trading party, they thought Kinney was responsible, and he had some trouble convincing the Mexicans he was innocent. He had nothing to gain by disrupting the lucrative trade with Matamoros, but Kinney was damned if he did and cursed if he didn't. If the Texans weren't after him, the Mexicans were. The three bandit gangs led by Ormesby, Yerbey and Hull managed to elude or fight off larger bands of Mexican troops until Hull's joining the Santa Fe expedition commenced the break-up of the gangs.

For a time news from the Corpus Christi region took center stage, with letters from one side or the other being prominently featured in Texas newspapers. A letter from J.E.L. Solomon, who was at Kinney's when Dimitt was captured, defended Kinney and his partner William B. Aubrey as being honest men, explaining part of the ill feeling against them was due to their shrewd business actions. Solomon said he had been in the area for six months, dealing with all parties, and had never seen anything to suggest Kinney had any dealing with the Mexicans other than normal trade.[33]

In mid-August, Kinney and Aubrey wrote a long letter explaining their conduct and replying to what were now charges of treason. The two men noted they had been on an exposed and dangerous frontier for two years, with no protection from their government, and had been required to hire from thirty to fifty armed men as a defense force. It was necessary for them to construct a log stockade and mount a twelve-pounder and two smaller cannon. They addressed the suspicions aroused by Kinney's visits to Mexico, noting these were nothing more than necessary business trips. The partners explained that most business coming from Matamoros had come to them, and this had led to envy from other traders. Widely printed, the letter did much to create the general opinion the men were innocent of treason.[34]

The various letters did not erase ill will in the region. On August 17 the San Patricio Minute Men and some Gonzales volunteers reached the tip of Padre Island and surprised a Mexican cavalry detachment. The soldiers, with their supplies and equipment, were brought back to San Patricio and held for exchange; the Mexican captain commanding the detachment wrote and suggested Dimitt be included in any prisoner exchange. The Texans became convinced after this deep raid that there were no further Mexican forces in Matamoros, and for a time there was quiet along the Gulf Coast. It would be nice to be able to report success in the efforts to exchange Dimitt and the three other Texans captured with him. Unfortunately, such is not the case. The Texans were carried into Mexico toward Monterrey. In Saltillo some of them escaped, and the Mexicans threatened to execute Dimitt if the escapees did not return. When he overheard the threat, Dimitt managed to obtain some morphine and committed suicide.

Even though Eli Chandler had remained busy during this time, his activities did not attract the widespread attention of the Kinney treason charges. The ranger captain was out again after Indians, leaving Franklin on June 4, 1841, with a forty-one man company, and moving up the Brazos River to the Cross Timbers, then to the divide between the Brazos and the Trinity. For three days the rangers crossed and followed various Indian trails. They camped the night of June 8, and the following morning captured a Mexican who told them there was an Indian camp in the vicinity. Chandler, afraid they might have already been seen by Indian hunters, left his packs with a seven-man guard and hurried to the camp.

They found two Indian women but an otherwise empty village. The rangers broke into squads and scouted the area, finding more women and children and a few men. By three in the afternoon they started back with twenty-four captives, one of whom told the rangers there were about sixty warriors in the band, all to meet at the camp for a big hunt. Chandler rode back to the deserted camp and found powder, lead, camp supplies, tools and sixteen horses. He left an old Ionie woman with a message they wanted peace; if the Indians would bring in any captives, Chandler would exchange them for his prisoners. As a gesture of friendship, he did not burn the supplies or destroy the camp.

When Chandler returned to his baggage guard he found the seven rangers had been attacked by many of the camp warriors. The Texans had not been caught by surprise and had managed to get to a ravine, organizing a typical defense by firing in relays, keeping a few loaded rifles for defense against a charge. Though heavily outnumbered, they successfully defended against several attacks and held their position, killing several warriors, including a chief, and wounding others.

Chandler was still considerably outnumbered and decided to return home, arriving June 18. His prisoners were a problem, one seldom faced by rangers, and he requested instructions about their disposition from the War Department. In a second message the same day, his official report, Chandler said his Mexican prisoner told him the camp was a mixed group, mostly Ionies but with some Waco, Caddo, Shawnee, Chocktaw and Kickapoo representatives. They were "making" corn between the Brazos and the Trinity and showed no disposition to make peace.

Chandler, like other commanders on the northern frontier, believed there was a major village somewhere on the upper Brazos or Trinity. In his report he mentioned he was going to rest his horses and go back and find this major camp. His Robertson County Rangers met the Milam County Minute Men, led by George Erath, at the Ionie village Chandler had just discovered. Lewis and a number of Austin volunteers joined the expedition.[35]

By general agreement, Chandler was designated commander, and the three units, composed of experienced frontiersmen who kept a spy screen well in advance of the column, moved up the Brazos. Erath said they had to contend with considerable sickness and moved slowly. The scouts found no trace of any Indian settlement or camp, and the expedition camped on the upper edge of the Cross Timbers, their supplies exhausted. Chandler and the other leaders decided to return as soon as the spies came back.

During the wait, Indians were seen near the ranger camp, and Erath and twenty men went to track them. He split his party into two squads, and one of them soon picked up a fresh trail. Following these prints, Erath came upon a party of either Cherokees or Kickapoos, who opened fire at close range from atop a rock cliff, killing A.T. Smith and grazing several other men. The rock barrier could only be approached from one side, and the Indian rifles kept the rangers at a distance. From a safe position Erath had his men open fire on any Indian who raised his head to fire. This sniping killed two Indians and may have wounded others. The other ranger squad arrived, having heard the shots, and shortly reinforcements came in from the main ranger camp. A ranger charge carried the cliff but the Indians slipped away in the woods, taking their dead and wounded.

The rangers buried their dead man and started back to the settlements. Erath split from Chandler on August 7, coming home by way of the Bosque, seeing no Indian sign on the way in. He was still convinced there was a big camp somewhere on the Brazos, but that only a major force could find it.[36]

Ironically, the big camp had been discovered some months earlier. While the various company commanders seemed to have been careful to submit reports on their scouts, these accounts were evidently not collated nor reviewed together by the War Department, no great surprise given the few clerks in the overburdened office. Chandler and Erath and Lewis were searching for a major Indian settlement in August that had been located in May!

The Texas Militia had also been looking for the fabled Indian camp. General Edward H. Tarrant, commanding sixty-nine men of the 4th Brigade, accompanied a scout by Captain James Bourland's company that left Fort Johnson and marched west to scout the headwaters of the Trinity

River. It was a small force to look for a camp containing hundreds of warriors.

Departing May 14, the militia unit marched for several days through the Cross Timbers, fording and refording various branches of the Trinity. They crossed several Indian trails, and on May 19 the tracks led to a deserted village. Certain there were Indians in the area, the troops did not burn the village, lest the smoke give them away, and instead used their axes to chop up anything of value.

The militiamen crossed the divide between the Brazos and the Trinity on May 21. Doubling back to the southwest they reached a ford on the Trinity, found fresh tracks, and sent out spies who located a camp three miles away. The men, dropping their blankets and packs and extra gear and forming in line, marched up and charged the village, routing the Indians and following them for a distance along a creek bottom. The Texans found another village two miles down the creek, with another in sight.

By now the horses were tiring and the company, less a few men left to watch the other village, suddenly began to face resistance. They had taken the villages by surprise, but the alarm had been given and warriors were swarming toward the militiamen from all directions. More and more muskets and rifles began to bear on the Texans, who were slowly advancing not against a distinct camp but an extended series of tepees and dwellings that they estimated ran for a mile and a half along the creek. The company was becoming scattered by their efforts to meet each attack, and General Tarrant began to worry about being cut off. He signaled a recall and began moving back to the first village, joined by the men guarding the packs.

Captain John B. Denton, Tarrant's aide, and Captain Bourland each took ten men to scout the woods. The two small units, joining about a mile and a half away, crossed a horseshoe bend in the creek and were startled to see a camp even larger than any they had seen that day. Under a dense fire from several directions Denton was killed and other men had their clothing torn by bullets. Captain Henry Stout, who had come along as an observer, and one of the enlisted men were seriously wounded. The Texans dismounted, started yelling with enough noise for fifty men, and prepared to charge on foot. The ruse worked; the Indians broke off and vanished in the woods. Bourland gathered up his men and casualties and retreated as quickly as possible.

The militiamen were in a dangerous position. Tarrant had taken a number of prisoners, which he did not want and could not guard, so he allowed the women and children to slip away. They took no male captives. From prisoners taken earlier they had learned there were a thousand warriors in the vast village complex. About half were out hunting or raiding, which may have saved the Texans. Most of the Indians were Cherokees, largely those driven out of Nacogdoches County, but there were also Seminoles, Creeks, Caddos, Wacos and Kickapoos in the settlements along the creek with an estimated three hundred acres of corn under cultivation. The area was a depot for stolen goods of all kinds, and the Texans uncovered huge amounts of molded shot and gun powder and a considerable weight of pig lead—the Indians seemed to have unlimited numbers of good firearms. The Texans even found all kinds of tools and bedsteads and feather mattresses.

Tarrant, fearful of ambush at a stream crossing and worried the warriors might discover just how small a force had attacked them and overrun his men by sheer numbers, led his men towards home as soon as possible before the still-scattered Indians could rally. About twenty-five miles out on the prairie the column stopped briefly to bury Captain Denton, and the rest of the return to their base was without incident. Despite their hurry to leave, the militiamen returned with three hundred pounds of lead and thirty pounds of powder, thirty brass kettles, twenty-one axes, seventy-three buffalo robes, thirteen pack saddles, two ladies' saddles, and three swords plus other items the report writer simply could not remember.[37]

The 3rd Brigade was also active during early June. The brigade commander reported to the president that members of his militia command under a Major Gage ran down a dismounted group of Indians and killed seven of the eight warriors. Earlier, the group's spies had caught up with a larger band and killed several, leaving the rest for Gage to find. These skirmishes were east of the Trinity, and the Texans believed the Indians were on their way to the big village complex discovered by Tarrant.[38] The brigades were in communication with each other, but no word of the village location reached any of the ranger companies. As previously described, Chandler and Erath were still looking for the place two months later.

The last few months of 1841 were relatively quiet, but Texas authorities were under no illusions this was a prelude to peace and quiet. Peter Hansborough Bell, who had served as Adjutant General several years earlier and who had a good idea of defense matters, was instructed to make a survey of the frontiers and submit defense recommendations to the president by August 30, 1841. Bell made a thorough inspection, traveling through the frontier settlements, talking to numerous people and conducting on-site inspections. He returned to Austin and sent in his report on October 4, 1841.

His lengthy observations, recommendations and inclosures carefully examined all aspects of defense of the western frontier. Bell paid considerable attention to traders and Mexicans in the frontier zone. He examined the possibility of closing down the trade, but came to the conclusion there were more reasons to keep the traffic going than not. His basic recommendation was to provide some form of protection to people trying to live on the frontier; without protection, the settlements would have to fall back. A key paragraph in his report recommended that the burden of defending the frontier be more equally shared rather than falling exclusively to the western counties. Bell also suggested forming a strong ranger-type command below San Antonio on the Nueces with jurisdiction all the way to the Rio Grande.

Bell spent some time in the Corpus Christi area and added his voice to those clearing Kinney and Aubrey of treason. He suggested that any ranger force in the Nueces-Rio Grande disputed territory could be supplied from Kinney's trading post, since Kinney had shown his willingness to support any force defending the people beginning to settle along the coast.

A short time before Bell's inspection visit, a Mexican band had attacked Refugio and then retreated. Bell reported that they had seemingly gone for good but could easily return if there was no protection in the area. Besides making a survey, Bell had the authority to form, abolish or reorganize minutemen companies. He found the Minute Men of San Patricio in poor shape and reorganized the company, ousting the commander and placing a Captain Cairnes, or Karnes, in charge to scout after the bandits who had raided Refugio. (This was not the Henry Karnes who had died the year before, and nothing much is known of this Karnes whose name Bell spelled Cairnes.) Bell instructed the new commander to scout east of the Nueces, but also gave him authority to move to the west side. He was not to do anything to invite attack.

Bell also reported that Kinney was supporting the San Patricio unit and suggested that the War Department might consider reimbursing him for this service. He regretted that a considerable quantity of goods taken from traders, chiefly horses and mules, could not be returned; despite government orders, the animals had already been distributed throughout the country. Bell was probably referring to goods and animals recovered from the various bandit gangs and held for proper identification. Victimized traders, however, were probably in no mood to await prolonged government wrangling![39]

Nothing much came of Bell's excellent recommendations—there was no money for anything other than minor projects. Whatever was left of the Regular Army was largely disbanded in 1841, and from then on the defense of the Texas Republic would fall to the ranger companies, the only remaining official military commands. Local minutemen companies, however, remained active.

Many of these companies considered themselves ranger units, and some of them drew pay. Captain Joseph Sowell led one such company, the Minute Men of Fannin County, and signed the muster and pay rolls for this "company of rangers." Sowell had a twenty-three man unit, including two lieutenants, which was mustered into service on July 17,

1841, but the command had fallen to fourteen men commanded by a sergeant when last paid on September 20.[40]

James H. Callahan had a company in Gonzales County serving in June and July 1841, then formed another unit in August which served through December 18, 1841. On one of his rolls, Callahan showed nineteen men as "spies;" the other nine were listed as "privates," an unusual classification for a ranger unit.[41] The Refugio Minute Men, listing some men as spies with others "detached as spy" and commanded by Captain John McDaniel, served during late 1841 and into 1842.[42]

As in earlier years, during 1841 various official ranger companies or ranger-type units served to defend Texas. The war with the Comanches continued, and several expeditions began breaking up the settlements of the Eastern Indians. Several captains continued to serve with distinction, but John C. Hays emerged as the preeminent leader. Other captains would come and go, die, move on or serve now and again, but from 1841 Hays was never really out of service for any length of time.

—6—

Invasion — 1842

As 1842 began, there was a lessening threat from the Eastern Indians scattered by the expeditions of 1841, but the Comanches remained a constant danger. The real worry, however, the threat on the Mexican border, led to congress' passing another joint resolution on January 26, 1842, establishing "a company of mounted men, to act as rangers on the southern frontier." A company was to be organized on such terms as the president deemed beneficial to the public interest. [1] The resolution did not designate a commander, but Jack Hays was selected. Whether the president, congress, or the Secretary of War and Marine appointed him is unknown, but Hays was a logical choice because the new unit was to operate on the southern frontier. No muster rolls for any of Hays' units for 1842 have survived, and what is known about his extensive activities is based on his few reports and the accounts of others. Based on these, this company was initially a small detachment.

The ease with which Texas could be invaded was demonstrated in March 1842 when a Mexican force under General Raphael Vásquez marched north and occupied San Antonio. Some of the citizens of San Antonio had been warning of a possible attack since late in 1841, so the attack did not come as a complete surprise. Hays began scouting the road south to Laredo in early March, apparently as a result of additional warnings. Ben McCulloch and Asley S. Miller, in San Antonio at the time, volunteered to act as scouts and rode west to check on the crossings on the Medina. In one of the reconnaisances that would later make him famous in the Mexican War, McCulloch counted the numbers in Vásquez' army but then blundered. Believing such a small force had to be an advance guard, he and Miller rode south to the Nueces, trying to find what they believed to be the main Mexican invasion force, and by the time they returned the invasion was over.

In the meantime Hays had dispatched Mike Chevallie and James Dunn to look for possible invaders, but both men were captured. Antonio Coy followed them, was also captured, and was roughly treated because the Mexicans evidently knew of his membership in Hays' company. The first definite news of the Mexican attack was brought by a courier, under a flag of truce, who gave the inhabitants until four o'clock to surrender the town. Hays met with the town leaders, and the matter was put to a vote. Fifty-three wanted to fight; fifty-four voted to leave.[2]

Following this introduction of democracy into a combat situation, a wild rush to destroy the considerable store of gun powder in the town took place. As many as 327 powder kegs were thrown into the river.[3] One man rode along on his horse, an open keg of powder under one arm, trailing powder behind him which another man lighted. The flame roared towards the rider, but fortunately the keg was empty before the fire caught up to the horse and rider. There was a reasonable explanation for this carelessness—most of the Texans were roaring drunk.

Knowing anything left in San Antonio would be taken by the Mexican troops, the San Antonians burned what they could not eat or drink. There were cigars and liquor for every man in town. When they finally decided to haul the artillery pieces to Seguin, many of the drivers could not walk and had to be tied to the ox-drawn cannon carriages or caissons.

John Twohig, a leading merchant convinced his warehouse would be looted, took a powder keg and laid a powder train to the rest of his stored gunpowder. He waited until most of the Texans had fled, watching from the end of the powder fuse. When town looters rushed over to break into his storehouse, Twohig calmly lighted the fuse and blew up his building then mounted his horse and followed the others.[4]

Vásquez entered San Antonio on March 5, leading a force

of five hundred soldiers, perhaps half that many armed
vaqueros, and some Caddo scouts. He found a stripped and
largely deserted town. After two days of looting whatever was
left, he started south again but released the three rangers
he had captured.

News of the invasion had spread along the frontier and
Edward Burleson, vice president of Texas as well as a
fighting frontiersman, gathered volunteers at Bastrop and
hurried to Austin. In view of wild rumors of another invasion's coming from Santa Fe, he planned to remain in Austin
until he had a firmer idea of the situation and sent couriers
in all directions to spread the news and scout out the
situation in other localities. He found Austin almost deserted; the government had fled to Houston until definite
word was received from San Antonio. Burleson collected all
the men he could and eventually marched down to San
Antonio but found a deserted town. He and his men stayed
for a time, living as best they could. They caught and ate a
number of pigs and took other property, belonging to Juan
Seguín, which would later be mentioned by John Jenkins as
a reason Seguín broke with Texas.[5]

Several companies hoping to be able to invade Mexico
joined Burleson in San Antonio. James H. Callahan, who
had earlier commanded a ranger company, was again in the
field, as was James H. Gillespie with a ranger-type unit.[6]
When nothing happened and with no food, most of the
volunteers returned to their homes. John Twohig and a few
other San Antonians returned to the town, but most stayed
away. The short raid, for it was no more than that, gave some
people a false sense of security.

Hays evidently lost some horses during the brief invasion, because Burleson sent him the following letter.

March, 1842

Sir: - I have issued an order to secure horses if
possible to forth[with] mount in the best possible
manner the balance of your command. You will
keep the most strict Vegulance [*sic*] and the Safety
of the Country depends on good spys. You will

report to me by the way of this place at Madam Calves Ranch all your movements strictly. You will send two or three of your best spys mounted on good horses as far west upon the preceding road and also the Laredo road at least to the Nueces and farther, if in your judgement they would not be captured. I have nothing new to inform you of Head Quarters except General Houston has made a declaration that he will carry the war into Mexico.

Yours respectfully
E. Burleson[7]

On March 17 President Houston wrote the *Galveston Adviser* of the events following the Vásquez attack. His report was current as of March 13, by which time Vásquez was well on his way south again. Houston reported the Mexican column was loaded down with plunder and marching only about eight miles a day, but "Colonel Hays is harassing them on their march." He pledged war would be waged against Mexico until the independence of Texas was recognized.[8]

This was one of the first communications by Houston indicating his intentions to fight an aggressive campaign against Mexico despite his awareness of the limitations of his country. He had mixed feelings on the subject, aware that an increased possibility of war with Mexico would hinder Texas' joining the United States. The slavery question was enough of a problem for the United States—the possibility of a war with Mexico was too much for the northern States to accept.

Houston thus began a series of communications that talked war, to a degree, while sumultaneously placing barriers to such a possibility. On March 18 Houston wrote of his plans to Brigadier General Alexander Somervell, a senior commander of the militia, and gave him instructions to wait before making any advances unless he was certain Mexico had mounted another invasion. The president was afraid that many farmers would rush to join an expedition, neglecting their spring planting and hurting Texas' economy.

He repeatedly cautioned the general about the necessity for discipline and strict control over any troops who signed up for an invasion of Mexico. Houston had always had a keen appreciation for security and accurate intelligence. He told Somervell to accept the services of two hundred men, well prepared to pass the summer as rangers and spies, to cover the country from San Antonio to Corpus Christi and westward. If Somervell could not enlist this many men, Houston wanted him to organize a corps of two companies of fifty-six men. Houston wanted Hays to command this corps, which was to report to Houston on a regular basis.[9] Houston subsequently sent a written order to Somervell to enlist these two spy companies for duty along the southern frontier.[10] He had evidently realized the impossibility of raising two hundred rangers on the frontier.

Despite much effort, little came of Houston's order to organize two ranger companies. The president himself wrote Captain Ephriam McLain on April 20, expressing his confidence in the former ranger and hoping he could form a fifty-six man company but also candidly mentioning that congress had made no provisions for paying the unit.[11]

Somervell sent out appeals to various leaders, inviting them to join him in San Antonio for an invasion of Mexico. These appeals were printed forms, with the name of the designated commander and the date written in by hand. One sent to Eli Chandler has survived.[12]

In the following months Houston also wrote numerous people in the United States, inviting volunteer companies to join in the attack on Mexico. He corresponded regularly with private citizens in Texas and members of his government about the proposed campaign, but the volunteers who responded to these appeals, and they came in some number, were not always suitable for military service even though they had come at their own expense, furnishing their weapons and equipment. Houston's grand plan began to fall apart even before it was fully developed, and on June 15 he complained of disciplinary problems with some of the volunteers from the States.[13]

Houston nevertheless continued with his efforts to raise more ranger units on the frontier. On June 18 he wrote a long letter to Ben McCulloch authorizing him to raise a fifty-six man command and again outlining his views on discipline and strict control of the troops.[14] If they accomplished little else, these appeals indicate that the government of Texas was aware of the acknowledged leaders within the frontier settlements.

Houston did not forget Indian allies and on June 21 issued what amounted to a safe conduct pass to Castro and a party of Lipans who had been visiting him and were ready to return to the Lipan camp near Austin. Houston stressed the past friendship of the chief and noted Texas might need them in a war with Mexico.[15] The Secretary of War and Marine reported on June 22 that Flacco and some Lipan braves had traveled to San Antonio to join Hays, but the ranger captain was scouting towards Laredo and the Lipans had finally given up and returned to Austin. The secretary mentioned the excellent work done by Flacco and other Lipans and their value to the spy service.[16]

Hays may have been scouting towards the border because of rumors of another invasion of Mexico. Mexican spies had reported to Canales in June 1842 that a Texas force near Corpus Christi contained four hundred infantry and fifty horsemen, plus an iron cannon at Kinney's ranch. The Mexicans were not immune to rumors and believed another strong Texas cavalry force was marching to attack Camargo.[17] For some months Mexican spies and agents had been active in Texas, ranging from the Nueces to the Brazos.[18] There had been a fight when a group of Mexican raiders surprised some Texans near San Patricio and killed a man they identified as Colonel Karnes,[19] who could have been the Cairnes or Karnes whom Bell had placed in command of the San Patricio minutemen.

Canales, the military commander of his region, was afraid the Texans would strike Mexico and decided to hit first. He formed an assault force from the troops in the various towns under his authority joined by a large group of armed *rancheros*. In a detailed report, Canales described how he attacked the Texans, drove them from their base camp into dense brush and battered them, killing more than twenty. Due to the density of the thickets, he was unable to completely destroy the group; however, his men captured several flags, including one of the Galveston Invincibles. The enemy shattered, he returned to Mexico.[20]

The Texas report of the action is considerably shorter. James Davis, the acting adjutant general of Texas, was over-all commander of a force of Texan and American volunteers based near Corpus Christi. Houston's appeals for American volunteers had not gone unanswered; New Orleans, Memphis and Mobile had volunteer companies in the area, and there were other units from Mississippi and Georgia. Most of the men in the area of Corpus Christi were Americans, with two mounted Texas companies. Ewen Cameron commanded a company of Mounted Gunmen in the two-unit battalion led by Major J.B. Hoxey.

In his brief report, Davis said his entire force did not exceed two hundred, including Cameron's Gunmen. This specific mention of the Gunmen suggests he considered Cameron's company as a ranger unit, different from his infantry companies. From his spies, Davis learned he might be attacked and shifted his men from their exposed camp near Corpus Christi to a strong defensive position in the brush. They left their camp baggage at the old camp.

About daylight they were attacked by Canales and the entire Mexican invading force which, they later learned from prisoners, consisted of two hundred Mexican troops and about five hundred *rancheros*. The fighting was very brief, perhaps twenty minutes, and the Mexicans broke away and abandoned the field. Davis said his men found only three bodies but many bloody trails made by bodies' being dragged away. He thought another thirty men had been wounded. He did not report any casualties among his own men. With Canales back across the Rio Grande, Davis considered his mission accomplished and disbanded his small force.[21]

With the disbanding of Davis' force, Hays and a few spies were all that officially remained for the defense of Texas. His handful of men based on San Antonio were left to protect the entire southern flank of the country.[22] The Texas Congress was aware of the republic's military weakness and passed another joint resolution on July 23 directing the president to accept one company of volunteers to range the frontier on the Trinity and Navasota rivers. The rangers were to equip themselves for a tour of not less than two months. At the same time congress authorized two companies for the southwestern frontier and set aside two thousand dollars to keep the companies in operation.[23]

Even before the joint resolution was passed, congress had already issued the orders for the formation of the two ranger units to protect the southwest. "Major Hays and Capt. Manchaca have received orders to raise men and act between the San Antonio River and the Rio Grande."[24] Passing the resolutions and issuing the orders were simple matters; raising the companies was more difficult. Hays formed a unit, or at least maintained the few spies that he already had, but the second company was never organized. Manchaca, who had served as commander of a spy company in 1836-1837 as part of Juan Seguín's regiment and who had also fought at San Jacinto, found it impossible to form a second unit. When it became clear to the Secretary of War and Marine that only one ranger unit was going to serve, Hays was instructed to increase his company to 150 men, all well mounted and armed. This force was to defend the entire country south to the Rio Grande.[25]

Hays could not have mustered an extra squad, much less 150 men, for reasons explained by the Secretary of War and Marine in his report for 1842. Rangers who had been serving for the past two years had become destitute in the service of their country. They had received little or no pay during these years, and had lost horses, weapons and clothing in the harsh frontier scouting. Men who did not have family obligations and who might have enlisted were too poor to pay for the horses and arms required to be accepted as rangers.[26]

This was not a new complaint. In an October 1842 letter P. Hansborough Bell had expressed the same views. He also had specific suggestions for the ranger force.

> I would respectfully suggest to your Department, the necessity of placing, as soon as may be practicable, on our Western frontier, one hundred & fifty or two hundred men—to be raised by Volun-

teer enrollment; or by draft; for the period of three
months; unless sooner discharged—to be well
armed; mounted and equipped; and in every manner provided so as to make them efficient Rangers
between the Nueces and the Rio Grande; and from
the Agua Dulce; or even from the Coast, and as
high up as the movements of the enemy may
require. . . .[27]

In the same report, Bell had recommended that the
government extend every liberality in supporting these rangers, because the burdens had fallen heavily on the western
citizens. He had predicted the western settlements must
contract in size unless they received some relief. No actions
had been taken on Bell's recommendations, and little developed from the proposals and resolutions and orders of
mid-1842. Hays and his few rangers comprised the official
army of Texas in the summer of 1842. Despite an impossible
financial situation, Houston continued to write letters concerning a counter-invasion of Mexico and lamenting the
sorry state of the volunteers in Texas. This state of affairs
continued throughout the summer, with no armed force
assembled, equipped or trained to invade Mexico or to repel
a serious attack from the south.

On September 14 Houston wrote Hays, addressing him
as Major Hays.

> You will receive despatches from the War Depart-
> ment, which will relate to your duties on the
> frontier. Feeling as I do for you a paternal anxiety,
> arising from uninterrupted friendship with your
> gallant father; I write to you unofficially; but will
> advise you, and you can if you will, estimate it in
> a two fold view.
>
> The situation of our frontier is very unhappy
> in its influences upon the prosperity of individu-
> als, as well as upon the general interests, settle-
> ment and growth of our country. To remedy exist-
> ing evils is a matter of primary importance to our
> situation. You are so situated that you can deter-

mine what course will be proper and safe to pursue. I have thought that advantage might result to
us if trade were opened to San Antonio and to such
other points as would be safe. In 1838 we had
friendship and commerce with Mexico, so far as
the frontiers were concerned, and had it not been
for the cow boys and Canales with his gang, we
would never have had any further troubles with
the inhabitants of the Rio Grande. But now, how
it would be proper to attempt the reestablishment
of trade will be for you to determine. . . .[28]

This somewhat strange communication certainly does
not read like the musing of a president bent on war. It does,
however, answer somewhat the question that has been
raised about the selection of Hays as a ranger captain when
there were more experienced men available. Hays certainly
benefited from his father's friendship with Sam Houston, but
he more than justified the confidence placed in him. The
respect Houston had for the judgment of the young ranger
is clearly shown by asking his advice on trading with Mexico
and even allowing him to make the decision on how to
reestablish the trade.

The problem of trade evidently worried Houston. The
next day he again wrote Hays, discussing the trade question
further and also the lack of intelligence, "If possible, send
me intelligence repeatedly, for I can hear nothing of what is
going on at Bexar, or of what your prospects are." Houston
closed by mentioning the English Charge d'Affaires had been
to see him and had strongly urged peace between Texas and
Mexico.[29]

The president's concern, almost obsession, about
prompt intelligence is understandable, but the letters Houston sent Hays were two weeks out of date when he wrote
them. His concerns about trade and peace were academic—
General Adrian Woll had issued a proclamation on August
30, 1842, to a Mexican force camped on the "left bank of the
Rio Bravo," announcing the second invasion of Texas. The
force was to march to San Antonio and reclaim the former
province.[30]

The Texans had no unit between the Rio Grande and San Antonio, even though they did have hints of possible trouble. One of the men who sometimes rode with Hays, William "Big Foot" Wallace, was probably responsible for alerting the Texans. Living in and around town, Wallace knew many of the inhabitants of San Antonio by sight, if not by name, and in later years he recalled that he had reported to Hays that there had been a number of strange Mexicans in the little town.

The rangers were also aware that there was little or no powder or lead available in the town. Stocks had been replaced following the Vásquez raid, but now the supplies necessary for fighting were again scarce. Hays sent Wallace and Nathan Mallon to Austin to buy whatever supplies of powder and lead could be found there.[31]

The two men reached Austin without trouble, but while they were there they helped bury the bodies of two men killed by Indians outside the town. They bought what supplies they could and started back for San Antonio, Wallace with a keg of powder wrapped in a blanket and tied to his saddle, and Mallon with some pig lead and a supply of percussion caps. The men were concerned about the recent Indian attack and the more than seventy miles of open country before they reached home. Because their horses needed corn, they fortunately decided to come back by way of Seguin where they found Hays and others with the news that San Antonio had been captured by Woll.[32]

Despite the rumors, and despite the ease with which Vásquez had taken San Antonio earlier in March, most of the Texans had gone about their business trying to make a living. On August 22 Sam Maverick and some of his friends had started back to San Antonio to attend the fall term of court. Concerned about his home and property's being abandoned, he had not brought his family back to town.[33] It was necessary to hold court to keep the judicial system from collapsing, and District Judge Anderson Hutchinson, considering the situation safe enough to travel, rode into San Antonio on Monday, September 5, 1843, prepared to open court.[34]

Nothing out of the ordinary occurred for several days.

Court opened as scheduled on September 9. Antonio Pérez, who had served well in several Indian fights and who had been as much a ranger as any man who claimed that distinction, warned Mayor John W. Smith in strictest confidence that a Mexican force of fifteen hundred soldiers was approaching town,[35] indicating he must have had accurate knowledge of Woll's advance.

Smith did not keep the information secret and told some friends. Late the following evening, September 10, a meeting was held with Judge Hutchinson presiding. About a hundred native citizens, led by Salvador Flores, joined some seventy-five other Texans headed by C. Johnson. A report by one of the men of seeing approximately one hundred horses north of the Presidio road was believed by the others to be the extent of the "invasion," just another band of marauders.[36] Nevertheless, just to be safe, the men at the meeting elected Hays commander and all vowed to resist any attack. Hutchinson decided to dismiss the grand jury, but he saw no reason to stop holding regular court sessions.[37] Hays took five men and, after directing the townspeople to stay calm until he or one of his spies returned with some word, started out in the night to locate any invading force. He also dispatched a courier to Gonzales, reporting what had happened and cautioning against panic but suggesting that plans for withdrawing might be in order in case the rumors of invasion were true. The message closed by noting fifty or a hundred brave men from Gonzales would be welcome.[38]

While this message was on the way to Gonzales, Hays and his spies were scouting south along the Laredo road. For once he was outfoxed; first going west then circling through the broken hill country north of San Antonio, Woll had been steadily advancing off of the main roads with a cumbersome little army of mixed infantry, cavalry and artillery including numerous supply wagons. Woll's masterful maneuver caught the Texans by surprise;[39] Hays was scouting south along the roads leading to the Rio Grande while Woll was already north of him and only three leagues from San Antonio. The Mexican general had spies in San Antonio from whom he had received reports of the ranger scouting trips. The last report Woll received was on September 10 when he was just north of town. He noted in his dispatches that the indiscretion of one of his agents with a woman in town had led to the inhabitants' knowing definitely of the invasion.[40]

On the morning of September 11, 1842, the people of San Antonio awoke to find a dense fog covering the town. Most of the Anglo Americans were staying in the Maverick house, a prominent location known as Maverick Corner, and could not see anything; but it soon became clear that Woll had surrounded the place with cavalry and was moving infantry along the streets. They could hear a band playing, and a cannon shot awoke anyone who was still sleeping. Unsure of what was happening, the men in the Maverick house let loose a heavy volley into the fog, causing thirty casualties among the troops massed in the streets. The Mexicans returned a volley, and for a time there was complete confusion. Manchaca, who had been staying with the men at Maverick's, scouted and returned cursing to report that Flores' men had run off after only a token resistance. When they finally realized they were opposed by over a thousand soldiers, with artillery, the Texans decided to surrender.[41]

Unable to locate any Mexican troops, Hays returned to San Antonio to find the town occupied by the enemy. He made two reports on September 12 concerning the capture of the town. The first was written near San Antonio and carried that designation. Addressed to the people of Texas, Hays stated he had put the citizens of the town in a position to defend San Antonio and gone to find the enemy, failed, and returned to find the place occupied and fifty-three citizens taken prisoner. He had examined the enemy camp and found it to contain thirteen hundred Mexican soldiers and two pieces of artillery. It was his belief they were the advance guard of an invading army. He would continue to scout them, and he asked for well-mounted men to join him for the purpose of spying.

Hays also noted he had captured a Mexican the same day who had told him the Mexican troops were going to fortify San Antonio and wait for reinforcements. The ranger recommended the prudency of a rendezvous at Seguin to repel any raiding parties the Mexicans might send out.[42]

Hays acted on his own advice and rode to Seguin the same day. It must have been much later in the day when he wrote his second, brief report to the Secretary of War and Marine repeating some of the details of his earlier message. Hays reported he had put San Antonio in good order and left with five men to find the Mexican force but had missed them because they had come around and entered through the mountains. He had attempted to enter town, but could not. After staying around San Antonio all of September 11, he had left spies behind and ridden to Seguin. He would try to watch for any approach to the "Guadaloupe."[43]

It must have been sometime after this that Wallace and Mallon rode into Seguin and learned of the capture of San Antonio. With a few others, Henry McCulloch had escaped from San Antonio, but most of the other male Anglo Americans—fifty-three of them—had been captured. John W. Smith, who had also escaped, managed to send a message with Mathew Caldwell, who rode to Seguin and began spreading the word by courier.[44]

Woll, in a clever and interesting move on his part, allowed his captives to send a message addressed to the citizens of Texas. Sixteen of the prisoners signed the letter, which said that they had made a brief resistance while still thinking the invasion was no more than another raid, that they had assurances they would be treated as prisoners of war, and that they would not have been taken prisoner had they not opened fire. The Mexican force was a formal army, determined "to conduct the war upon the most honorable and chivalrous" terms. The Texans requested that any Mexican officer or soldier captured by the Texans be treated accordingly.[45]

Hays' reports were carried by courier to as many settlements as possible. By three in the morning of September 14, a rider had brought the news to LaGrange, going by way of Gonzales. A committee in LaGrange immediately sent a rider to San Felipe with the news.[46] A messenger brought the word to Houston on Friday, September 16. The *Telegraph and Texas Register*, a weekly newspaper printed on Wednesdays, was out of date when the story appeared on September 21.

The newspaper printed a dispatch from Mathew Caldwell, requesting help. Caldwell said he had 125 men and was awaiting for his strength to double before marching on San Antonio. He reminded everyone that the Texans had previously needed only this many men to take San Antonio in 1835. He urged people to remain in their homes, because he thought they were safe enough, but he did need powder and lead. He closed: "The enemy must be whipped, we have them where we want them."

In response to these pleas, many an old fighter started for the scene of action. Reverend Z.N. Morrell and others in Gonzales gathered up all the ammunition and supplies they could find and headed for Seguin, leaving instructions for any other volunteers reaching Gonzales to follow. Arriving in Seguin, they found others had already formed and elected Mathew Caldwell their leader.[47] Caldwell selected ten men with the best horses and sent them as a reinforcement to Hays, now back on the Salado Creek eight miles east of San Antonio. There was little news from the invaders, other than the fact they were still in San Antonio. John Smith had managed to sneak into town and discovered the prisoners had already been moved. It did not seem the Mexicans were preparing to depart.

Morrell, switching from preaching to rangering without difficulty, was one of the ten reinforcements sent to join Hays on the Salado. He and several others left accounts that fill out the meager details of the official reports. Hays made several attempts to sweep around San Antonio in the following days, going north and then cutting back south to see if another Mexican force was coming to reinforce Woll. Unable to accomplish a complete sweep, he turned to scouting south along Salado Creek, a considerable barrier to east-west travel. While checking to see if the Mexicans had moved east towards the settlements, Hays' men discovered tracks of a mounted force heading towards Gonzales.[48]

Caldwell, reorganizing his men into a more formal command structure completed on September 17, placed Captain James Bird in command of sixty men from Gonzales and Seguin. Forty cowboys from Victoria made up another company with Ewen Cameron as captain. Thirty-five men from

Cuero were led by Captain Daniel B. Friar, and another twenty-five from LaVaca were commanded by Captain Adam Zumwalt. Forty of the men with the best horses served as a spy company under "the worthy Capt. John C. Hays." The total force of 202 men again elected Caldwell major by acclamation. C.C. Colley, receiving twenty more votes than John Henry Brown, was elected adjutant.[49]

From the writer's description in the newspaper article, Cameron was leading what can only by described as a ranger company. He had either kept his company together after the fight near Corpus Christi earlier in the year, or had formed a new one to meet the new emergency. Hays' designated spy company contained the men with superior mounts, members of his company augmented by men who had been rangers or who had frontier experience.

It seems likely Hays came back to take part in the reorganization, which was completed around two in the afternoon of September 17. He obtained enough men to bring his company to forty, and Mathew Caldwell's entire command of 202 men started for the Salado, arriving around midnight.

Other units had been watching for any move eastward by the Mexican army in San Antonio. James D. Owen had reported from Victoria on September 16 that intelligence had reached him that there were Mexican troops on the lower road. He had received a report of forty enemy in Goliad the night before. A spy sent to a *rancho* near deserted Goliad had found Mexican troops, and the ranch hands in high spirits holding a fandango. The spy had brought back wild reports of the size of the Mexican army, but Owen believed these were exaggerated although his spies had found signs of mounted men in and around the town. Owen told the Secretary of War and Marine he and others would fight long enough to allow the families and wagons to get out, but he was not too concerned because no large Mexican force could advance due to the extremely muddy roads. They could whip back smaller raids.[50]

During this period Hays and his men, without giving away their strength or where they were camped on the Salado, had been keeping a close watch on San Antonio.

They made several sweeps close to the outskirts of town one day, capturing some Mexican horses, and were chased for a time by forty enemy cavalry but escaped a fight. The Texans were literally starving because Hays would not allow them to risk disclosure of their position by hunting. He explained the problem to his hungry men and then asked Preacher Morrell to talk to them.[51]

The increasingly desperate situation of Hays' spy company was resolved when Henry McCulloch joined them bringing thirteen reinforcements and plenty of food. McCulloch, like his brother Ben, was an experienced frontiersman and a veteran of San Jacinto. Even though Henry McCulloch brought his own men, Hays was beginning to be better known; when the two groups combined they elected Hays commander of the spy company.[52]

The overall commander of the forces, Mathew "Old Paint" Caldwell, was ready to fight, a brave action on his part because he had only recently been released on parole from Mexican captivity. There is little doubt he would have been executed if again captured. He sent Hays and a few men to scout the town and see if they could draw out a few Mexican horsemen.

Hays took three men, including Morrell, rode completely around San Antonio, and was able to capture a prisoner on the sweep. When Morrell took another prisoner in full view of some of the Mexican troops, bugles began blowing, Mexican officers began yelling orders, and the soldiers rushed for saddles and weapons. The Texans galloped back across the prairie to their main camp with news that the original thirteen hundred invaders had been reinforced by another three hundred soldiers.[53]

Hays returned to San Antonio to try again to draw out the enemy horsemen. Caldwell reported:

> This morning at 10 o'clock I sent Capt. Hays near San Antonio to make a feint; on the enemy and then fall back to my position; which had the desired effect; and Capt. Hays was pursued by about 600 cavalry. . . .[54]

The ranger came close to ending his career that September morning. As the men in the scouting force approached San Antonio, they saw a considerable Mexican force awaited them. Woll seemed to have his entire cavalry command in the saddle. What had started as a ruse to draw out some horsemen for target practice ended in a frantic race for life to get back to the shelter of the Salado and the Texas rifles.

James Nichols, who was in the ensuing fight, described the Texas position as being in front of Salado Creek, which served as protection from a rear attack. In the 1840s Texas streams and rivers had considerable water flow, and Nichols described the Salado as thirty to forty feet wide in spots with a depth of twelve feet. The east bank of the creek was generally higher, but both banks were high enough to provide shelter and concealment. Nichols identifies two other terrain features that figured in the selection of their position by Caldwell, John Smith, Hays and several others; at each end of the position there were ravines running into the main creek. Hays and his spies were to hold the northern ravine; Nichols and a detachment had the duty of guarding the southern flank and the ravine there. The five-hundred yard distance between the two ravines spread thin the remaining defenders. Another description of the position describes it as running straight east and west and mentions only a southern ravine which twenty men had been designated to hold.[55]

Hays, remaining ahead of Woll's cavalry, led his detachment to a ford about a half mile above the hidden Texans, crossed, and rode down the east bank to the main defensive position before they could be cut off or run down. The rangers dismounted and took their places in the line. The ground to their immediate front was heavily wooded, the pecan trees hindering a mounted attack.[56] The Mexican cavalry, too well trained to run into an unknown situation, pulled up before they were in range of the Texan rifles and remained in formation approximately four hundred yards from the creek, their brightly uniformed troops in sharp contrast to the somberly clad Texans. It must have been around eleven o'clock in the morning.[57]

For a time nothing happened. The cavalry commander

sent back word of the location of the Texans and an estimate of their numbers, although his estimate could not have been very accurate. Probably aware of the ambush the Texans were trying to achieve, the Mexican commander stayed well in the open. The Mexicans, despite their superiority in cavalry, made no serious effort to scout the flanks of the Texans.

As soon as he could, Woll arrived with at least four hundred infantrymen, artillerymen to serve two cannon, forty Cherokees led by chief "Cordaway" (Vicente Cordova), and a hundred volunteers from San Antonio.[58] While the Texans watched the newly arriving forces deploy and then rest from their forced march from town, Caldwell made his final plans and gave his troops a short talk.

He then asked Morrell to address the men, probably expecting a short prayer. Reverend Morrell never confused his loyalties. This day he was not a Baptist preacher but a Texan with a rifle defending his country, and he was not inexperienced in such matters. Morrell told his friends not to fire until they could see the whites of the eyes, to take care and shoot low, and to first kill every man who carried a sword or wore an officer's hat.[59] When he finished his brief address, the Texans deployed along the bank and waited. While not specifically stated by any of the participants, the few men armed with shotguns must have been formed as a reserve. All of the riflemen, the bulk of the force, were on the firing line.

The Mexican artillery opened the fight, but the canister and solid shot did nothing more than rip the trees above the Texans. The huge pecan limbs torn off by the artillery fell among the men, startling some of the horses but doing no real damage. Seeing they were firing high, the gunners lowered the elevation of the cannon barrels and shot into the ground. The defenders dropped below the banks and watched the dirt and rocks blow over their heads in a loud demonstration that caused no injury.

When the Mexican infantry advanced, the Texas rifles cut into the formations long before the enemy's smoothbore muskets were within their firing range. The defenders fired in relays, dropping below the bank to reload. Initially charging in platoons of about fifty men, running across the front of the Texas line, the Mexican infantrymen fired as they approached but caused no damage. Their heavy losses caused this strange tactic to be abandoned.[00] As Morrell remembered in later years, all the Texans really had to fear was a flanking movement which would allow the Mexican force to fire down along their line. The Mexican commander did attempt one flanking maneuver, but he was unable to conceal the movement of his troops. The Texans with shotguns were moved hastily to the exposed position, hiding until the attacking force was only thirty feet away, then their close-range, shattering blast of buckshot tore the Mexican unit into shreds. The flanking attack simply melted away.[61]

The small band of Cherokees, slipping among the trees, was the only enemy unit that managed to come to close quarters with the Texans. In a sharp fight, often hand to hand, they were beaten back and lost several warriors. It was generally agreed that Wilson Randle of Seguin killed the notorious Vicente Cordova in this fighting.[62] A quick count showed eleven dead Cherokees, and the Texans turned back to defend against other Mexican charges. Each attack was easily stopped.[63] With long breaks between most of the charges, the battle was not a continuous engagement, and the Mexicans took time to collect their dead and wounded. Woll made no effective use of his cavalry, and why he did not send them wide to the flanks to attack the Texans' rear was never explained. Most of the Texans were on foot, and Hays and McCulloch's few horsemen could not have made any decisive resistance to the over two hundred enemy horsemen.

The Mexican infantry resumed the frontal attack, advancing, halting, firing, reloading and moving forward again. Most of the time they overshot. The Texans were well sheltered, both while firing and while reloading, and easily turned back each rush. Each charge was halted farther away from the creek bank while the Mexican dead piled up among the trees. During one halt when the Mexican horsemen left the field leaving the infantry in position, the Texans heard distant musketry and rifle fire and then considerable cannon fire. They began to worry someone coming to reinforce them had been caught in the open.[64]

During the final, halfhearted charge, the defenders became so contemptuous of the Mexicans they sat atop the bank and fired among the trees. They suffered their only fatal casualty when some of the Cherokees again crept among the trees and opened fire, but a few other Texans were wounded. The Mexicans finally called for a truce until six o'clock to carry off their wounded.

As the Mexicans began retreating towards San Antonio, Caldwell had a difficult time keeping his men in place. They were still heavily outnumbered, and he was worried about the enemy artillery. Despite carrying off many of their injured men, the Mexicans left sixty dead and wounded near the creek bank. Most of the wounded died during the night.[65]

When Caldwell wrote his report that night, he did not have any clear idea of what had happened out on the prairie and made no mention of the small arms and cannon fire they had heard. A company of men led by Nicholas Dawson had been cut off when they had run into the rear of the Mexican force fighting Caldwell. The men had ridden for eighty miles, pushing their horses to reach the Texans with Caldwell. Suddenly surrounded by enemy cavalry, they could neither run nor effectively fight on their exhausted mounts. They fired into the nearest cavalry but were soon under heavy cannon fire. A few attempted to surrender and were shot. One of the men in the company, known only as Griffin, a slave of Samuel Maverick's who was armed only with a mesquite limb, fought until he was cut down.[66]

Ben McCulloch, Clem Hinds and Eli Hankens of Hays' detachment made a scout at dusk and found the site of the battle, but it was becoming too dark to identify any of the mutilated bodies. Uncertain if any of the corpses was Morrell's son, believed to be riding with Dawson, the Texans spent a restless night.

Some time during the dark hours, a hundred men from Bastrop reached Caldwell. This event marks the first mention of Sam Walker in Texas history and the ranger story. Recently arrived in Texas, Walker had served in the Seminole Campaign in Florida and had considerable military experience. When news of Woll's invasion reached him, Walker joined a local ranger company led by Jesse Billingsley and headed for San Antonio. Halted by darkness and uncertain of Caldwell's location, the company commander sent Walker ahead to find the Texans. He managed to locate Caldwell's men and was sent back to bring up Billingsley's reinforcements.[67] A similar scout a few years later in the Mexican War would make Walker a national hero.

About ten the next morning, Caldwell received the news, probably from Hays' spies, that the Mexicans had started leaving San Antonio.[68] After a short consultation, Caldwell led his combined force towards town. Morrell was extremely worried about his son, but there was no word in town so the minister and some of his friends rode out to the scene of Dawson's fight. Even though some of the bodies were so mutilated thay could not be recognized, Morrell was certain his son had not been killed. The boy had to be a prisoner, another reason for Morrell to go after the retreating Mexicans.

Hays had his own reasons for chasing the Mexicans; several of his rangers had been captured when San Antonio was overrun. All the Texans were concerned about the more than fifty men, now on their way to Mexico, who had surrendered to Woll. Despite gallant efforts, however, they would not be able to rescue the prisoners.

Reinforcements began arriving in San Antonio almost as soon as Caldwell's band reached the town. Jesse Billingsley and a small detachment were first, but turned back to recover the bodies of the men of Dawson's company and return them to their homes. The exact sequence and names of individuals or unit commanders are uncertain, but some good men were catching up to the chase. Ben McCulloch was late in hearing the news, but came as swiftly as possible. William Eastland was in the group. John H. Moore arrived with a considerable force. The Texans started west after Woll, heading for the Medina. The only known reinforcements joining the Texans after their departure from San Antonio were one hundred men from LaGrange who arrived while the Texans were camping for the night on the banks of the Medina.[69] The LaGrange men must have been the last sizable reinforcement, because Morrell recalled that the original two hundred men had increased to five hundred by Tuesday morning September 10.[70] Most of the men were on foot, with Hays and his men acting as scouts and advance guard.

The retreating army made poor time, slowed by the large number of carts and wagons they had loaded with wounded and everything of value in San Antonio. Woll, who had learned or suspected that Caldwell would be reinforced, had piled his injured on anything he could find that moved and had slipped out of town during the night of the fight on the Salado. His losses were never accurately determined; Morrell later claimed he had heard Woll admitted to six hundred casualties.[71]

Thomas Jefferson Green, a former member of the Texas Senate and Congress from Bexar, later wrote one of the best accounts of the Woll invasion and the Somervell expedition, most of it based on his personal participation. He believed Woll left San Antonio with approximately two hundred wounded, most of whom died on the way back to Mexico.[72] In his reports, not always models of fact, Woll noted his command "scarcely numbered 500" after leaving San Antonio, but earlier he had sent back two escorts for prisoners and wounded, possibly 199 men.[73] If these guards are subtracted from what he said he had before any fighting, 288 soldiers remain unaccounted for, presumably casualties.

The Texans had no way of knowing the extent of Woll's losses, or that now their own forces may have been numerically equal to the Mexican army. They did know they were heavily outnumbered by the Mexicans in cavalry, and that they had nothing with which to counter the enemy cannon. Ironically, far from insuring victory, the increase in their numbers had brought about a split in the Texas force. John Henry Brown, who took part in these events as a young man and who was later to write a history of Texas, stated that the combined force chasing Woll was 489 men, not far off of Morrell's estimate of five hundred. Brown also stated the command was divided into two battalions with Caldwell as colonel, John Moore as lieutenant colonel and James S. Mayfield as major.[74] Neither Nichols nor Morrell mention the division of the command. Both agree that agitation by Moore and Mayfield resulted in Moore's being voted commander, an occurence not mentioned by Brown. Whatever the chain of events, there is no doubt that Caldwell no longer had any firm control over the force.

On the evening of Wednesday, September 21, the Texans caught up with the Mexican rear guard at a crossing on Hondo Creek west of the Medina. Even though the ford was protected by a Mexican cannon and a detachment of troops, Hays wanted to advance against it at once and requested any mounted men who could be spared. He wanted enough men to bring his detachment up to one hundred, but there were not that many riders with good horses in the slowly advancing Texas force. Hays did not hesitate. Morrell, mindful of his captive son somewhere in the Mexican column, again gave the few horsemen a challenging talk.[75]

Taking what few men he had, tired horses or not, Hays led a charge across the ford and up the slope towards the cannon, whose gunners failed to allow for the sloping ground and overshot the charging Texans. Before the artillerymen could reload, the horsemen were past them, killing the gun crew with pistols and shotguns and scattering the infantry reserve. One of the Texas was slightly wounded, another's horse was killed. None of the infantry stayed to make a fight, and darkness brought an end to the skirmish.[76]

Different men saw the Hondo Creek fight in various ways. One said Hays and his horsemen killed thirty gunners, wounded thirteen, and held the cannon for a time before heavy reinforcements came up and forced him back across the creek.[77] These figures must have included the infantrymen, because a cannon crew would have been significantly smaller than thirty in number. Caldwell, unfortunately skipping over this part of the campaign in his report, wrote only that Hays made an attempt to take the cannon and could not be supported due to the "heavy" ground and tired horses.

Nichols is not so charitable. He said Hays went galloping up the slope thinking he was leading a charge rather than a "forelorn" hope. William Eastland had been given command of some mounted men and waited in a ravine to support the ranger attack but was shortly recalled. The bulk of the Texas force was formed in another ravine by Moore who, rather than taking the offensive, prepared to receive a Mexican attack! What could have been the end of Woll's army turned into a major embarrassment.

Both sides went into camp for the night, with the Mexican camp marked by extensive cook fires. Accounts of what happened during the night vary from writer to writer. Morrell said Ben McCulloch scouted the enemy camp and returned to recommend waiting for dawn to attack. When it was light enough to see, the Texans found the Mexican force had slipped away and marched another six miles.[78] Nichols claimed Henry McCulloch made this scout. He wrote that Hays became suspicious of the bright fires and lack of noise and took Ice Jones with him to check the enemy camp only to find the Mexicans had slipped away, leaving the fires as decoys.[79]

Caldwell reported he found the Mexicans the next day, drawn up for battle on the open prairie where his men would be exposed to artillery fire. His men were tired; horses were exhausted; supplies were running out, especially powder and shot, and he deemed it prudent to retire.[80] For a fighter, Old Paint Caldwell wrote a diplomatic report, but in actuality he had prudently not attacked or continued the pursuit because of a disastrous split within the various groups that now comprised the Texas army.

Mayfield, who led the Bastrop County volunteers, took a strong stand against further action and spoke at some length about the futility of following the Mexicans, now obviously in full retreat. Even though he conveniently failed to mention the prisoners in Woll's army, his remarks fell on generally receptive ears. Most of the men who had fought in Caldwell's band at Salado, or who had joined in the initial pursuit, had left families unguarded and homes unprotected. They were tired from long marches, little food, and only snatches of sleep. The countryside was muddy, the few horses broken down. There was almost no ammunition in the column.

Morrell countered these arguments with an impassioned plea for continuing the chase. The captives must be released; Dawson's men had to be avenged. This time Morrell was unsuccessful; too many men voted to turn back, and those who voted to stay were not enough to make any serious pursuit. Preacher or not, Morrell was honest enough to admit he never forgave Mayfield for breaking up the Texas force.[81]

The Woll invasion was over, but recriminations and arguments would continue for a long time. Nichols blamed Caldwell for not retaining his independent command over the original force that had fought on the Salado. He stated that Hays had retained command of his company, even though generally operating under Caldwell. When Hays' fighting force from Salado was joined by the forces under Mayfield and Moore and the various other commanders, the original fighters were outnumbered and outvoted on matters of command and procedure. Caldwell lost control of the Texans. Mrs. Maverick later noted that Caldwell was troubled by not being able to catch Woll and by being blamed for the failure of the pursuit. She always thought he died from grief.[82] Whatever the cause, Old Paint had rushed to the defense of Texas for the last time. He returned to Gonzales and died on December 28, 1842.

Contemporary writers spent considerable time and ink discussing the Woll invasion. Their conclusions do not always agree with the conclusions of later historians. There was some speculation that Santa Anna had ordered the invasion as part of the continuing effort to cause trouble and discord in Texas, or that it may have been a cover to allow discontented Mexicans the chance to return to Mexico. About two hundred families did return with Woll. There was talk that the invasion was a scheme to stop the autumn's judicial session in San Antonio, where the district court was to hear numerous creditors against Juan Seguín, and that Woll's raid was made to put an end to the case and keep Seguín's lands from being seized by creditors. Tom Green wrote that one of the reasons Seguín left Texas was a belief that the western frontier was collapsing, a belief also advanced as an excuse for Antonio Pérez, firmly loyal earlier, to desert and join Woll's army.[83]

No action was taken against any of the remaining natives in San Antonio, even though some had actually fought with Woll at the Salado. Only those who left were censured. A few,

Manchaca for example, continued to fight with the rangers. For the most part, however, any feeling of cooperation was gone, and there was no longer a significantly large mingling of Anglo-American and Spanish names on the ranger muster rolls.

Of the various accounts of the invasion, none is more interesting than Woll's almost daily reports, referenced earlier, to his superiors in Mexico. He sent an initial, rather brief summary of the Salado fight about midnight on September 18, reporting that he had pursued a considerable force of Texans who had had the audacity to attack the city, chasing them out to the Arroyo del Salado. There he fought with three hundred Texans until a force came from his rear. He immediately sent three squadrons and a light field piece to fight these new arrivals. His horsemen and cannoneers killed 120 and captured fifteen, then turned back and scattered the Texans on the Salado, inflicting great loss. Because his men had been out all day and were hungry, he had returned to San Antonio.

The next day, September 19, Woll made a terse report saying he had sent Lieutenant Colonel D.C. Bravo with twenty-five soldiers and thirty-three *defensores* from the Rio Grande to escort his wounded from the battle of the previous day.

A day later he dispatched a long, detailed account of the fighting along the Salado. In this longer version he reported he had sent Antonio Pérez, now a lieutenant colonel in the Mexican army, and twenty-five *defensores* of San Antonio reinforced by sixty regular cavalrymen, to chase Hays. They were later followed by another 130 horsemen, while Woll followed with his infantry. He stressed that his instructions forbade him from fighting in woods, but he nevertheless decided to advance. Woll mentioned that the enemy troops were commanded by Colonel Caldwell. According to Woll, his men were attacked by the Texans, who were repulsed. When he was certain no reinforcements were coming from Seguin, Woll attacked the Texans.

It was then he learned that a large force was approaching, and he sent several squadrons and a field piece to combat these new arrivals. His men killed 120 in a fifteen-minute skirmish, and then returned to help the others finish off the Texans on the Salado. They were unable to complete the destruction because the Texans had fled deep into the woods. Woll collected his wounded and returned to San Antonio about ten that night. He regretfully reported he had twenty-nine soldiers killed and fifty-eight wounded. They initially observed sixty Texan bodies in the woods, but the wounded had been carried away. Woll estimated the Texas losses had been severe, though he could find no more than five bodies in the woods on a later check.

Woll listed one captain killed and five other officers wounded in the fighting. He cited most of the Mexican officers for their gallant conduct, declaring the Texas prisoners were astonished and full of admiration for the way his soldiers had fought.

On September 20 he made another report, mentioning he was leaving Bexar, and on the same day he noted he was camped on the left bank of the Medina. A considerable number of the families in Bexar had joined him, along with their flocks and possessions piled on 150 carts. The next day he was still on the Medina reporting the death of one of his wounded officers.

Woll sent a dispatch from his camp on the Rio Grande on September 22, reporting on events of the past few days because he had evidently been too busy to write each day. He gave his version of the Texan attack on his rear guard: the haughty Texans had rushed his rear guard with a hundred men but were repulsed and lost a captain and many horses.

Woll has an interesting note to the report of September 22. He told of repulsing the Texans at the Hondo ford and riding back to his camp on the arroyo. On the way he was challenged by a Captain Hays, who took off his hat and called him by name. Hays supposedly asked him to approach and talk. Despite the pleas of his aides, Woll said he rode back and took off his hat and returned Hays' salute. Two treacherous Texans fired at him from a distance of thirty yards but missed, whereupon "the aforsaid Hays projected himself into the most dense [part] of the forest, defaming god and insulting me and calling me a coward."

It would be interesting to know how Woll knew Hays' name. Woll had a good idea of events in the Texas camp, mentioning that five "San Antonio Mexicans" including Antonio Coy were riding with the Texans. Woll concluded his series of dispatches and reports by saying the Texans had broken into small bands and given up the chase.

Throughout his reports, Woll displayed an almost pathetic eagerness to remain in favor with his immediate commander and the Mexican government—Santa Anna. He constantly overstated the Texas strength and the terrible losses he inflicted on each force opposing him. Just like the Texans' reports of this campaign, Woll's dispatches often raise unanswered questions. Woll mentioned several times he was to stay in Texas only a month but never said why, or who, gave him the instructions. He also made a point of not fighting in woods, again without explanation. Despite Woll's initial proclamation, it is clear the Mexicans were not trying to conquer Texas; Woll's larger command was no more attempting a permanent stay than had Vásquez' smaller force. Today, with the advantages of time and research, it is clear Woll was following orders of the Mexican government to make a strong reconnaissance in force to determine if the Texans were gathering an army to invade Mexico—hence the time limitation on his stay north of the Rio Grande.

If the campaign was considered over by Mexico, it was not closed in Texas. Even though he had not caught up to Woll, Caldwell planned to resume operations later. He concluded his own report by saying his men had gone home and would reassemble in thirty days. It is not known how many returned to carry the war into Mexico but Edward Burleson, with hopes of leading the attack, set October 25 as the date to rally in San Antonio. Various groups and individuals started for the town before that date. Sterling Brown Hendricks, a well-educated lawyer from Alabama who had arrived in Texas in January 1841, was one of the men who came to fight. He and Tom Green would write the two basic accounts of the expedition against Mexico.

A company commanded by Captain Samuel Bogart reached San Antonio too late to chase Woll, but his eager volunteers from Washington County decided to remain in the town until the new army could be formed. They waited eight weeks.[84] Bogart and his men could have saved themselves incredible hardships had they been able to foresee what was ahead of them. Just reading the "orders" forming the expedition would have warned the more astute of trouble.

On October 3, 1842, President Houston wrote Brigadier General Alexander Somervell about a possible invasion of Mexico.

> Sir—Your official communication from San Felipe, under date of 29th Ultimo, reached me late last night. I seize the first opportunity to communicate my orders.
>
> You will proceed to the most eligible point on the Southwestern frontier of Texas, and concentrate with the force now under your command, all troops who may submit to your orders, and if you can advance with a prospect of success into the enemy territory. you will do so forthwith.

Even though Houston mentioned he intended to "communicate my orders," he never gave Somervell a *direct* command to do anything. What seemed an order had a qualification.

> You will receive no troops into your command but such as will march across the Rio Grande under your orders if required by you so to do. If you cross the Rio Grande you must suffer no surprise, but be always on the alert.

Houston cautioned Somervell about the necessity for discipline and control of his troops, for maintaining security and observing the rules of civilized warfare. In closing, he told Somervell he could "rely upon the gallant Hays and his companions" and desired that he obtain his services and cooperation.

Nothing is said about the strength or composition of the possible invasion force. There is nothing about pay, provisions, equipment, ammunition, where to invade Mexico, or what the force was supposed to do after invasion. The closest Houston came to any logistical support was, "You are at liberty to take one or two pieces of ordnance now at Gonzales. For my own part I have but little confidence in cannon on a march." The only real specific is the suggestion to contact Hays and make use of his ranger detachment. Nothing was said about Hays' actually being part of Somervell's command, and apparently no specific orders were dispatched to Hays on the subject. It was a missive guaranteed to bring about failure.[85]

As president, Houston had more on his mind than a possible invasion of Mexico, which he probably considered nothing more than a raid to restore pride among the Texans. Santa Anna's thrusts were an occasional nuisance, but Indian raids were a daily threat. As always, Houston sought to solve the Indian problem by diplomacy. In October he sent commissioners to make a treaty with the scattered Eastern Indians, meeting at a Waco village. His letter to Eli Chandler to raise a detachment and escort the commissioners shows Houston kept his eye on possible ranger commanders and knew which ones to tap for critical missions.

The dangers in Indian treaty negotiations were fully appreciated by the Texans; one of the commissioners even wrote on the back of Houston's letter that it might be wise to increase the ten or fifteen men proposed to twenty. Trouble was possible not only from the Indians but also from those Texans who did not want peace. Chandler was equal to the job; he raised seventeen men, served for twenty-five days, and brought everyone home safely.[86] He must have had other problems, or recognized the threat of danger, because he thereafter remained close to home and took no part in the expediton forming near San Antonio.

Captain Bogart and his company managed somehow to exist in and near San Antonio while waiting for the expedition to start. He was worried that the town might fall to another Mexican attack and talked with Hays about a guide for a patrol he wanted to send to the Nueces River. The guide was not furnished, but Bogart sent his men anyway. They followed Woll's route to the river but found nothing. Thereafter Bogart kept spies out to prevent another surprise.

Just what Hays was doing during these weeks is unknown. Hendrick's narrative suggests that the ranger was doing very little, certainly not near San Antonio. Other accounts contain no mention of Hays. By the end of October several units had assembled about the town, but Somervell did not arrive until February 4, a month after Houston wrote his letter. Accompanied by his adjutant general, John Hemphill, he began a leisurely organization of the rabble.

Tom Green noted, with some disgust, that the general spent more time being entertained than in training troops. The people doing most of the wining and dining were the same people who had been so attentive to Woll when he was in command of San Antonio. By now there were almost no Anglo Americans left in town.[87] Hendricks estimated there were twelve hundred men in and around the town at this time. Somervell wasted another two weeks in forming the men into companies; what should have been done in hours took days; a day of work somehow stretched into a week. Many men became bored or disgusted and went home, and no effort was made to stop desertions. Neither was any effort made to explain what they were doing or what their commander planned.

The men had come to invade Mexico, not sit. They had left families unprotected, and their main occupation was farming not fighting. Willing to take time to fight and to face hardship and danger when necessary, they were not willing to sit about town doing nothing. They would not wager anything on an incompetent commander, and many such as Green and Hendricks had early doubts about Somervell. The force continued to shrink. The invasion of Mexico was doomed before it ever left San Antonio.

Somervell eventually divided his companies into two regiments and, remembering Houston's suggestion, contacted Hays. Hendricks remembered that Hays requested Bogart's men join him as a second spy company. At this time Hays had a detachment of eighteen men, while Bogart led a sixty-man company. The Washington County men naturally wished their captain to command both units, but Hays was senior, actually the only officer in an official position. His company was a special command, and he evidently intended to keep this independent status.

To keep some semblance of peace, Somervell had an agreement that, whenever Hays went forward with any of his men, an equal number of Bogart's troops would accompany them. When Hays was absent, both units would be commanded by Bogart. It was an unsatisfactory arrangement. Bogart was urged to seek election as commander of one of the regiments being formed, but he declined. He believed he could do more good as commander of his spy company.

Bogart and Tom Green were either assigned or assumed the important task of shoeing the horses; the Somervell expedition was basically a mounted force. Efforts to obtain powder and lead from the town citizens failed; the Texans did not have silver for payment. Green, bitter about the lack of money and supplies, noted that the large herds abandoned by the citizens of San Antonio who had fled with Woll were not confiscated. The Texans took enough animals to feed themselves, nothing more. For the most part everyone was out hunting deer, then tanning hides to make pantaloons and jackets. The weather was changing, and there was a growing chill in the air.[88]

The organization of the command did not really change anything. Somervell still wasted time, and the actual move towards Mexico seemed as far away as ever. Finally, on November 13 he started the troops for the Medina River where they camped for almost two weeks waiting for a cannon and their commander to arrive. When both the gun and the commander finally reached the command, Somervell decided not to take it with him! Most of the troops were thoroughly disgusted and dispirited.

The men began to encounter the first real signs of winter, with cold rainy days made worse by a chilling wind. For some reason the column struck out across country rather than taking the Laredo road. Texas roads were sorry in wet weather, but at least they crossed known terrain. The Texans marched blindly into a huge bog, which extended for miles, and floundered in the deep mud for almost three days before finally reaching firm ground. Many horses were lost in the efforts to get clear, and most of the remaining animals were in poor condition. It was the first of several disasters, and the worst.

Hendricks wrote a factual, reasonably objective account of this campaign, but his comments on the bog are blunt:

> Whether General Somervell is to be blamed with this is not for me to say, but it is said by going the Tuscosa for eight miles below our encampment, we could have struck the Laredo road without travelling over any bad or boggy ground. Captain Hays, however, was the pilot and between him and General Somervell lies the blame!

Green had little to say about the bog, other than that Somervell decided to surprise Laredo by a flank move, and a seven-day march stretched into seventeen days. He did mention that the horses were "damaged."[89]

After the days in the bog, tempers were on edge when the straggling, now partially dismounted column finally reached a place to camp. Hays was absent on a scout, and Captain Bogart ordered the remaining men in the spy company to bivouac with his company. A Lieutenant McLain in Hays' detachment refused to let the rangers move, and several of them started cursing Bogart, who withdrew. When Hays returned, Bogart went to the ranger camp to discuss the awkward situation. General Somervell and Hendricks attended this meeting, as did a number of rangers. Despite the presence of Somervell, some of the rangers began berating Bogart. McLain, probably Ephraim McLean, a former ranger, was especially abusive and was ably supported by a Sergeant Stokes. Seeing he was wasting time, Bogart left, followed by Hendricks, and later preferred charges against McLain and Stokes. Somervell promised to hold a court martial, but his promise was the end of the matter except that the general lost a little more respect.

The expedition, falling apart, never had a chance. As early as November 19 the Acting Secretary of War M.C. Hamilton wrote Somervell a blistering letter, noting that the war department had not received any communications from the commander. Hamilton noted he had received reports of men allowed in camp, or even mustered into service, who had no intention of going to Mexico. Such men were consuming food and supplies. Hamilton ordered Somervell to determine if he had force enough to carry out the objectives of the campaign so late in the season. If so, he was to move immediately; if not, he was to disband the force.

In his letter Hamilton discussed several matters that may explain some of Hays' actions. The ranger had been authorized to declare martial law in Bexar County, if necessary, and had broad powers as commander of the western frontier. The war department had expected that Somervell would form his command east of San Antonio, and that Hays would have an independent command west of town. When Somervell moved, Hays would report to him and act under his orders; but if Somervell did not cross the Rio Grande, or disbanded his force, Hays was to revert to his old status and could even raise three ranger companies.[90]

Hamilton's letter could help explain why Hays consistently acted in a semi-independent manner. There is nothing to explain what arrangement Hays had with Somervell, or what orders, if any, the general might have given him. Hendricks is the authority about Hays' detachment being increased to sixty men. Some of these new men may have been the ones cursing Bogart, men whom Hays did not have time to integrate properly into his experienced rangers. Whatever the facts, on November 30 Somervell assigned Hays' unit as the spy company and designated Bogart's company as the leading company within the column, a position of honor.

When the column started out the following morning, Bogart's men refused to follow the spy company. They galloped after the reinforced ranger company, and the two commands trotted side by side for several miles. Finally a raging Somervell galloped up and halted the comic opera performance. He forced Bogart to take the second place in the column, at which point most of the Washington County men decided to return home. They finally agreed to stay, fearing their departure might jeopardize the success of the expedition.

The Texans marched for several days without incident.

Hays and his rangers, moving a day ahead of the column, were definitely performing as the spy company. The others followed their tracks, spotting the remains of their camp fires from time to time. Hays may have been continuing to have disciplinary problems, because the column passed one area burned over by fires that had not been properly extinguished. His old companies would not have been so careless. On the night of December 2 Somervell had a message from Hays saying the ranger, with Flacco and another Lipan, had gone to scout the Mexican border, leaving the rest of his men on the west bank of the Nueces. Hays' message is the first mention of Lipans' scouting with the rangers.

The Nueces was not a large stream, but it was in flood stage and crossing was hazardous. Somervell seemed to exercise no more command over the river crossing than he had over previous activities, and Bogart is credited with devising the plan to make a makeshift bridge to allow the command to cross the rushing waters without undue trouble. Safely across, the column camped on the west bank to await word from Hays.

Supported by some Lipan scouts, Bogart's company was sent forward on December 5 to locate Hays. Flacco and another Indian rode into camp the following day and reported Hays had gone down to Laredo and captured two prisoners. The ranger had scouted the river and found no Mexican troops because the main enemy forces were either downriver in Guerrero or upriver at Presidio. Hays had hurt his horse capturing the prisoners and was camped only eighteen miles away.

Bogart, already on his way to join Hays, was overtaken by the rest of Hays' men who told Bogart that the entire Texas horse herd had stampeded, delaying the march, but that the spies and Bogart's company were to continue. A careless sentry lost Hays one of his prisoners, and the rangers made a forced march to Laredo fearing the man would alert the Mexicans.

Somervell sent the two scout companies, supported by other troops, to cut off any Mexican forces trying to reach Laredo. By now the Texans were moving in a dispirited manner, and the column could not cross the highwaters of the Rio Grande without boats or rafts. Hays and Bogart were the only commanders who led their companies into Mexico. Eventually joined by Somervell, who left the main force to check on their progress, the little column paraded through the streets of Laredo, flying their flag. There was no resistance, and the Laredo authorities placed the town at the disposal of the Texans. Somervell made out a requisition for needed supplies and clothing, then led his men out of Laredo.

The bulk of the Texas army never crossed into Mexico, creating additional grumbling. By now, there was almost open rebellion among some of the senior officers. Some of the requisitioned supplies were sent from Laredo to the Texans on December 9, but this happy event was marred by news that some sixty men had entered Laredo on their own and engaged in looting. Despite the prompt arrest of the men and the return of most of the stolen articles, the previously cooperative Mexicans became sullenly hostile. Another group of Texans rode down to the river and found the bank lined with armed *rancheros*. A supposedly friendly Mexican guide led other Texans on a rambling, aimless search for water, and rumors began to fill the camp about Mexican reinforcements on the move.

Somervell started the column on a series of short marches, changing camps from time to time. This was little more than a ruse to return north, and was so seen by many in the column. The Texans stopped to debate the course of action to follow. Colonel Tom Green, the Brigade Inspector, resigned in disgust and joined Hays as a private soldier![91] Somervell assembled the entire command and announced he was willing to proceed with the campaign—whatever that meant—even if only a part of his men remained. Hendricks estimated there were still 730 men in the column, but after the discussion 230 elected to return home and left on December 11. Despite this reduction in numbers, for the first time the remaining Texans had a definite goal and plan; they would go down the east bank of the Rio Grande until opposite Guerrero, cross and take the town.

By December 14 the Texans had marched to within six miles of the Mexican town, where they found several ranches and a large herd of sheep. They captured the shepherds and learned there were no Mexican troops in Guerrero. When they approached the river bank opposite the town, the main column stayed hidden in the thick brush while the scout companies rode down to the Mexican shore and managed to swim some of the horses to the Mexican shore. Using two canoes, additional men and baggage were ferried across. It was slow work; after three hours only forty-five of Bogart's men and thirty-five from Hays' company were in Mexico. The men turned their horses loose to feed on corn that had been pulled down and piled on the ground.

Because Guerrero was well back and out of sight from the Rio Grande, the Texans placed a sentry on the crest of a sharp rise in the ground near the river. Bogart and Green rode up the slopes to scout the town but saw a considerable Mexican force galloping towards them. Wheeling, the Texans started back for the water at a run. Green's horse slipped and fell, but he managed to get the animal up and running again before he was caught. For some unstated reason, Green had a red streamer or flag tied about his waist which he unrolled and waved at the Mexicans who must have thought this a signal and halted, fearing an ambush.[92]

The sentinel, atop the rise nearest the river, had seen the chase and given the alarm. The surprised Texans hastily grabbed their mounts and weapons and formed in the gullies at the foot of the slope, but Bogart came up and ordered them to form below the crest. His men formed the front rank with Hays' group just behind them. The size of the Mexican force was concealed by a small knoll, but the Texans later learned there had been four hundred horsemen chasing Green and Bogart.

Some of these actions had been seen by the Texans on the opposite bank, and many began crossing to the Mexican side both with and without their horses. After some time the entire Texas expedition, less sixty men guarding the baggage and the remaining horses, was across and prepared to fight.

There were vigorous efforts to convince Somervell to advance, but he hesitated and finally refused. By the following morning the Mexican cavalry had vanished, but the *alcalde* of Guerrero and his aides called on Somervell and offered to surrender the town and cooperate in any manner providing the place was not plundered. The general agreed and submitted a modest request for supplies and more clothing, becoming more critical as the weather worsened, to be delivered about a mile from Guerrero. Even with snow and sleet and freezing temperatures, the Texans had a good night, feasting on a hundred and fifty sheep.

In a heavy rain, a cold, wet and miserable group of Texans went to the selected delivery site which, selected by the Mexicans in open terrain commanded by several hills, had all the markings of a trap. Artillery on the rises could have swept the creek bank where the supplies, mostly worn out clothing, were dumped. Even though there had been clear agreement on furnishing one hundred horses, the Texans found no animals. Another night on the wet ground left the invaders in a sour mood and the Texans, except for the men in the two spy companies, returned to the north side of the Rio Grande. Somervell instructed Hays and Bogart to enter Guerrero and demand five thousand dollars in place of the hundred horses, or else Somervell would march on the town with five hundred men.

Hendricks said the small force entered town as directed. If his memory was correct only fifty-two Texans, some on special duty but a few others refusing from fear to join the mission, rode into the city of five thousand and paraded through the streets to the main plaza. The Texans immediately placed sentries on the roofs overlooking the plaza while they presented their demands to the *alcalde*. Lined up around the plaza, the Texans were surrounded by at least four hundred curious townspeople who seemed awed by the invaders and brought them cigars, sweets, and corn for their horses. After more than an hour had passed the *alcalde* came out and regretfully informed them that, because Mexican troops had been quartered in the town, they had no more than seven hundred dollars and certainly nothing approaching five thousand. The Texans took the seven hundred dollars and the *alcalde* and rode down to the river bank to confer with the general.[93]

In one of the few times he showed any emotion, Somervell flew into a rage when the rangers returned. He sent the *alcalde* back to town with the money, and his subsequent failure to order a march on Guerrero, as threatened, put an end to the campaign. The following day, December 19, his adjutant general issued Order No.64, evidently the only one of many such orders to survive, which simply said the troops belonging to the South-Western Army would march to the junction of the Frio and Nueces rivers and thence to Gonzales where the force would disband.

This order was all that was needed to break up the column. The force simply fell apart and about two hundred men decided to go home. The approximately three hundred others had come to fight and joined the standard of Colonel William S. Fisher, who became the new commander. Green, reverting from private back to his officer rank, became another of the leaders. Besides their desire to continue the campaign against Mexico, many of the men had other reasons for breaking with Somervell; in addition to his dismal command presence, he had promised an equal division of any animals taken in the campaign, a pledge he did not keep.

Field conditions, much less combat, have always taken a toll on cavalry mounts, and by now many of the Texans were dismounted and the rest riding broken down horses suitable only for walking. It seems evident that many of the Texans hoped to obtain decent mounts for the long ride home, as well as provisions.[94] Six of the eleven company commanders refused to return with Somervell although not everyone in their units stayed with them. Fisher, aware of the desire for mounts and loot, cautioned those going with him to distinguish between plunder and legitimate spoils of war.[95]

The smaller column with Somervell began straggling north while the slightly larger group with Fisher crossed into Mexico and marched on Mier. The adventures of this ill-fated group are not part of the ranger story, but Sam Walker, William Wallace, John McMullen and James L. Truehart, all probably from Hays' company, fought at Mier. William Eastland and Ewen Cameron, though not acting as rangers, led parts of companies. Eastland would later be executed after drawing a black bean, a sad end for a gallant ranger commander. In the fighting in Mier, the Texan rifles caused blood

literally to flow in the streets, but again there was a failure
of command. Injured, Fisher listened to tales of heavy reinforcements and agreed to Mexican offers of safe conduct.
Instead of honorable treatment, the prisoners endured a long
captivity in Mexico and the loss of each tenth man in the
celebrated drawing of the black and white beans. Many of
the Texans survived and returned home to balance the
books, in their own fashion, during the Mexican War.

Those who did not march on Mier got back home as best
they could. It was a difficult march, cold and wet with both
men and horses suffering from lack of food and rest. The
men lived on whatever game could be shot. The men remaining from Bogart's company marched for San Antonio. Hendricks said they ran into Flacco and a few Lipans whose
warning of a Mexican party at a nearby rancho kept the
weary Texans from stumbling into an ambush. Bogart and
some of the others became lost and wandered through the
brush until they finally reached the Nueces near the Laredo
road. There is no further mention of Hays and his men in
Hendrick's narrative, other than that he started back to San
Antonio.

In his final report, Somervell seems to be recounting a
completely different series of events. He dismissed the march
home by saying they crossed the Nueces with considerable
difficulty. On January 1, 1843, near the river, the captains
still with him were ordered to go to their rendezvous locations and disband their troops. Bogart's men, still a proud
company, reached San Antonio on January 4 and had their
first real food and taste of bread in twenty days. The men
were in rags, the animals worn down. These Texans had
done their best in an impossible situation. If not rangers in
the official sense, this spy company had served in the best
ranger tradition.

The various accounts of the Somervell expedition do not
reveal much of what Hays was or was not doing on the long
march down and back. Hendricks and Green are specific
about the times and places when Hays was with the column
as well as a few times when he was on specific assignments,
but much of the time he and his men are unaccounted for.
The ranger company was evidently no more cohesive than

other units when the decision to return was made.

Ben McCulloch, who does not appear prominently in any of the accounts, was with Somervell and at first stayed behind with Fisher's command. Green said McCulloch and "some choice spies" went into Mier and talked with the alcalde and some Americans living in the town. He came back and reported that Canales had gone but heavy Mexican reinforcements were expected shortly.[96] Ben McCulloch, too experienced to stay and become involved in a fight that no longer had any purpose, turned back and headed home.

Somervell's report helps explain some of Hays' actions, or what often seems to be a lack of action. On November 19 Somervell's acting adjutant general forwarded a list of the eleven companies that made up the command, a total of 630 officers and men not counting the commander and his staff officers.[97] It is interesting to note that Ewen Cameron had a fifty-one man company in the expedition, though they did not operate as rangers or spies. The most interesting feature of the listing, however, is that Hays is not included.

Somervell does not shed any light on this murky picture. He was not the first, or last, commander to try to make the best of a miserable performance in an after-action report. He blames the eventual failure of the command on not having enough troops, explaining he would have required at least a thousand men, rather than the less than seven hundred he had, for what he had planned. Once on the march, he explains away their performance by describing the breaking down of the horses in the bog, a misadventure caused by a sudden rainstorm as they moved from one road to another "rendering the whole region almost one entire bog." The horses were so injured they were never able to travel at speeds required for the rapid moves needed in the campaign.

Somervell continues his report with a general account of the major actions of the expedition. He describes the capture of Laredo and his displeasure over the looting that followed. He mentions Hays and Bogart and their actions in crossing the Rio Grande. Once again, he stressed the heavy rains that fell while the Texans were near Guerrero. Somervell explained they retreated from the Rio Grande to feed the horses. The debates, the bitterness, the breakup of the command are not mentioned other than that it would have been an act of imprudence to stay longer, and that some stayed in camp while he and the rest departed.

The final report includes a list of the units that returned with Somervell. Bogart's company is mentioned, but once again Hays is not shown.[98] Somervell must have considered Hays as being under his general command yet not part of the expedition. Once the command broke up Hays reverted to his official position as frontier commander, a dual status which may partially explain the insubordinate actions of some of his men, and returned home on his own.

There is a final footnote to this generally sad chronicle. On the way home, sometime after warning the Texans about an ambush, Flacco was murdered. There are several suspected individuals or groups, but exactly who killed the Lipan scout has never been conclusively determined. Houston wrote a beautiful letter to the Lipans, but the damage was done and the splendid cooperation ended between the small tribe and the Texans. For whatever reason, the Lipans blamed someone in San Antonio for Flacco's death, and they became very hostile in their dealings with the town.

The closing months of 1842 included actions that involved rangers, either in an official role or acting on their own in scouting missions. During their long history, the rangers have been called upon for some strange missions; one of the earliest of these missions resulted in the so-called "Archives War." The Vásquez raid had brought about the removal of most governmental functions from Austin, but Sam Houston had more pressing matters on his mind after that first invasion and left the archives in the capital city. Later in the year he decided to remove the records to a safe location in Washington-on-the-Brazos.

Turning to dependable Eli Chandler, Houston tasked him and Thomas I. Smith to carry off the archives. The president cautioned the two men there was to be no bloodshed, even though the citizens of Austin were determined to hold the national records and had formed a vigilante unit to guard the precious documents and ledgers.

Moving with characteristic swiftness, Chandler caught the vigilantes off guard, loaded the mass of papers, books and ledgers in several wagons, and started out of town. Mrs. Angelina Eberly was the only citizen watching, and she ran to a signal gun to fire a shot to alert the townspeople. What was rapidly becoming a comedy took an ironic turn when Captain Mark B. Lewis gathered some men, rolled out another cannon from the arsenal, and started in pursuit, a former ranger chasing another ranger and prepared to wage war over several wagon loads of paper.

Lewis and his men soon caught up with the slow moving wagons, at the crossing on Brushy Creek not far from Austin, and fired a few warning shots. Chandler, who had his orders and certainly did not wish anyone shot, surrendered gracefully, and Lewis and his triumphant vigilantes rode back to Austin with the republic's records.[99] This was the last service for Lewis; in one of the violent episodes of the time, he killed a man in Austin in July 1843 and shortly thereafter was shot and killed trying to escape from the authorities.[100]

One of the last scouting actions of the year occurred in mid-December when a company from Victoria made a raid into the disputed Nueces territory where a Mexican *rancho* had been a trouble spot for some time. Known as New Bahia, or Carlos' Rancho, it had served as a base for raids against Victoria. During both Mexican invasions, armed men had been seen at the *rancho*. Travelers told of seeing Mexican soldiers there and believed it to be a spy center.

Captain J. Owen gathered a 120 man volunteer company, camped near the *rancho*, and gave the people there two choices: gather up everything they owned and move to Mexico peacefully, or be driven out! They excepted the family of a José María, who was known to be a loyal Texan, and invited him to move to Victoria with them. The others saw the futility of resisting and moved to Matamoros. For a time, there was talk of another Mexican raid to punish the people of Victoria, but nothing came of the threats.[101]

It is doubtful if many Texans mourned the passing of 1842. The year had seen two invasions and a counter invasion. Good men had died, and many others would spend terrible time in Mexican captivity. True, they had done their fair share of killing and had beaten back Woll's attack, but that did not completely balance the scales. At least there were no more major attacks from south of the Rio Grande.

The two Mexican invasions demonstrated again the need for military units in being to meet an invasion, whether from Mexico or by Indians conducting large-scale raids. It was plain by now that Texas could not afford a regular army, but there was also considerable doubt concerning the adequacy of the militia system for anything other than campaigns that could be planned for and organized over a considerable period of time. Towards the end of the year, a report by the Secretary of War and Marine outlined the problems with the militia system and proposed the formation of a permanent force of two infantry and two cavalry companies to control marauders and delay any invasion until the militia could form. His remarks on the condition of the militia are too lengthy to include in detail, but they describe a disorganized, or completely unformed, body of men. The law which allowed drafted men to obtain others to serve in their stead, and the custom of electing officers, had both caused major problems already and showed promise for creating future troubles.[102] The four companies proposed by the secretary were never formed, and for the remainder of the Texas Republic the ranger units would be the only military force actually in the field.

—7—

Only the Rangers - 1843

The generally unfavorable events of 1842 convinced the Texas Congress and other officials that something drastically new must be done to protect the republic. Use of volunteers to repel an invasion was inefficient, and Texas had done nothing to hinder the ease with which a Mexican army could march north. There was no regular army, and volunteers from the threatened towns were all that stood between Texas and another Mexican invasion or a second giant Comanche raid. All of the republic's defenders came from the more sparsely settled western counties, while the heavily populated eastern areas made no contribution to defense even though the men of the east were just as patriotic and willing to fight as were the men who served in the spy companies or those who turned back Woll. They were simply too far away to hear of an attack, rally and march to Goliad, Victoria or San Antonio in time to be of service. Agreeing on the futility of trying to revive a regular army, the Texas Congress set about trying to establish a formal, organized militia with designated commanders to allow the entire country to take part in repelling an invasion.

On January 16, 1843, congress passed an Act for the Defense of the Frontier. Part of the act declared a state of martial law between the Nueces and the Rio Grande while hostilities still existed between Texas and Mexico.[1] The provisions of this act do not bear directly on the ranger story, but a second act passed the same day authorized the formation of a spy company for the protection of the southwestern frontier and allocated five hundred dollars to support it.[2] The act stated the company would be in service until the provisions of the militia act could take effect. Houston had considerable reservations about the act of January 16, partially about the proposed location of the militia units and very much about the cost of the new organization. His refusal to sign the act[3] was the end of the militia, but the spy company authorization was not cancelled.

As usual congress designated no commander, but Jack Hays became captain of the new spy company although no orders or directives survive indicating how he was selected. Muster and pay rolls for 1843, however, show him as commander of the company authorized in January as well as leader of the unit during several reorganizations during the year. For the entire year Hays was the only formal military commander, and his rangers the only formal military force, authorized by law in Texas! In a proclamation, for which he had congressional approval based on the act of January 16 even though it never became law, President Houston declared martial law in the Nueces-Rio Grande country and forbade any armed forces to operate in the region except those commanded by Major John C. Hays.[4]

Muster and pay rolls show that Hays' company remained active during most of the year. The first command, for February and March, shows an activation date of February 20, which would have allowed time for the congressional authorization to be formalized, the news to reach Hays in San Antonio, the recruitment of men and the formation of the detachment. Hays had problems forming the unit; at the end of nine days all he had recruited were two privates, and it was not until March that he was able to enlist thirteen other rangers. It was not a very impressive command—fifteen privates and Hays—and most of the familiar names are missing although R.A. Gillespie is shown and Frank Paschal, who is listed on the earlier 1841 rolls, was back. Despite the growing gap between the Mexican-born inhabitants and the Anglo Americans, M. Eschalara is listed as a guide.[5] Considering the devastated condition of San Antonio, it is no surprise Hays had difficulty finding suitable recruits. The two Mexican invasions had caused many families to leave the city, and the pool of men qualified for ranger service was small.

The rangers served through March 1843 and reenlisted for April,[6] but their accomplishments during these months are unknown. While they were undoubtedly active, whatever they did was completely overshadowed by another major Texas expedition.

The most prominent military effort of 1843, the Snively Expedition, was to be the last of the invasions and counter-invasions waged between the Republic of Texas and Mexico. The formation of the force followed ranger organization and method of equipment, and at least one ranger captain, Eli Chandler, was an important leader.

In historical retrospect, the march against the Santa Fe Trail is considered little more than a foraging raid by mercenaries, but in the accepted conventions of the 1840s it was a legitimate affair. Jacob Snively's proposal to intercept and capture a Mexican trading caravan going from St.Louis to Santa Fe—the property of *all* Mexican citizens was considered a lawful prize—was sent to the Texas government and received the approval of President Houston. In a letter dated February 16, 1843, Snively was notified his request had been granted. He was to operate under certain conditions, the most important being that the force would not exceed three hundred men. Cost was always a decisive factor in Texas' military operations, and Houston believed such adventures should pay for themselves.

> The expedition will be strictly partisan, the Troops composing the corps to mount, equip, and provision themselves at their own expense, and one half of all the spoils taken in honorable warfare, to belong to the Republic and the Government to be at no expense whatever on account of the expedition.[7]

One of the members of the expedition, Steward A. Miller, left a graphic word picture of how his companions were armed, an account that would describe a typical ranger of the time.

> The most of the men are hardy Frontiersmen, inured to toil and danger, & the use of arms. They

are furnished generally with a rifle, breace [*sic*] of
pistols, & Bowie Knife, many of them have a pair
of holsters & several brace of pistols besides. That
such men thus accutred, equiped, and determined
should effect the object of their tour is almost
beyond doubt.[8]

Unfortunately for the Texans, Miller's prediction did not
come true. Although the raiders came close to one Mexican
trading party, they never managed to cut off any appreciable
body of men or goods. They crossed into American territory
and collided with a United States Army unit protecting the
Mexican traders. Not wishing to fight Americans, some of the
Texans broke away and others gave up some of their weapons. Disputes over whether to continue or return home
caused the expedition to split, ending any chance of capturing a Mexican caravan. After considerable hardship and
encounters with Comanche warriors, the bulk of the Texans
returned home.[9]

Unlike the preceding year, 1843 was not a time of campaigns
and battles; there were no more major fights after the Snively
Expedition. The rangers undoubtedly kept busy, or else the
Texas government would not have allowed Hays to keep his
company in service, but documenting his actions is difficult.
In his only surviving report for 1843 he referred to earlier
reports he had submitted, but none of these can be found.
Although he must have been active, only a newspaper
account of his capturing three spies indicates any scouting
in the summer of 1843.[10]

Jim Nichols claimed he started out the year with Hays
and described Hays' applying for a new company because of
Indian attacks. Nichols listed Calvin Turner, John Rogers,
William Deadman, James Rogers and himself as members
of this unit, and recalled that Wallace was the first lieutenant
and Ad Gillespie the second lieutenant.[11] Once again the
difficulty of remembering names and events years afterward

becomes a problem; of all the men listed by Nichols, only Gillespie and James Roberts are listed on the February-March 1843 roll which shows Hays as the only officer and Gillespie as a private. Big Foot Wallace was still a prisoner in Mexico and not even in Texas.

While he did not always remember the correct names, Nichols did describe certain events and actions that are worth noting. He said Hays moved away from San Antonio early in 1843 to avoid the spies that watched every ranger move. In their new camp, the rangers engaged in training to improve their riding and shooting skills. Posts were placed in the ground and the rangers galloped by, shooting at the wooden stakes with their rifles, then using pistols at close range. Later they used round targets, and Nichols claimed they were able to hit the marks most of the time.

Considerable time was devoted to improving their riding skills. The rangers had long recognized the superiority of grain-fed American horses, but a good horse was no guarantee of superior horsemanship. Even though most of the men were good riders, Hays wanted them to learn Comanche riding skills. Nichols describes how they practiced running at full speed, leaning down from the saddle and picking up a rifle, a coat, a hat, or even a silver coin![12] Such training had a serious purpose; a dropped weapon needed to be recovered quickly without dismounting and remounting. Wounded comrades needed to be quickly gathered up and removed from the field.

The rangers had taken a superior weapon, their rifle, and adapted it to frontier combat. They had developed tactics to fit the enemy and the terrain. Now they borrowed from their Comanche and Mexican foes to refine horsemanship for battlefield conditions, including adoption of the heavier Spanish bit to enable them to control their mounts with one hand during spirited charges, leaving the other free for weapons.

There was little Indian fighting in the early part of 1843. Nichols describes one scouting expedition's chasing a party of Comanches which had stolen horses near San Antonio. The rangers followed them to the Medina. After a running fight, with some Indian casualties, the Comanches ran into the brush and abandoned the stolen animals. Hays and his men gathered up the horses and started back but the Comanches, trying to regain the lost mounts, rallied and dogged the rangers almost to San Antonio. The rangers nevertheless managed to get most of the horses back to their owners.[13]

Nichols, concluding his account of life with Hays, described how he had an opportunity to obtain some property, asked for a release, was replaced by Kit Acklin, identified by Nichols as Ackland, and left the company.[14] Again there is a conflict with records and muster rolls; Acklin does not appear on any 1843 rolls, although he was to become extremely active the following year.

With little Indian activity, the rangers were faced with the task of protecting traders on the Laredo and San Antonio road as well as from marauders near the growing settlement at Corpus Christi. A Mexican bandit named Agatone (Agaton) was the leader of many of these forays and the chief antagonist of the rangers. Openly defying Houston's proclamation of martial law, he went where he pleased and in late April was near Corpus Christi with a force estimated at one hundred to three hundred Mexican soldiers. When his spies reported that Hays had gone to the Rio Grande, Agatone sent a seventy-man detachment to intercept the rangers on their return.

Hays and his fifteen men had been scouting the Rio Grande settlements and were on their way back with a considerable herd of horses and mules "captured from the Mexicans on the Rio Grande," as one newspaper explained. Agatone's men caught up with Hays along the Nueces but hesitated to attack and hid in the river bottoms. During the night they managed to stampede the animal herd, but Hays had his men's mounts under guard in another location and saved them. Unable to pursue the scattering bandits and animals in the dark, the chagrined rangers returned to San Antonio.

The paper continued the account of this adventure by

noting Hays was "excited to renewed activity" and planned to return to the border. In the same article the writer said Ben McCulloch had raised volunteers for a raid on the Rio Grande settlements, and a Captain Walls of Victoria was gathering men to take action against the bandits near Corpus Christi.[15] If anything came of these two efforts, however, it was never reported. Other Texas bands did range, doing their bit to avenge the recent Mexican invasions and collect a little plunder along the way. A party of western volunteers raided a Mexican settlement near Matamoros and returned with one hundred horses; another band intercepted Mexican smugglers and "collected" four thousand dollars in specie. Such successes induced others to engage in similar enterprises.[16]

President Houston was opposed to such raids by either side. His opposition to any military activity outside the Texas border explains his lukewarm support for the Somervell Expedition. Undoubtedly he desired peace with both Indian and Mexicans to help the effort to join the United States. Not all Texas officials agreed with him, thus furthering some of the famous early-Texas political feuds. The letters to the press by Thomas J. Rusk, a leader of the "invade and revenge" faction opposed to Houston, certainly encouraged men to "volunteer" for raids into the Nueces territory and even into Mexico.[17]

Despite the shattered economy along the western frontier, commerce between Mexico and Texas increased during the summer of 1843. The *Telegraph and Texas Register* reported in the June 14 edition that there were thirty-one loaded wagons waiting to leave the Rio Grande for Bexar, and an equal number waiting to go south. The editor wondered how long Agatone would be allowed to roam the Nueces area boasting he would try Hays before a court martial, and suggested Hays might be planning a court of his own.

The same edition of the paper contained a brief article about a large war band of Comanches that had raided to Aransas Bay, captured two families, then moved towards Camargo. The writer speculated that a successful earlier raid had encouraged this band to attack Mexican settlements along the Rio Grande.

These sporadic attacks came at a time when Houston was making a major effort to sign peace treaties with all the Indian tribes. Commissioners met with all the settled Indians that could be reached at the Waco village and sent scouts and interpreters to some of the known Comanche camps. These commissioners and their Delaware scouts had a frightening time, expecting to be killed each day, but were finally spared by the Comanche chiefs. Despite the talks, none of the Comanches came in to sign peace treaties.[18]

The peace talks must have had some impact, certainly with the settled Indians, because attacks in the Austin area decreased as the year progressed. Continued attacks by Agatone and his marauders, however, were probably the cause of Hays' ability to increase the strength of his detachment. His muster roll for June-July 1843 lists thirty-seven privates. Most of the original 1843 unit signed up again. Frank Paschal left to campaign successfully for election to the Texas Congress later in the year, but Eschalara was on the roll, Mike Chevallie reenlisted, and Ben McCulloch became an official ranger after several years of rangering on his own. Hays now had a group of men who would stay with him during much of the next two years, a cadre of men who would polish and define the ranger tradition.[19]

The expanded company was in action in short order. When an Indian band rode into the outskirts of San Antonio and killed a farmer working a field near the Alamo ruins, the townspeople first believed Lipans near Seguin had committed the crime. They had been experiencing trouble with the Lipan tribe since Flacco had been killed, but Hays was convinced Comanche riders were to blame because their trail led north. He and his men followed the tracks but never caught up with the Indians.

A short time earlier Hays had used his powers as Commander of the Frontier to arrest three suspected spies of the brigand Agatone, whose agents in all the frontier settlements were difficult to spot among the local citizenry. Hays went to great lengths to elude these agents, not always successfully; in this particular case he simply shot the three men.[20]

Hays still had twenty-five rangers on the September 1843 muster roll but was feeling the effect of limited finances. Lack of financial support was an enemy he could not fight. Most of the time he managed to field patrols in the Nueces country, keeping the bandits moving and uncertain of his location or intentions. Pérez, another brigand, was reported in mid-August to be on the Medina with one hundred men, and Hays took fifteen rangers, probably all he had in camp, and located the outlaw camp on a small stream west of the river.

The Mexicans spotted the rangers and started shooting. The Texans returned fire until the robbers hurriedly broke camp and moved downstream. Hays followed cautiously, aware of the differences in numbers and watching for an ambush, and for a time there was a running fight heading out onto the open prairie. When the Mexicans fired the grass the rangers stopped, unable to see in the dense smoke. Believing the fire was a cover for an attack, the rangers pulled back and took a defensive position but, by the time the smoke cleared, Pérez had managed to break away.[21]

Newspaper accounts show Hays scouting in the Nueces-Rio Grande country during the final months of 1843. In late September traders reported seeing the rangers all the way from the sources of the Nueces down to San Patricio, scouting for any Mexican troops on the border. By early November trade had slowed between Bexar and the Rio Grande settlements because the merchants and traders were afraid their goods would be confiscated on entering Mexico. Victoria, once a flourishing town, was partially deserted and only a few stores remained open.[22]

In early November Hays returned from his last scout of the year. During the month he had run onto a Mexican party including Leandro Garza who, with Antonio Pérez, was one of the two primary Mexican spies most wanted by Texas. In the brief fight, Garza was wounded but managed to slip away into the brush. The rangers also met a number of Mexican scouts along the Nueces who promised friendship and pledged to aid Hays in recovering stolen property. They told the rangers that the semi-regular scout companies which the Mexican government had along the Rio Grande were being disbanded, and that less support was being given the bandits. They thought trade would improve during the coming year. Chances for better trading conditions were considerably enhanced when traders killed Agatone in late November.[23]

The only Hays report that survives from 1843 was written at this time. The ranger reported he had been on a scout to the Leona, having heard rumors of an enemy camp on the stream. Reaching the stream, some thirty miles east of the Nueces River, he found a camp abandoned about three days earlier and started out, not knowing if the camp had been a group of traders or, more likely, a bandit hangout. Not all the campers had left the area, and the rangers captured several laggards who talked freely, saying the Mexican general who had sent them had recalled them for discharge. The Mexican ranging companies had either been discharged or furloughed for six months, and several hundred troops and two cannon had been recalled to the interior of the country.

Military conditions were not much better in Texas. Hays informed the Secretary of War and Marine that he had been forced to furlough his company, because he no longer had funds to pay them, and had also incurred debts of five hundred dollars for which he was personally responsible. He stated that he had used every means to save money and had accounted for all his funds in his previous reports.

In his letter Hays was optimistic about Indian affairs because there had been no Comanche raids on the western frontier in several months. The danger was from Mexican bandits and raids from south of the Rio Grande. He was afraid that Mexico's disbanding its frontier companies would throw men out of work, with the only employment being robbery. As had others, he suggested the formation of a well-mounted force, not necessarily large, to guard the frontier and keep the marauders in check. Such a command could be maintained at small cost to the government and would provide security to the frontier settlements.

In a closing paragraph Hays suggested that whoever had command of this force should be given instructions on how to treat former citizens of Texas who had defected to Mexico but were now returning. Some of these people had already arrived in San Antonio, and Hays was afraid they were capable of harm to the republic. It was the first time anyone had publicly addressed the status and treatment of individuals and families who had changed sides after the Vásquez and Woll invasions.[24]

By mid-November the rangers were out of action, a casualty not from enemy actions but from lack of funds. It would not be the last time dollars rather than bullets stopped the force, a recurring problem for the remainder of the century. When the spy company had been established at the beginning of 1843, the paltry sum of five hundred dollars had been set aside for expenses, but exactly what other monies had been provided during the year is not clear although considerable funds must have been made available to keep and expand the company. On one occasion President Houston directed the acting treasurer to transfer $520.29 to the Secretary of War and Marine for Hays' company,[25] an odd sum probably for payment of a specific voucher. Payrolls alone were enough to put the unit out of action in a short time; the August-September 1843 payroll for twenty-five men amounted to only $1,236.00, somewhat short of the rate of a dollar a man per day. Where Hays acquired the additional money he needed is unknown, and it is a miracle he managed to keep the command going as long as he did.

Even though only one of his reports for 1843 has survived, quite a number of Hays' supply and service requisitions and vouchers are safely stored in the archives and give some hint of how the rangers, though broke, kept active. Local merchants, recognizing Hays as a man of honor to be trusted, cooperated with the men they saw as protectors and friends and provided what was needed, trusting Hays to pay when money was available.

For the rangers, on constant patrol, shoeing their horses was a big expense. In August James Goodman did thirty-six dollars worth of horseshoeing and arms repair, and William Small presented a bill for $34.50 for additional shoeing in October. These bills were paid in full a year later on December 28, 1844.[26] William Elliott's bill for $11.37 for supplying the company in May and June with various medical and general supplies—rope, chain, soap, chloride of lime, quinine and other pills—was paid on December 28, 1844, when Hays obtained money from some unknown source.[27]

Nathaniel Lewis, another San Antonio merchant, supplied Hays with gunpowder and coffee, both frontier essentials. His October 1843 bill for $102 was paid in full on April 20, 1844.[28]

The November 28, 1843, edition of the *Telegraph and Texas Register* contained an article on Hays, believing he had left Seguin and was on the way to Washington-on-the-Brazos. The newspaper article reveals how well known the young ranger had become in a few years; more and more he was the leader mentioned in the press. For now, however, Hays was out of the ranger business, not in a hurry, breaking his trip in Seguin and visiting with friends during the holidays. He was entertained in Seguin by the Calvert family, among many others, and his rather long stay in the town can be explained by his having met Susan Calvert earlier in San Antonio. It was the beginning of a courtship that spanned several years. Hays left Seguin, reluctantly it can be assumed, to continue on to Washington-on-the-Brazos with Frank Paschal, G.T. Howard, W.G. Cooke and Antonio Menchaca. The still-young ranger had earned his respite from the hardships of frontier life. It was well he rested in Seguin, because 1844 would be an eventful year.

—8—

The New Colts - 1844-1845

Hays remained in Washington-on-the-Brazos through early January 1844, but he evidently still had sources of information on the border because he informed President Houston that four bands of Cherokees had crossed the Rio Grande at San Fernando. Mexican traders had sent him word the Indians had been encouraged by Manuel Flores. [1]

Despite the shortage of funds, the Eighth Texas Congress realized the need for some form of protection on the southern and western frontiers, and on January 23, 1844, it passed an act creating a new ranger command, "An Act Authorizing John C. Hays to raise a Company of Mounted Gun-men, to act as Rangers, on the Western and South-Western Frontier."[2] Unlike earlier legislation, this act was very specific, designating Hays as commander with the rank of captain, and a lieutenant to be elected by the forty privates in the company. The captain was to be paid seventy-five dollars a month, the lieutenant fifty, and privates were allowed thirty dollars per month.

The command was to be organized by February 1, 1844, or as soon thereafter as possible. Time of service was to be four months with pay every two months, however the president could extend the time of service in an emergency. As before, each man would furnish his horse, arms and equipment. The act was comprehensive, designed to meet at least some of the needs of the time, and resulted in a splendid ranger company. Years of experience were finally combined with a new weapon to develop an advanced tactical system.

Muster and pay rolls for this company have survived and indicate Hays was unable to meet the February 1 activation date. The bulk of the unit signed on February 25 with Hays as captain, Ben McCulloch elected as lieutenant, and twenty five privates.[3] Additional men in March and a few joining in early April finally brought the command to the authorized strength of forty privates and two officers. Ben McCulloch was a skilled frontiersman who had commanded his own companies. Many of the enlisted rangers had served with Hays in earlier units; Mike Chevallie was back and Frank Paschal, congressman or not, reenlisted. Sam Walker, having escaped from a Mexican prison, managed to return to join Hays and began a brief career that would make him famous.

Hays did not wait in San Antonio until his company was at full strength. A brief story in the *Telegraph and Texas Register* for March 6, 1844, reported him scouting between Gonzales and LaGrange a fortnight earlier, sometime around February 20, accompanied by Colonel Wm. Cook (William Cooke) Major Howard and Frank Pascal (Paschal). They encountered four or five Mexican marauders along a stream called Peach Creek. During a chase they lost the bandits in the creek bottom but captured a horse. The Mexicans must have been active in the area because the newspaper also said it was "believed" Captain Ben McCulloch was "after" the men with a volunteer company from Gonzales.

This brief newspaper account does not answer the question of what Hays and his three companions were doing in the vicinity of Gonzales. Although Paschal had or would shortly rejoin the rangers, Cooke and Howard were not members. McCulloch's attempt to capture the marauders with a volunteer force suggests the band was known and considered a danger. It seems likely Hays gathered three old friends who could be trusted in a fight and rode over to do whatever they could.

Returning to San Antonio, Hays continued enlisting men and had his unit in good shape my mid-March when he left again after a group of Texas outlaws who had raided ranches near San Antonio and headed north towards the Colorado with nearly two thousand head of cattle. Newspaper accounts do not mention any contact with the thieves but do reveal the rangers were not limiting their actions to fighting

Indians and Mexican raiders.[4]

A rumor Woll was again marching on San Antonio created a near panic, but spies soon dispelled the rumor and peace returned to town. The news that Hays was raising another ranger company, however, and that a law was being considered to punish people who had fought against Texas, caused a number of Mexican-born San Antonians to leave for the Rio Grande.[5]

Hays had the best company he had ever assembled, well mounted and trained, and during this period they found a solution to the recurring problem of defense against the Comanche use of archery at close range. The rangers obtained a number of the Colt five-shot revolvers.

There are claims that individual rangers had Colts at an earlier date, but no contemporary accounts support their widespread use before 1844. The rangers must have had the revolvers at least long enough to become familiar with the often-tricky repeaters. From several documents, this acquisition can be dated in late 1843 or early 1844. In a letter to the Colt factory dated November 30, 1846, Sam Walker wrote:

> The pistols which you made for the Texas Navy have been in use by the Rangers for three years, and I can say with confidence that it is the only good improvement that I have seen. The Texans who have learned their value by practical experience, their confidence in them is unbounded, so much so that they are willing to engage four times their number.[6]

E.W. Moore, who was largely responsible for the 1839-1840 navy purchase of Colt revolvers, stated the rangers received Colts from the disbanded navy "after being in service upwards of four years."[7] This agrees with Walker's account, suggesting a late 1843 or early 1844 date of issue. In the preceding chapter Nichols described in some detail how Hays trained his company in late 1843, but he mentioned only pistols and undoubtedly would have noted a major change in weapons had the Colts been issued at that time. Early 1844 seems likely for the first major issue of Colt revolvers to the rangers, but there are no records of just when, how many or where the delivery took place. It did take place, however, and American history changed.

Around June 1, 1844, Hays and fifteen men left camp near San Antonio and rode north to the area between the Pedernales and the Llano rivers to investigate signs of Indians and to try to determine which tribes were causing trouble. Hays did not go farther because of the ongoing talks and negotiations; he may have had orders not to excite the tribes. Recrossing the Pedernales on their return, the rangers took a break near a stream later identified as Walker Creek. Most of the men dismounted to rest their horses, unsaddling or loosening the cinches. Hays had a four-man patrol, well back protecting their rear, which soon galloped in to alert Hays they were being followed. The ranger had his men back along the trail as soon as they saddled their horses.

The years of scouting and fighting had not been wasted. The men, not new hands rushing eagerly after easy game, rode cautiously and soon spotted the Comanches who had been trailing the rear guard. If it had been only a few Indians, they would have fled upon seeing fifteen armed men, but these Comanches turned and rode away at a slow pace, drifting towards some woods. The experienced rangers did not become excited and dash after them.

Attempting to encourage the rangers to charge after them into the woods, the Comanches slowly circled, edging closer to the edge of the timber, but Hays kept his men in a walk and moved up the side of the stream. Their ploy having failed, the Comanches galloped into the woods and vanished, but soon a considerable body of Indians began forming along the crest of a slight hill. The rangers halted and counted from sixty to seventy warriors riding back and forth waving their lances and shields and shouting challenges, dashing down the slope a few paces then wheeling back into line.

The game went on for a time, the Indians trying to goad the rangers into firing at long range from which their padded shields could stop spent balls. Once the rangers fired, the Comanches thought they could rush down the slope, showering them with arrows and engaging them at close range with their lances. In earlier days Hays would have led his men to the shelter of the stream bank and prepared for a defensive fight; today he held his ground then rode at a walk towards the hill.

First visible as they rode forward up the gentle slope, when the rangers came to the steeper base of the hill they were out of sight of the Comanches for a few critical moments. A few curious Indians rode down the slope to see what had happened but could not view the Texans, whom Hays had led at a gallop around the hill for a charge up the slope to attack the surprised Comanches on their flank. The rangers fired their rifles into the massed Indians, emptying a number of saddles. The melee moved down the slope onto the level ground, and in a matter of minutes the Comanches rallied into formation and turned to charge the heavily outnumbered rangers.

In the confusion of close combat, no man that day took the time to consider that the rangers were altering tactics and history or that the West was being changed by a Yankee inventor and a band of frontiersmen. Mounted combat was starting down a new path, but these rangers were probably wondering if they had placed too much trust in the five-shooters.

The Comanches had no such doubts; they had maneuvered the rangers into the open with empty rifles, outnumbered them by at least four to one, and were now facing only the rangers' little pistols and a few knives. Only this time the little pistols fired...and fired...and fired again, toppling brave warriors to the ground. The Comanches could face anything but the unknown; they broke and fled out of range.

Although shaken, the Comanches were Lords of the Plains, The People, and they rallied again in an attempt to ride over the rangers. Sam Walker and R.A. Gillespie, ahead of the other rangers, were surrounded and lanced but finally broke away. Peter Fohr was killed outright, W.B. Lee sustained severe wounds and Andrew Erskine was slightly hurt, but the little repeaters continued to fire and the Comanches again fled out of range. The fight was not continuous in all quarters of the battlefield, and some of the rangers managed to change cylinders. Despite his wounds, Gillespie even reloaded his rifle.

By the time the fight had stretched over three miles, there were still at least twenty Indians able to fight, double the number of still-effective rangers. Hays, who could see a chief yelling at his warriors, getting up their courage for a final attack, doubted if the rangers could survive another close-quarter battle. He asked if anyone had a charged rifle and Gillespie nodded, dismounted, and rested his rifle on a huge boulder. The sharp report of the rifle cut off the end of the chief's war cry. The brave fell out of the saddle.

It was too much, even for Comanches. The rest of the warriors broke away, each trying to escape and making no attempt to carry away their dead and wounded. Injured warriors who escaped made it on their own. The rangers, with many wounded or dead horses and too tired to pursue, reloaded their weapons and looked after their wounded. Hays camped on the field while preparing the injured men and horses for the ride back to San Antonio.

The second day after the battle four Comanches rode up, almost blundering into the camp, undoubtedly trying to locate any wounded from the fighting and unaware the Texans were still in the vicinity. A group of the best-mounted rangers chased after the Comanches and killed three of them although the fourth escaped in the brush. The rangers returned to San Antonio by easy stages, taking care of the wounded men, and arrived sometime before or on June 16, 1844, when Hays wrote a report of the engagement. The original has long been lost but was printed in the House Journals.

> REPORT of the Battle of Walker's Creek,
> fought by Capt. J.C. Hays, in June, 1844.
> San Antonio, June 16, 1844
> Hon. Secretary of War and Marine,
>
> Sir, On the first of this month, I left camp, which was near this place, with fifteen men, for the purpose of scouring the country, and, if possible, to ascertain what tribe of Indians were committing so many depredations.

I proceeded a north course, as far as between the Perdenales and Llano. After scouring the country, and wishing to go no further, on account of the negotiations that were going on, I concluded to return; although I saw sufficient sign of Indians to have induced me to proceed farther up the country. But having an eye single to my instructions, I deemed it prudent to return.

When on Walker's Creek, about fifty miles above Seguin, when encamped, a party of Indians made their appearance, numbering about ten, and endeavored to draw me out. I immediately ordered my men to saddle, and prepare to fight; for I could have no doubt but that their intentions were hostile. After being mounted, I proceeded slowly towards them—they, at the same time, using every art and stratagem [sic] to throw me off my guard, and induce me to give chase to them. They, however, did not succeed in their design. I then fell into the timber, and moved up the creek about a quarter of a mile, when I discovered their number to be between sixty and seventy. After ascertaining that they could not decoy or lead me astray, they came out boldly, formed themselves, and dared us to fight. I then ordered a charge; and, after discharging our rifles, closed in with them, hand to hand, with my five-shooting pistols, which did good execution. Had it not been for them, I doubt what the consequences would have been. I cannot recommend these arms too highly.

The fight, which was a moving one, continued to the distance of about three miles—being desperately contested by both parties. After the third round from the five-shooters, the Indians gave way; but, whenever pressed severely, making the most desperate charges and efforts to defeat me.

I however, charged their ranks; and, with a courage that is rarely displayed my men succeeded in routing and putting them to flight—killing twenty on the ground, and wounding, at the lowest estimate, twenty or thirty more.

The second day after the fight (having re-mained where the fight took place on account of my wounded,) a party of four made their appearance. I immediately ordered six men to give chase to them; thinking at the same time, that they had embodied, and presumed to give me another fight. My men, at the word, mounted their horses, and pursued them about a mile, when they came upon them and killed three of them—the fourth having evinced a disposition to escape, if possible, from the first.

My loss was, one killed (Peter Fosh) and three badly wounded, but not mortally, and one slightly. Two were wounded with lances and two with arrows.

The party consisted of Camanches [sic], Wa-coes [sic] and Mexicans.

I will take occasion to say, that my men evinced no dismay; but, on the contrary, would dare them to come to the charge.

Your obedient serv't
JOHN C. HAYS,
Commanding S.W. Frontier.

RECAPITULATION

Loss of <u>Mexicans</u> and Indians, killed on the ground, 23—Wounded, most of them badly, 30. My loss was, killed 1—Peter Fosh. Wounded badly, 3, S.H. Walker, R.A. Gillespie, and W.B. Lee. Wounded slightly, 1, Andrew Erskine.

J.C. HAYS,
Com. S.W. Fron.[8]

In some manner, whether a printer's error or in Hays' original report, the dead ranger was identified as Peter Fosh rather than Peter Fohr. Let the record show that Peter Fohr was one of the early rangers with Hays, with documented service from January 1841. He is listed on most of Hays' muster rolls from that date until his death in 1844.

The fight attracted much attention in Texas, although at the time there was not much significance attached to the use of Colt revolvers. The *Houston Morning Star* carried a long account of the fight, supposedly based on an interview with Hays.[9] The newspaper story, which generally agrees with Hays' official report though with considerably more detail, could have been the basis for later versions of the battle.

Word of mouth and personal letters further spread the news. T.G. Weston wrote Sam Houston on June 16 before the newspaper account was printed and mentioned the encounter, but without much detail although he must have talked to some of the participants. From what he could gather, the Indians had cut the ranger trail or at least come on some of them from the rear.[10]

Mrs. Maverick described how Hays visited her on June 20 and told her of a big Indian fight on June 8. Her tale follows the general outline of events in both the report and in the newspaper stories and includes mention of the good work done by the new revolvers. She included the incident of Gillespie's killing the chief—not mentioned in Hays' report for some reason—and correctly identified the dead ranger as Peter Fohr.[11]

Rufus Perry, a member of Hays' 1844 company, gave to John H. Jenkins what he described as an eyewitness account.[12] His version is of interest because it is the only version by a participant other than Hays' own report. Perry specifically mentioned the new revolvers, "Here Colt's five-shooter was first used—two cylinders and both loaded." In general his version follows Hays' and the newspaper accounts. Perry mentioned the five Indians' trying to lure the rangers into an ambush, and how Hays ignored them and instead charged the main body. He recounted how the Indians charged the rangers, riding through their line two or three times until the Indians began to give way under the repeated revolver fire but not retreating until one of the rangers killed a chief. A running fight took place for ten miles during which Walker and Gillespie, each trying to kill an Indian, rode ahead of the other rangers and were cut off and lanced.

Perry's account of the second day and the location of the fight differ from Hays and the newspaper version. He recalled that Peter Fohr and Andrew Erskine had been left as camp guards when the main party went to chase the Indians and were alone in camp the second day when five Indians attacked them. The two men killed all the Indians, but Fohr was slain and Erskine wounded.

Perry's location of the fight, on the Pinta Trail near the head of Salado Creek, is puzzling. Hays reported the engagement as being about fifty miles above Seguin, many long miles north of the head of the Salado. The Pinta Trail, the name given to what became the road connecting San Antonio and Fredericksburg, ran northwest from San Antonio and away from Salado Creek. Henry (Henri de) Castro, new in San Antonio and still unfamiliar with Texas terrain, thought the fight was near Corpus Christi![13] There is no need to mention all the various versions of Walker Creek, other than to note the location of the fight was often a controversial feature.

Because Hays himself said the battle was near Walker Creek, this discussion of location may seem excessive to a contemporary reader who might be tempted to simplify the controversy by merely locating Walker Creek on a map. Unfortunately there are five Walker Creeks, and none is near what is believed to be the general location of the engagement. The rangers were scouting in new and largely unknown territory. Hays possibly even named the creek on the spot; if so, the name did not last.

The Walker Creek fight, or the Pedernales fight, or Hays' Big Fight as it is sometimes called, received scant notice after the initial publicity. One of the few contemporary, printed accounts appeared following the Mexican War; in Samuel Reid's *Scouting Expeditions of the Texas Rangers* the author describes this battle, evidently having talked with some of the participants. In all major details his account is the same as those printed in Texas immediately following the action. After this publication, however, most writers and historians appear to have overlooked the impact of this battle.

The ranger use of Colt revolvers in significant numbers

completely changed frontier combat. No longer would the Texans have to fight a controlled battle, always keeping some rifles charged and depending on terrain as much as on firepower for success. Hereafter they could meet the Comanches in the open, fighting while mounted and matching the deadly Indian bows with their own deadly form of close-range weapon. Despite the somewhat fragile Colt, even if outnumbered the rangers could hope to beat the Indians.

Hays acquired yet another area to patrol when Henry Castro began settling a considerable colony of mostly Alsatian immigrants west of the Medina River. The project had the full support of the Texas government, and Hays sent the following letter to Anson Jones.

San Antonio de Bexar, 21st July, 1844

Dear Sir,—I have to acknowledge the receipt of your esteemed communication by Mr. Castro, and assure you that I will do every thing in my power to enable him to effect his object (the establishment of his colony) as soon as possible.

The small force that I have under my command will not be sufficient to afford the colonists much protection in their new settlement. I think, however, if my force was increased to 15 or 20 in addition to my present numbers, they could proceed to the lands and commence their operations in safety.

Mr. Castro is now in this city, and will proceed immediately to the settlement. He has been detained a short time in consequence of my inability to accompany him, caused by a severe spell of sickness, from which I have but recently recovered.

I have the honor to be, very respectfully,
Your friend and obedient servant,
John C. Hays[14]

Evidently Hays had not recovered enough to travel when Castro decided to inspect his grant. In his diary Castro noted his departure from San Antonio on July 25, 1844, to visit his grant escorted by five men, including James Dunn, from Hays' company. After scouting much of his land, Castro and his party returned to San Antonio on July 31 with two of the rangers sick with fever.[15] Returning to San Antonio, Castro discovered that agents, "much seconded by a desperate character by the name of Rump, who belonged to Captain Hays' company of rangers," were trying to talk some of his colonists into leaving him and joining new German settlements northwest of San Antonio.[16] Hays' muster rolls list a John Rahn and a John Rhum in the unit, one of whom is possibly the ranger referred to by Castro. If so, evidently no action was taken against him because both of the names Rahm and Rhum continued to be listed on rolls through the end of 1844.

Meantime Hays again had the threat of Mexican invasion to worry him. Like all good commanders, he tried to obtain the best-possible intelligence of the enemy and maintained a network of spies along the Rio Grande. In late July 1844 he wrote the Secretary of War and Marine that one of his spies had uncovered Mexican plans for a mounted, six-hundred-man force of three divisions to invade Texas and capture San Antonio. If repulsed, the first division was to retreat, followed by the second, then the third to maintain a "constant annoyance." Hays' mention that the agent's report had been confirmed by a gentleman who could be trusted suggests he also had American traders in Mexico working for him. The attacks were scheduled to start in August.[17]

Fortunately for Texas, Mexico had too many internal problems to mount any serious attacks, although small scale raids continued to be a nuisance. A rumor of such a raiding party caused Hays to send Rufus Perry, Kit Acklin, John Carlin and John Dunn to check the area south of the Nueces on Turkey Creek.[18] While never specifically designated, Perry was probably in charge of the detail. All four rangers were experienced frontiersmen, tough physically, which accounts for their survival in a classic ranger scout. Their fight with a large Comanche band shows what ranger life could be like on the Texas frontier in 1844. Starting from their camp near San Antonio, the four men reached the Nueces River on August 12 and scouted along the river.

Wishing to take note of any tracks or trails in the vicinity, Perry sent the other three ahead to make camp and instructed them to camp on high ground where they could see Indian or Mexican intruders. When he finished his scouting, Perry found they had unsaddled and were instead preparing to camp on the river bank. Why Perry did not insist they move, especially when he thought he had found fresh Indian tracks, was never explained. He was worried enough to leave his horse and go to a small hill close by to check out the countryside, but seeing nothing he returned to the camp.

After eating supper Carlin and Dunn took the horses down to the river and watered them. It had been a hot day and the cool water was tempting; the two rangers undressed and went swimming while Perry and Acklin were resting back at the camp. With no warning, the camp was overrun by a group of Comanches. Acklin managed to fire one round while running for the shelter of the brush; Perry reached for his rifle but dropped it after being hit in the shoulder by an arrow. He ran for his horse, drawing his revolver and firing at the charging Indians, but a second arrow hit him in the temple and a third shaft struck his hip, going through his body. Somehow Perry reached back and pulled this third arrow out through his back. He fired again and fainted from loss of blood.

When Perry regained consciousness his first thought was to kill himself rather than be captured, but to his surprise he was alone. Thinking the bloody ranger dead, the Indians had run by him searching for the others. Perry managed to get to his feet and walked to the river bank where he saw the two naked rangers who had heard the shooting and crossed to the far side. When they saw Perry, Dunn and Carlin swam back. Acklin, who had hidden in the brush then doubled back to join them, asked the two rangers to take up the seriously wounded Perry on one of their horses, but they considered Perry as good as dead and refused. They let him hold on to one of the animals and assisted him to the opposite side of the river.

Perry fainted again, and all three left him in the belief he was dead. They took his rifle and revolver, then the two mounted rangers also deserted Acklin. Sometime later Perry came to and sat up on the river bank. Acklin had tugged the arrow from his shoulder, but Perry still had to stop the bleeding from his several wounds. He managed to crawl under a pile of driftwood and debris, washed up by floodwaters, where he was out of sight while the Comanches again checked the river bank. If they did see his tracks, they apparently believed he would soon be dead and saw no point in risking their lives in the closely piled tree limbs. Perry found mud and leaves in the bank and managed to stop the bleeding.

That night he hid in a hollow tree then spent the next day trying to regain some strength, unable to move farther than the river bank for water. Feeling a little better, he started that night for San Antonio, over a hundred miles away. He was afoot, without food, badly injured and weak from blood loss, but he managed to walk or crawl a few miles at a stretch before collapsing to rest. He knew that he must not stop to sleep because he would never get up. Fortunately he found water along the way, but his only food was a few mesquite beans and three prickly pear apples. Perry reached San Antonio in seven days!

Despite his condition Perry arrived in town a day before Acklin, who had also survived on beans and pears. Their arrival caused a sensation in San Antonio. Dunn and Carlin, in better shape though burned by the hot August sun, had reached town several days earlier with news their companions had been killed.[19] Hays and others censured the two rangers for leaving their companions, but no other disciplinary action was taken against them.

Perry was weeks recovering from his wounds. Vouchers for board and treatment and pay for Frank Paschal to stay with him show he was out of service until October. Ben McCulloch was also sick for ten days at this time and was also treated by Paschal.[20] Even though he remained on the muster and pay roll through September 1844, Perry is not on the new company roll for October-December 1844 although he did survive his injuries to become a ranger captain in 1874 when the Frontier Battalion was organized.

During this period the rangers performed a variety of tasks. McCulloch drew special pay for carrying dispatches to Washington-on-the-Brazos in late August. The Texas government was still in Washington, following the flight from Austin after the Mexican invasions of 1842, and the rangers were the only safe way to transmit official dispatches to and from the temporary capital. In December McCulloch submitted another voucher for travel to and from Washington "on business for the company." In June Tom Lyons and Alfred Berry traveled to Corpus Christi and back to San Antonio on official business and were reimbursed in October when money became available, even though Berry was no longer a member of the rangers by October. Hays also received reimbursements when a number of old vouchers were cleared on October 28.[21]

A new muster roll for the rangers was begun on October 29, to run through the end of 1844, but Hays began to have serious money problems. He furloughed one ranger on November 14 and let go three more on November 19. On November 29 Hays cut eight men and had to reduce by another three men in December. His company dropped from thirty-seven to twenty-two.[22]

During the latter months of 1844 and most of 1845, Texas newspapers did not print many stories about Indian raids or Mexican invasion plans. The major interest in the press was the issue of annexation by the United States, including the reactions of the British and French to such a move. By 1845 it was clear Mexico, torn by civil strife and with Santa Anna forced from office, was in no condition to mount a serious attack on Texas. Rival generals were using their troops to fight each other rather than the Texans. Comanche raids were again devastating entire areas in Northern Mexico; one Mexican newspaper complained that the reconquest of Texas was being hampered by these attacks and suggested the "perfidious Texans" were somehow behind the Comanche raids.[23]

Although the Comanches were raiding mostly in Mexico, thus removing much of their threat from Texas, there were still occasional forays from south of the border and by Indians after horses along the Texas frontier. On November 23 a band of Indians, probably Comanches looking for horses, stole the son and daughter of a Mrs. Simpson and headed north. Volunteers started on the trail immediately but the Indians passed the children to a mounted band. All of the Indians escaped when a heavy rain washed away their tracks, and a well-armed party searched for days but found no trace of the children. They did encounter several groups of friendly Delawares who told them the Comanches had been raiding along the Rio Grande. The Delawares had a Mexican boy who had been sold to them by some Comanche raiders, but the lad had been well treated, liked his new friends and refused to leave them.

One of the men on the scout sent a full description of their search to a newspaper, describing the country they crossed. He reported that a hostile band was camped high up on the Clear Fork of the Brazos and suggested that an expedition should move against them as soon as the spring grass was up.

> A company of rangers, similar to the gallant corps
> of Hays, is absolutely required along the line of
> frontier extending from the Colorado to the Trinity.
> Let Congress but appropriate the direct tax of the
> Western Counties to this object, and it is done.[24]

Later in December another band, suspected to be Lipans, stole horses near Seguin, but a posse chased them and killed two, wounded others and recovered the animals. Yet another Indian raid was able to escape with seventeen horses from the neighborhood of General Burleson.[25]

These isolated incidents revealed the continuing need for more frontier protection than Hays and his company could provide. In addition to volunteer units created for a specific emergency, several of the frontier areas established semi-permanent companies. Henry L. Kinney formed a ranging company to protect his interests and those of the people now living near him in the Corpus Christi area.

In June 1844 Kinney and some of his men had a fight with Indians who had raided the area. The Indians retreated, riding away in a crescent-shaped formation with their wounded and their stolen horses in the center. The chief rode from side to side, giving signals by cries and a whistle, but was wounded by Juan Ruiz, Kinney's clerk, who rode up behind the chief and shot him with a shotgun. Other warriors grabbed the seriously injured Indian and kept him in the saddle. Seeing they were being cut down one at a time, the Indians dropped to the ground and pretended to flee.

These Texans did not have the experience of the rangers and took the Comanche bait. Nine of the men, positioned three to four hundred yards in advance of any support from the rest of the company, opened fire and emptied their rifles in one volley. The Comanches quickly remounted and charged the nine men, who had dismounted to reload.

Kinney yelled for them to mount and ride back to the shelter of the main body, but they were either too far away to understand or did not realize their danger. While they were reloading, the Indians rode over them, shooting arrows and using their lances. One man saw them and bolted but was run down and lanced to death. Another Texan shot an Indian near him, then threw his empty pistol at another and mounted his horse but was shot with an arrow. The archer was killed by another member of the company. The injured man's horse carried him out onto the open prairie, where he died.

Juan Ruiz, one of the nine men cut off by the Indians, became separated from his horse, and Kinney and others tried to distract the Comanches from the surrounded man. Kinney galloped through the Indian circle and managed to swing Ruiz up behind him, but as he turned to force his way clear a Comanche rode behind him and thrust a lance completely through Ruiz, slightly wounding Kinney. Unable to hold the dying man in place and still control his horse, Kinney was forced to let go of his clerk and dropped the dying man to the ground.

With the support of more of his men, Kinney was able to break free with only a slight wound in his back. He had two bullet holes in his clothing and arrow gashes on his rifle stock. There were a number of Mexicans in Kinney's force, one of whom died shortly after the fight. Another was injured. A man identified only as Berry was wounded, and others not listed by name were also killed or wounded. The Comanches lost six killed and a number wounded, but they managed to carry away all their casualties including their chief, who must have been killed or desperately wounded because he dropped all his weapons and equipment. Two days later a detail went out to bury the Texan dead and found all the Comanche arms and trappings, indicating the Indians had not returned to the scene of the fight.[26]

In August 1844 the Secretary of War and Marine authorized Kinney's unit as a regular ranger company with a strength of fifty-six men. A joint resolution of the Ninth Congress appropriated $2,349 to pay the expenses of this new company.[27]

An event in late 1844 reveals much about the level or riding and shooting skills possessed by the rangers and other frontiersmen. It also demonstrates the sometimes confusing and blurred lines between peace and war that occurred between the Texans and the Comanches. A great contest was held outside San Antonio on the prairie by the San Pedro Springs, the site of the first settlement of the town.

Everyone who could that day walked or rode northwest to the springs for the festive occasion. The riding contest must have been well advertised because many of the riders, Texan, Comanche and Mexican, arrived from long distances. After the spectators had assembled, the riders took their places. On one side was a long line of brilliantly decorated Comanches. Opposite them was a line of plainly clad Texans and a number of Mexican *caballeros* in their slashed trousers, decorated jackets and sombreros.

When everyone was in place, a young Mexican galloped between the lines and rode several hundred yards out onto the prairie, leaned down to place a spear on the ground, wheeled, and rode away. He was barely clear when the last Comanche in line jerked his horse to one side and rode back a hundred yards, turned his mount and galloped towards the spear. Without slowing he scooped up the shaft and held it aloft then jerked his mount about and galloped back to replace the spear on the ground without breaking stride or leaving the saddle.

Without a word or command, one of the Texans repeated the trick, then every man in both lines picked up the spear without stopping or dismounting. The judges then placed a glove on the ground, but all the contestants picked up the small glove as easily as they had the spear. A board with a target drawn on the wood was then placed in the ground. One of the Comanches gave a war cry and rushed at the target, clasping his bow and several arrows in his left hand, and hit the target twice as he rode by. Every Indian hit the target at least once, but each of the Texans and Mexicans was also able to shoot a pistol ball into the board as he galloped by.

Because these games had not eliminated anyone, the judges let the contestants do whatever they wanted in "free style" riding, galloping along the prairie, dropping to the ground, vaulting back into the saddle, riding backwards, leaning down to snatch rocks, grass or twigs. They simulated firing under the neck of their mounts, changing sides under the horse's neck.

Just how points were awarded is unknown, but at the end of this stage ranger John McMullen was being considered the winner. In the final event, breaking wild mustangs, the contestants had to take a length of rope, select a mount and ride it broken, or broken enough to ride and control. McMullen was the first to try and rode back with a somewhat subdued mount. Not all were willing to try this event.

Accounts of this event vary in some details, but all agree John McMullen was the winner. This is not surprising; he was a skilled frontiersman and rider, a veteran of the Somervell campaign and a recently returned Mier prisoner. Second and third place finishers vary with the story teller. In one version, Kinney from Corpus Christi was second with a Comanche third. In another account a Comanche warrior called Long Quiet was second, Kinney third, and Señor Don Rafael, a Mexican from the Rio Grande settlement, fourth. The winners received decorated pistols and knives as prizes, and all the Comanche participants received gifts.[28]

As they had for the past few years, the Texas Congress began the New Year by again attempting to provide for frontier defense. Another act for the protection of the frontier was approved February 1, 1845.[29]

Hays was appointed to command a company, but bitter experience had shown a single company was not sufficient to patrol the frontier much less protect it. Accordingly, smaller detachments were authorized. Roberts and Milam counties were to have ten-man units each commanded by a lieutenant; Travis County was allowed fifteen men and a lieutenant; due to its exposed position Bexar was authorized thirty men and a lieutenant; and Goliad and Refugio were to share fifteen men and a lieutenant. Hays was to be commander of both his company and the Bexar detachment but would also command if any or all of the detachments were concentrated in an emergency.

Pay was established at seventy-five dollars for the captain and thirty dollars for each lieutenant, with the privates each drawing twenty dollars a month. The sharp drop in pay, for the lieutenants and privates, from the year before reveals the condition of the treasury, but the government did set aside ten dollars a month per man to pay for ammunition, horseshoeing, medicine, forage and subsistence.

There are no records to show if any of these smaller detachments were organized, but Hays wasted little time forming his new company. Service began on February 12, 1845.[30] He evidently had little trouble finding good men; R.A. Gillespie became the new lieutenant and many of the earlier rangers reenlisted. "Big Foot" Wallace was a member, one of the few times he is listed on a ranger muster roll, and John McMullen joined. At least two thirds of the men had been in previous ranger companies.

The unit was active during the year, though without the bloody battles that had marked earlier days. Because official reports have not survived, most of its actions are known only from secondhand accounts, largely newspaper stories, and from vouchers for service. Hays made one trip to Corpus Christi in late March 1845 to check on reports Comanches were gathering on the Rio Grande for a raid into Mexico.[31] On March 25 the Texas auditor certified and the comptroller approved Hays' entitlement to a credit of $5,412.05 out of the appropriation for the defense of the frontier. That the rangers remained active is indicated by a bill in the amount of $136.50 for shoeing horses in February thru July. The smith furnished fifty-eight pairs of shoes, reset many more, and repaired two coffee mills.[32] It is interesting to note the developing levels of government in early Texas in which every voucher was carried to the penny then checked and audited. The cumbersome system would prove to be a gold mine for later historians.

Nathaniel Lewis, one of San Antonio's pioneer merchants, again supplied the rangers with a variety of goods. One bill he submitted was for foodstuffs—coffee, sugar, salt, bacon, beef, rice, flour, corn meal and beans—for a total of $732.19. During the same period, Hays ordered 532 bushels of corn for the company horses, six kegs of powder, lead and percussion caps and four bags of buckshot. This last item indicates the rangers continued to make use of shotguns. In addition, a medicine chest was selected by "Sergt Myers by order of Col. Hays." It must have been a rather fancy chest because its cost was $47, a considerable sum for the time. Sergeant Myers does not appear on muster rolls for this company. One voucher lists two bottles of wine, a coffee mill and a pistol belt. An interesting item is "papers vermillon for Comanches;"[33] the rangers must have kept on hand a small stock of goods for trading or for rewards.

Lewis seemingly stocked everything except medical supplies. It is easy to think of these early rangers as superhuman, but they did get sick and needed such remedies as could be provided in the 1840s. These included pills of various kinds, quinine, emetics, saltpeter, sulphur and calomil. Most of the medical supplies were purchased for specific rangers, listed by name on the vouchers.

According to newspaper accounts Hays, acting as a diplomat rather than warrior, was involved in an incident with Indians in late August. A large Comanche band, as many as 150 according to the *Telegraph*, intercepted some Mexican traders on "San Pedro," probably near San Antonio, killed one, and captured five others as well as much livestock. Hays managed to talk with the Comanches and obtained the release of the captives and the stock. He caught the Indians at the right time; although they were always interested in plunder, this time they seemed more interested in buying guns to fight Kickapoos and were willing to release their prisoners in hopes of speeding a possible arms sale. They also had a very ingenious proposal for Hays: since the Texans were trying to kill Mexicans, and since the Comanches were also Texans, why not let them kill the Mexicans? The ranger was wise enough to refer this proposal to his superiors.[34]

Hays escorted the Secretary of War and Marine to Corpus Christi and back in late September, signing the voucher on September 26, 1845. The secretary personally approved and signed the voucher the following day. A day later, on September 28, 1845, the company, forty-two enlisted men with Hays and R.A. Gillespie, was paid off and discharged.[35] Although the rangers would soon be back, this time in the service of the United States, their discharge in September 1845 makes a convenient and logical place to close the story of the early rangers.

The rangers had finished their last months of service to the Texas Republic in routine patrolling, but it did not diminish the importance of their achievements. Patrolling the frontier continued to be important because it kept the Indian and Mexican raiders at a distance. The rangers no longer had to prove themselves; long before 1845 they had become a feature of frontier life and were admired throughout the republic. Although few in number, they made a contribution to the republic far in excess of their numerical strength and far outweighing the small sums spent on their upkeep. Without the rangers, be they labeled spies, mounted gunmen or volunteers, the frontier settlements and individual farmers might easily have been driven back into the eastern counties. How Texas might have developed in such an event is speculation, but the republic certainly would have progressed in a different, and slower, manner.

In the United States, seemingly limitless open country enabled the country to expand and grow. The Republic of Texas also had vast territories throughout which the small ranger companies were able to keep the Comanches at a distance, preventing the devastation that stifled growth in Northern Mexico. Ranger units had taken part in driving the settled tribes out of East Texas and from the fertile lands of the Brazos, Colorado and Trinity rivers. Perhaps not acceptable today, these actions nevertheless opened huge tracts of land for settlers. The rangers had also managed to maintain a degree of peace between the Nueces and the Rio Grande, allowing at least some trade between the frontier towns and Mexico.

Texas developed rapidly in the years between 1835 and 1845. Settlements became hamlets, then towns, and the estimated population of 30,000 in 1830 reached 100,000 within a few years. By the time union with the United States was being seriously discussed, perhaps another 50,000 people had become citizens. In the December 25, 1839, issue of the *Telegraph and Texas Register*, the editor complained that too many lawyers, physicians, clerks and graduates of universities in the United States were coming to Texas when it was farmers who were needed. Even though he may have been correct in saying many of these new immigrants would be disappointed, the young republic *was* changing from a land of riflemen and farmers to a nation of varied interests, trades and professions. The climate and soil of the eastern counties made them suitable for a plantation economy, and a large slave population became part of Texas. The majority of farmers, however, operated small plots and depended on their family members for workers.

Texas was still a wild country, but there was a very early

effort to establish schools at all levels. Churches grew in
number and membership. A surprising number of newspapers were published during the republic years and would
later become treasure troves of information about the rangers. By and large, their editors were among the strongest
supporters of the para-military rangers.

Despite considerable opposition from anti-slavery ele-
ments in the United States, Texas joined the Union on
December 29, 1845. Some in the United States had opposed
the union with Texas, fearing it would lead to war with
Mexico, and their fears were soon realized. Seeing the conflict
as certain, the United States dispatched General Zachary
Taylor with military troops to a camp near Corpus Christi,
then south to the Rio Grande. Texas had formed a number
of ranger companies during this transition period, but Taylor
refused to allow any of them into the army. Later, after the
initial battles with the Mexican forces opposite Matamoros,
he accepted a company organized by Sam Walker because he
had no other horsemen familiar with the brush country and
none able to engage in guerrilla warfare. Walker became a
national hero when he rode through the Mexican lines and
returned with news that troops besieged by the Mexicans
could hold out. During this early period of the war, John Price
also had a ranger company supporting Taylor.

Taylor finally called on Texas for troops, and two
mounted regiments and one infantry regiment joined his
army. The 1st Texas Mounted Rifle Regiment, organized in
the western part of the state, was largely composed of men
with ranger experience. Hays was elected as colonel, Walker
as lieutenant colonel, and Chevallie as major. Ben McCulloch commanded one of the companies with John McMullen
as lieutenant. R.A. Gillespie and Chris Acklin also led companies. Too old to serve under United States Army Regula-
tions, Eli Chandler nevertheless organized a company and
fought anyway. Kinney rode down from Corpus Christi and
served as a staff officer. They were rangers in fact, if not
name, and everyone soon called any Texas unit a "ranger"
command. As before, they supplied their own mounts, saddles, clothing and weapons. There was one important difference—now they were paid regularly.

The ranger use of rifles, horse management, and above all the Colt revolver created a sensation among the rest of the army. The Texans were the only effective mounted force, taking over courier duties, train escort, advance guard and counterguerrilla missions. They could operate deep in Mexico, scout possible roads, and locate water. Every man in the army who wrote any type of memoir had some comment on the wild rangers. Their lack of uniforms and frequent demonstrations of lack of respect for anything not Texan often caused grumbling in other commands, but there was no quarrel with their conduct in battle nor with their efficiency. Without them, the campaign in Northern Mexico would have been even more difficult and might have had a different outcome.

To the United States Army, the Texans demonstrated the value of repeating firearms and, in the process, brought Sam Colt out of financial ruin and enabled him to reestablish his manufacture of firearms. The army also saw a new form of mounted combat which prepared it for the arduous years ahead fighting the Plains Indians.

Few of the men who had been ranger leaders during the republic and in the Mexican War continued on active service after the end of the war in 1848. Only Rufus Perry spanned the decades to serve again for a few months in 1874; the others turned to a variety of pursuits, many searching for fortunes in California, but their departure from the ranks was not the end of the rangers. As a state within the Union, Texas turned over military defense responsibilities to the United States Army, and much of the U.S. Cavalry was stationed in Texas in the years before the Civil War. After the Mexican War, and again following the Civil War, however, Texas found it necessary to bring back the ranger companies. In each succeeding era the rangers were to equal the legendary fighters of the republic days, possessing improved weapons but still furnishing everything they used including their horses and saddles and lacking uniforms, badges or flags. They were slowly to evolve from soldiers of sorts to peace officers, but the customs established in the 1820s served them through the century.

And down to this day.

APPENDIX

Battles—or Legends?

The early rangers had the not always desirable distinction of becoming legends in their own time. They, like most Texans of the day (and today), enjoyed a tall tale, especially one on themselves. Nothing was more fun than regaling an outsider with stories of epic adventures made up on the spot, and the stories tended to improve with each retelling. Although few of the men would lie about their own deeds at the time, they had no qualms about embellishing a comrade's actions. In later years an old ranger might help out a newsman or historian by improving a trifle on what had happened. It became a matter of pride to have been associated with Hays or McCulloch or Chandler, to have been at San Jacinto or along the Salado. Who would not have wished to help turn back the Comanches at Plum Creek? The number of men who rode with Hays grew through the decades—though not all of them can be found on muster rolls.

During the 1880s several writers collected stories from men and women who had lived through the wild days of the Texas Republic. They performed an invaluable service, and if properly used their work fills in many a gap in the often brief official reports. They seldom had access to records, reports or official papers, however, and they made little or no effort to crosscheck the recollections they transcribed and printed.

The task of the historian is to gather all possible source materials on a period or event or person, to collate these often conflicting accounts, then to write a readable narrative that is as accurate and unbiased as possible. Judgments are permissible, providing they are based on the morality of the period in question rather than current morality. In accomplishing this task, a few legends are shown to be just that, or at best extremely suspect, and the historian occasionally feels a sense of sadness.

While I was collecting materials on this history of the early rangers, accounts of several of the battles involving Hays and his men did not ring true even though some of these stories have been told so long they have been accepted as gospel and printed without question in recent reference books and biographies. At least one suspect "battle" is commemorated by a bronze marker. Conflicting dates, or no dates, failure to find the names of men who fought on any roster, and superhuman conduct were some of the features that aroused my doubts. The most compelling doubts were raised by the lack of any mention of these fights in contemporary sources.

Hays' epic lone stand at Enchanted Rock is the oldest of these questionable fights. Although some details in the various accounts do differ, there is a general similarity in the versions of this battle. The earliest version dates from the Mexican War and was printed in Samuel Reid's account of his experiences with McCulloch.[1] In all the various accounts, in 1841 or 1842 Hays and some of his men are either scouting or surveying near Enchanted Rock, a granite hill north of present-day Fredericksburg, when Hays becomes separated from the others and is cut off by Indians. He dismounts from his horse and manages to run to the top of the rock, where he holds off the attackers for one to four hours until his men finally manage to fight their way up and save him.

In the various stories, the shape of Enchanted Rock plays a key part in Hays' ability to fight for some time against superior numbers. Wilbarger, in his account of the fight, describes Enchanted Rock as "the apex of a high round hill very difficult to climb. In the center of this rock there is a circular hollow sufficiently large to allow a small party of men to lie in it, and its perpendicular sides formed an effective breastwork." Writing a few years later, Sowell had a similar account, "It was of large, conical shape, with a depression at the apex something like the crater of an extinct volcano. A dozen or more men can lie in this place and make a strong defense against largely superior numbers, as the ascent is steep and rugged."[2] More recent accounts have some variation of the above, with the shape of the rock, or other natural features, giving Hays an advantage. All tales indicate he could easily shoot at one Indian, turn about and scare others. Only when he was faced with overwhelming numbers did his position become critical, but fortunately his men arrived and drove off his attackers.

Reid's book was first published in 1847, only a few years after the fight was supposed to have taken place. No newspaper reported this fight, and no official report can be located. No contemporary account by a participant or writer has survived. Hays' actions for 1841 are fairly well known. He left few reports and no muster or pay rolls for 1842, but it was a busy year and his activities are fairly well documented elsewhere. It is unlikely he could have been away for an extended period of time, engaging in such a daring skirmish, without some mention by the men with him or by himself.

The only other early mention of the fight is in John Caperton's manuscript on the life of Hays,[3] a tribute written after Hays and Caperton had gone to California after the Mexican War. Caperton, who had not served with Hays during the time of the Texas Republic or during the Mexican War, first joined the ranger in 1848 for an expedition to locate a land route from San Antonio to El Paso. Although Caperton had no first-hand knowledge of Enchanted Rock, or of the first revolver fight also covered in the manuscript, it would be logical to assume Hays told Caperton of these events, as well as of other details of the republic days. If so, it seems strange that Hays would not have also mentioned a major fight in Bandera Pass, another disputed battle that will be examined later. It seems likely, however, that it was Reid rather than Hays who served as Caperton's source. An examination of the Caperton accounts shows he was familiar with Reid's book, mentioning it by name. Caperton's accounts of Enchanted Rock and Hays' revolver fight are similar to Reid's stories, and neither Reid nor Caperton mention Bandera Pass. Caperton had access to Reid's book and likely lifted the Enchanted Rock encounter.

A sentence towards the end of Reid's account is critical in evaluating this battle—or legend. "'This,' said the Texian, who told us the story, 'was one of *Jack's*' most narrow escapes....'" It is easy to visualize one of the rangers spinning a tale to entertain the Louisiana lawyer-turned-ranger. Hays had actually been up along the Pedernales River surveying land claims at various times, and the ranger may have turned some scamper across Enchanted Rock into a tale that would one day be cast in bronze.

Obviously Reid never saw Enchanted Rock. Neither did later retellers of the story of the fight ever visit the "battle-field," which is not a rocky hill but a solid granite mass, the second largest such formation in the United States. There is no natural fortification atop the hill, no trench. No boulders dot the surface. There *are* shallow depressions where the stone has flaked away—depressions perhaps deep enough to protect a man's ankles. None of the features described in the tales can be found.

The top of the rock is a broad, slightly sloping field approximately five hundred feet in diameter. The sides of Enchanted Rock do not drop evenly and regularly, nor is it difficult to climb. Many areas are shielded from view atop the hill. From any location at the top, Hays would have been able to fire on only one or two Indians at a time while others could have charged him unseen until they were upon him. There are so many covered routes to the top that no one man, or even several men, could have possibly whirled and circled enough to have threatened a substantial party of attackers. The only way Hays could have survived was for the Indians to have come at him one at a time, and Indians did not fight in such a suicidal manner.

A second fight included in many biographies, histories and reference books is a major battle between thirty and forty rangers and a hundred Comanches in Bandera Pass in 1841 or 1842 or 1843. Like Enchanted Rock, Bandera Pass is a known landmark, a natural gap through the hills north of the town of Bandera commonly used in the 1840s as a route through the hill barrier. It has a long history and was the site of an earlier battle between Indians and the Spanish.

The printed versions of the fight at Bandera Pass are not as early as Reid's retelling of the Texian's yarn about Enchanted Rock. Reid mentions nothing about this battle, which would certainly have been a major encounter and thus likely to be retold by the rangers. Neither does Caperton mention Bandera Pass, although he describes the first revolver fight and several other skirmishes that can be identified with known fights. The earliest account of the Bandera Pass fight seems to be by Thomas Galbreath, as told to Sowell.4 The earliest accounts of the supposed fight are all in Sowell, published roughly a half-century after the event.

The various recollections agree to some degree. Hays and his company were scouting along the Medina River, moving north when a large Comanche war party ambushed them as they rode through Bandera Pass, a five-hundred-yard long break in the hills. Thrown off balance by the sudden attack, the Texans began to waver, but Hays rallied them. "Steady there, boys," he exclaimed. "Get down and tie those horses. We can whip them."[5] The Indians had firearms as well as their traditional weapons, and the fight ranged from bow and arrow and rifle fire, at a distance, to hand-to-hand fighting with knives and lances. The rangers suffered considerable loss, and the fight was in some doubt until the Comanche war chief was killed. The Indians gradually retreated, taking their casualties with them. The rangers, with their five dead and six wounded, fell back to the south end of the pass where there was a large water hole. Two of the wounded rangers were taken to San Antonio for treatment.

Galbreath does not have a specific date for this engagement, but he claimed he joined Hays after the ranger had returned from the Somervell expedition in 1843. Hays supposedly had thirty to forty men in the battle, a figure that agrees with the version of B.F. Highsmith as also told to Sowell. Existing muster rolls show Hays had a company of thirty-plus men for a short period in 1841 and during June-July 1843. The 1842 rolls have been lost. He commanded a large company during parts of 1844, but none of the accounts of Bandera Pass is as late as 1844.

There are a number of questionable points in Galbreath's story as told to Sowell. He said he was wounded in the battle, but he is not listed on any of Hays' extant muster rolls. He recalled that Lee Jackson was killed, but neither Lee Jackson nor the George Jackson mentioned by Creed Taylor can be identified. Galbreath said he had not been in the company long enough to know all the men, but he does mention some participants besides Jackson. He lists Sam Walker, but Walker did not join Hays until 1844. Sam Lucky (Luckie) was described as wounded and can be found on some 1843 rosters, but none of the rosters shows him as wounded. Ben McCulloch, Andrew Erskine, R.A. Gillespie and Mike Chevallie, all in the battle according to Galbreath, served with Hays at various times in 1843. James Dunn and Kit Acklin (Ackland) are listed among the wounded; Dunn was with Hays during June-July 1843, but Acklin did not join until February 28, 1844.[6]

Another account of this fight was given by Benjamin F. Highsmith.[7] The main difference between his version and Galbreath's is in the date he gives; Highsmith's date in the spring of 1841 presents yet another problem. The general details of this engagement as remembered by Highsmith, and most of the names he gives, agree with Galbreath. He even cites almost the same speech by Hays. Like Galbreath, he could not remember many of the names because he had recently joined the company.

Creed Taylor, supposedly in the fight, left another account of the action and mentions a more specific date of June of 1841.[8] His version is generally the same as the other two, with Walker in the fight and Acklin's killing the Comanche chief, but he recalled that Hays had only twenty-five men. Walker, as mentioned earlier, was not in Texas in 1841, and Acklin did not join Hays until 1844. Other events of Hays' rangers in 1841 are fairly well documented, and it is difficult to fit a major battle into what is known of that busy year even if the inconsistencies in names were to be resolved. Furthermore, Creed Taylor is not listed on any of Hays' 1841 muster rolls; although he did see service during the Woll invasion, he cannot be connected with any ranger command during the republic years.

Taylor mentions that Andrew Erskine had a five-shooter. This was earlier than the period after Walker Creek when the repeaters were in general use by the rangers, but Taylor could have bought the weapon himself. This mention of the Colt raises the distinct possibility that Taylor was confusing Bandera Pass and Walker Creek. In addition to the death of Jackson, Taylor recalled that a Peter Fore was slain, Walker thrust through with a lance, and Erskine among the wounded. If Peter Fore is changed to Peter Fohr, Taylor's casualty list and type of injuries begins to resemble the Texan losses in the fight at Walker Creek. Comparing Taylor's memoirs with known events casts doubt on this particular fight. He *was* in the Mexican War, but his version of his service reads more as fiction than fact. Taylor confused events and participants and often remembered that it was he who accomplished actions usually credited by historians to others.

Nevertheless, despite confusion over dates and names, there are possible explanations for some of the discrepancies. Jackson, Galbreath, and even others, for example, could have joined up with Hays on the march, thus not showing on any muster roll. It does not seem likely that three accounts of a fight would remain if there had been no fight, but all three acccounts were recorded by the same writer, Sowell. The Galbreath and Highsmith versions have troubling similarities despite the difference in dates. Taylor's story is considerably different, but he was also being recorded by Sowell. The accounts in Sowell do not constitute a clear-cut source, just as Reid's hearing of Enchanted Rock is not reliable, and the possibility that Sowell had this story from either Galbreath or Highsmith and influenced the recollections of the other two cannot be overlooked. It is also interesting to note that Wilbarger does not mention Bandera Pass.

The primary indictment of the Bandera Pass battle is the lack of any contemporary account. By 1843 Hays was the premier ranger leader, and his activities were covered by Texas newspapers. Much of what we know of his actions during 1842 and 1843 is from press dispatches, and ranger actions in 1841 are quite well documented. It does not seem likely the rangers could engage in a major battle, lose five killed and six wounded, and not have something printed in the press. Two wounded men were supposedly brought to San Antonio for treatment, but if so surely someone would have mentioned the fact in diaries, letters or memoirs. The big revolver fight on Walker Creek and the misadventures of the four rangers in 1844 were mentioned by several people in town. Why not a major battle at Bandera Pass? John Salmon Ford, who served with Hays in the Mexican War and who collected much material for his memoirs,[9] has a great deal of information on Hays' scouts and fights, but he makes no mention of Enchanted Rock or Bandera Pass. John Holland Jenkins' memoirs, one of the best collections of colonial and republic tales, does not mention either fight; the several references in the footnotes of his book are supplied by the editor and have obviously been derived from later accounts of the fight. It is also worth noting again that Caperton makes no mention of any fight at Bandera Pass.

Galbreath's account of another fight in or near the Nueces Canyon is also of doubtful accuracy and is probably a garbled version of Walker Creek.[10] Details of yet another of Hays' fights are mixed in, but the main outline of Galbreath's Nueces Canyon battle is clearly the first revolver fight at Walker Creek.

It is not a pleasant task to suggest that respected pioneers suffered memory loss, or embellished wild tales to satisfy the authors who were taking down their life story, or wished to be a large, or at least larger, part of something momentous. Early Texans were not the first to recall events in a more favorable light than actually shown in the encounter. Pointing out marked discrepancies in accepted works is not a sure road to popularity, particularly if the discrepancies are in Texas' hallowed ranger accounts. Legends have indeed grown up around Hays and other early rangers, but the reality of their accomplishments is not diminished by pointing out the doubtful status of the legendary fables. The position of the first rangers is secure enough to withstand carping about the few fights that likely never took place.

After all, there were enough and plenty that *did*.

FOOTNOTES

CHAPTER 1 — COLONIAL TEXAS

1. J.W. Williams, *Old Texas Trails*, edited by Kenneth F. Neighbors (Burnet, Texas: Eakin Press, 1979) has a carefully researched study of these trips through Texas, comparing old accounts and records with the actual terrain.

2. Ibid., 111-19.

3. T.R. Fehrenbach, *Comanches* (New York: Alfred A. Knopf, 1974), 214-20.

4. Ibid., 153-235, covers this period in detail.

5. Eugene C. Barker, *The Life of Stephen F. Austin* (1926; reprint, Austin: University of Texas Press, 1985), 31. When Moses Austin passed through Nacogdoches in July of 1821, there were thirty-six people in the town.

6. Barker, *Stephen F. Austin*, contains a detailed examination of this period in Texas history.

7. Ibid., 41.

8. Ibid., 43-80.

9. J.H. Kuykendall, "Recollections of Capt. Gibson Kuykendall," *The Quarterly of the Texas State Historical Association* (hereafter *TSHA*) vol.7 (1904), 30-31.

10. Barker, *Stephen F. Austin*, 96.

11. Kuykendall, "Recollections," 31. This election was for the Brazos district. Earlier in November, the Colorado settlers elected John Tumlinson as *alcalde*, Robert Kuykendall as captain, and Moses Morrison as lieutenant. Barker, *Stephen F. Austin*, 88.

12. Barker, *Stephen F. Austin*, 96-97.

13. Eugene C. Barker, "The Government of Austin's Colony, 1823-1831," *The Southwestern Historical Quarterly* (hereafter *SHQ*) vol.21, no.3 (1918), 232-33.

14. The basic account of this incident is in J.W. Wilbarger, *Indian Depredations in Texas* (1889; reprint, Austin: Eakin Press and State House Press, 1985), 204-5. Wilbarger, however, places the incident in 1824. He also lists John J. and Joseph, or Joe, as the brothers rather than the sons of the murdered man. D.E. Kilgore, *A Ranger Legacy* (Austin: Madrona Press, 1973) 26, 35-39, correctly identifies the often-confusing members of this large family.

15. Kilgore, *A Ranger Legacy*, 21-32. Kilgore has a detailed account of this unit, including photocopies of pertinent documents.

16. Barker, *Stephen F. Austin*, 91.

17. Ibid., 92.

18. Ibid.

19. The details of these military operations are outside the scope of this book. Barker, *Stephen F. Austin*, 94-95, contains considerable detail; Kuykendall, "Recollections," 35-36, describes events from Kuykendall's perspective.

20. Barker, *Stephen F. Austin*, 117.

21. Kuykendall, "Recollections," 38.

22. Barker, *Stephen F. Austin*, 145.

23. Ibid., 163.

24. Ibid., 261-65, covers Terán's stay in Texas and his recommendations in full.

25. Ibid., 265-83, covers in detail the effects of the 1830 act and Austin's efforts to work within the law's restrictions, preserving peace yet still allowing immigration.

26. John Henry Brown, *History of Texas* (St. Louis: L.E. Daniell, 1892), I:182-83.

27. Barker, *Stephen F. Austin*, 351-52.

28. Ibid., 348-49.

29. Ibid., 396.

30. Ibid., 396-400.

31. Ibid., 408-9.

32. Ibid., 416.

33. Eugene C. Barker, ed., "Journal of the Permanent Council," *TSHA* vol.7 (1904), 249-62.

34. H.P.N. Gammel, *The Laws of Texas 1822-1897* (Austin: The Gammel Book Company, 1898), I:513.

35. Ibid., 525-27.

36. Ibid., 543.

37. Ibid., 924-25. At this time rangers were required to have "weapons" without specific types' being mentioned. However, even this early, potential recruits had to have a "good horse." It was not until December 5, 1836, that a "good rifle" and a brace of pistols were required.

38. Ibid., 600-1.

39. Walter Prescott Webb, *The Texas Rangers, A Century of Frontier Defense* (New York & Boston: Houghton Mifflin Company, 1935), 24.

40. Andrew Jackson Sowell, *Texas Indian Fighters; Early Settlers and Indian Fighters of Southwest Texas* (1900; reprint, Austin: State House Press, 1986), 808.

41. Noah Smithwick, *The Evolution of a State, or Recollections of Old Texas Days* (1900; reprint, Austin: University of Texas Press, 1983), 82.

42. Ibid., 80-81.

43. Ibid., 82-87. The following incident is based on his account.

44. This version of the incident is based on Smithwick's account. Wilbarger, *Indian Depredations*, 220-22, generally supports Smithwick,

clearly setting the action in January 1836 and mentioning that "Mrs. Sarah Hibbins" had just returned to Texas from a visit in Tennessee. John Henry Brown, *Indian Wars and Pioneers of Texas* (189?; reprint, Austin: State House Press, 1988), 88-90, has a slightly different account. According to Brown, Tumlinson told him of the chase and fight, saying he took "eighteen rangers, the first ever raised under the revolutionary government of Texas," on the chase for "Mrs. John Hibbins'" children. He generally agrees with the other versions, except in three details: Tumlinson said *he* killed the Indian, not Rohrer; Lieutenant Rogers was with the small party that chased down the Indians with the Hibbins boy; and the mule carrying the child was killed. Tumlinson also mentions he had two men wounded. Whether the different versions are faulty recollections years after the fact, or ego, will never be known.

45. Brown, *History of Texas*, I:537.

46. Sam Houston, *The Writings of Sam Houston 1813-1863*, 8 vols. edited by Amelia W. Williams and Eugene C. Barker (Austin: University of Texas Press, 1938), I:398.

47. Walter Prescott Webb, Editor-in-Chief, *The Handbook of Texas* (Austin: The Texas State Historical Association, 1952), I:938.

48. Smithwick, *Evolution of a State*, 87.

49. Ibid.

50. Ibid., 88. This section is based on his narrative, 87-96.

51. Ibid., 90.

52. Ibid., 91.

53. Ibid., 92.

54. Ibid.

55. Ibid., 108.

56. Henderson K. Yoakum, *History of Texas* (New York: Redfield, 1855), II:180-81.

CHAPTER 2 — THE EARLY REPUBLIC

1. See Fehrenbach, *Comanches*, for a modern telling of this story.

2. Houston, *Writings*, VII:4-5.

3. Robert E. Davis, Editor, *Texana* (Waco: Texian Press, 1963), I:57-58.

4. Gammel, *Laws*, I:1112-14.

5. Ibid., 1134.

6. Smithwick, *Evolution of a State*, 108.

7. Ibid.

8. Ibid., 112.

9. Ibid., 113. In other sections of his book, 118-19, Smithwick was not overly complimentary of Coleman, saying he had been a lawyer in civilian life and was only a staff officer at San Jacinto.

10. Ibid. According to a payroll for a later command of Andrews, the officer's name was Micah, not Michael.

11. Ibid. Smithwick later praised Andrews as a fine officer.

12. Ibid., 113-15.

13. Ibid., 116-17.

14. Ibid., 123-40, covers his stay with the Comanches and return to the company.

15. George Bernard Erath, *The Memoirs of Major George B. Erath, 1813-1891* (1923; reprint, Waco: The Heritage Society of Waco, 1956), dictated to Lucy A. Erath.

16. Erath, *Memoirs*, 12-40.

17. Ibid., 47.

18. Ibid., 47-48. Coleman's actions suggest he did act as overall commander at least in some instances.

19. Ibid.

20. Ibid.

21. Ibid., 49. Erath's account of the scout and fight follows on 49-53.

22. Ibid., 53.

23. Andrew Jackson Sowell, *Rangers and Pioneers of Texas* (1884; reprint, Austin: State House Press, 1991), 41-42.

24. Webb, *Handbook*, II:622-23.

25. S.S. Wilcox, "Laredo During the Texas Republic," *SHQ* vol.42, no.2 (1939), 83-107. Smith's report was written in San Antonio, March 27, 1837.

26. Houston, *Writings*, II:76-78; *Journals of the Fourth Congress of the Republic of Texas 1839-1840* (hereafter Journals of the Fourth Congress) (Austin: Von Boeckmann-Jones Co., n.d.), II:197.

27. *Mirabeau Buonaparte Lamar, The Papers of Mirabeau Buonaparte Lamar*, 6 vols. edited by Charles Adams Gulick, Jr., *et al* (1921-1927; reprint, Austin & New York: The Pemberton Press, 1968), IV: Part I, 229-30.

28. Gammel, *Laws*, I:1334-35.

29. Brown, *Indian Wars*, 50-51.

30. Karnes' later service is covered in Chapter Four.

31. Wilbarger, *Indian Depredations*, 361-67.

32. Anson Jones to John Forsyth, December 31, 1838, printed in *Journals of the Fourth Congress*, III:21-22.

33. Gammel, *Laws*, II:15-20.

34. Ibid., 29-30.

35. Ibid., 48.

36. Ibid.

37. Ibid., 84-85.

38. Ibid., 93.

39. Lamar, *Papers*, II:402-3.

40. Ibid., 468.

41. Gammel, *Laws*, II:48.

42. Erath, *Memoirs*, 56.

43. *Journals of the Fourth Congress*, III:89. It is of interest to note these units were listed as "Rangers."

44. *Muster and Pay Rolls, Republic of Texas,* based on sworn statements on November 16, 1879, when descendants were claiming pensions.

45. *Muster and Pay Rolls,* Capt. Panthers Comp'y of Shawney Indians, 25 Nov 1838 to 20 Dec 1838.

46. *Muster and Pay Rolls,* Jan 25-Feb 25, 1839.

47. *Muster and Pay Rolls.* Muster Roll of Capt. Lewis Sanches' Company of Mounted Gunmen, June 15, 1839 to July 22, 1839.

48. *Journals of the Fourth Congress,* III:88.

49. Smithwick, *Evolution of a State,* 154.

50. Capt. J.H. Moore to Secretary; of War, March 10, 1839, printed in *Journals of the Fourth Congress,* III:108-10.

51. John Holland Jenkins, *Recollections of Early Texas* (Austin: University of Texas Press, 1958), edited by John Holland Jenkins, III, 183.

52. Smithwick, *Evolution of a State,* 156.

53. This account is based on Moore's report, see footnote #50 above. See also Smithwick, *Evolution of a State,* 154-57; and Jenkins, *Recollections,* 183-87.

54. There are several later accounts of this scout and engagement (Jenkins, *Recollections,* 178-81; Wilbarger, *Indian Depredations,* 367-71, Brown, *Indian Wars,* 70-73), but this version is from Brookshire's official account of May 31, 1839, printed in *Journals of the Fourth Congress,* III:110-11.

55. Burleson to Albert Sidney Johnston, March 2, 1839, printed in *Journals of the Fourth Congress,* III:112-13.

56. This is the same Andrews who had commanded a company in the Coleman rangers, one of the companies formed by Lamar's call in February 1839. A single payroll in the ranger papers in the State Archives, showing the company was paid for services between March 10-June 10, 1839, is the only official reference to Andrews. The payroll refers to the company as Texas militia, which may have been a way of insuring payment. By whatever name, they were rangers and were so considered by contemporaries.

57. Burleson to Albert Sidney Johnston, May 22, 1839, printed in *Journals of the Fourth Congress,* III:112-13.

58. Lamar, *Papers,* II:522-23.

59. Report of the Secretary of War for 1839, printed in *Journals of the Fourth Congress,* III:77.

60. Ibid.

61. Ibid., 78.

62. Report of Gen. K.H. Douglass to Albert Sidney Johnston, July 16, 1839, printed in *Journals of the Fourth Congress,* III:115-16.

63. Ibid., III:103-4. Final report of Gen. Douglass.

64. Ibid., III:88-89.

65. *Muster and Pay Rolls,* Captain Tipps, 13 July to 5 August, 1839 and Captain Todd, June 28, 1839 to August 5, 1839. Rusk was a private in Todd's company from June 28 to July 9, when he was elected colonel of the Nacogdoches regiment and became one of the senior

commanders! The workings of the militia and volunteer system of that day seem very strange to a soldier today.

66. *Muster and Pay Rolls.*

67. *Journals of the Fourth Congress,* III:18. The report was dated October 25, 1839.

68. *Ordnance Papers, Republic of Texas.* Undated requisition, with cover latter to Quarter Master General, dated December 21, 1839.

69. *Journals of the Fourth Congress,* III:46.

70. Brown, *Indian Wars,* 73-74.

CHAPTER 3 — TOOLS OF THE TRADE

1. See John G. Dillin, *The Kentucky Rifle* (Washington, D.C.: National Rifle Association of America, 1924) and Henry J. Kaufman, *The Pennsylvania-Kentucky Rifle* (New York: Bonanza Books, 1960) for detailed descriptions of these weapons.

2. Charles E. Hanson, Jr., *The Plains Rifle* (New York: Bramhall House, 1960). A recent summary of the various rifle types is in Louis A. Garavaglia and Charles G. Worman, *Firearms of the American West* (Albuquerque: University of New Mexico Press, 1984).

3. Garavaglia and Worman, *Firearms,* 38-39, 48-49.

4. Smithwick, *Evolution of a State,* 82.

5. Joseph M. Nance, "Brigadier General Adrian Woll's Report of his Expedition into Texas in 1842," *SHQ* vol.58, no.4 (1955).

6. James Nichols, *Now You Hear My Horn* (Austin: University of Texas Press, 1968), 62-64.

7. John C. Duval, *Early Times in Texas* (Dallas: Tardy Publishing Co., Inc., 1936), 51-54.

8. Woll makes a distinction between "pistols," probably holster pistols, and "pocket pistols," but does not mention any manufacturers.

9. The story of the Colt revolver has been told by countless writers. *A History of the Colt Revolver* (New York: Bonanza Books, 1940) by Charles. T. Haven and Frank A. Belden is still one of the best, not only for detail on individual weapons but for the mass of documentary material on the testing and selling of early Colts.

10. *New Orleans Picayune,* February 1, 1838.

11. Haven and Belden, *Colt Revolver,* 261.

12. *Journals of the Fourth Congress,* II:124. Official reports and documents refer to the Colts as "Patent Arms."

13. Ibid., 124-25.

14. *Ordnance Papers,* Republic of Texas, Hockley to A.S. Johnston, October 18, 1839.

15. Ibid. An undated memorandum signed by John Ehlers showing funds still owed the Patent Arms Company by the Republic of Texas as of December 16, 1844, is the only source listing the various arms sales made to Texas by Colt.

16. Ibid.

17. Ibid., memorandum March 11, 1840.

18. Ibid., ordnance return of the 1st Infantry, May-June, 1840.

19. Ibid. On May 20, 1840, armorers in San Antonio submitted bills for repairing "8-shooter" and "patent rifles." A Charles Daniels was paid $9.00 on July 5, 1840, for repairing two Colt rifles belonging to Captain Lewis' company, and on September 15, 1840, was paid $144.00 for working on several Colt rifles. These are just several of similar vouchers in the *Ordnance Papers* which indicate people on the working level had started calling the weapons after their manufacturer, and only infrequently used the term "Patent Arms."

20. Ibid., Statement of Arms and Ammunition, September 30, 1843.

21. Ibid., Auditor's Office, February 29. 1844.

22. Nance, "Woll's Report."

23. Haven and Belden, *Colt Revolver*, 268.

24. George Wilkins Kendall, *Narrative of the Texan Santa Fe Expedition* (1844; reprint, New York: Harper and Brothers, 1856), I:253-55.

25. Lamar, *Papers*, IV: Part I, 231.

26. Nichols, *Horn*, 64-65. Thomas Green used a Cochran at the battle of Mier in 1842, Thomas J.Green, *Journal of the Texian Expedition Against Mier* (New York: Harper and Brothers, 1845), 83.

27. *Muster and Pay Rolls*, Captain Lewis Sanches, June 15-July 22, 1839.

28. Smithwick, *Evolution of a State*, 97.

29. Nance, "Woll's Report."

CHAPTER FOUR — COMANCHES

1. James K. Greer, *Colonel Jack Hays, Texas Frontier Leader and California Builder* (New York: E.P Dutton & Co., Inc., 1952). This material is a considerably abridged version of Chapter One.

2. Harry Cage to Saml Houston, Nov 29,1837. *Andrew Jackson Houston Papers*, Texas State Library.

3. Records of the Texas General Land Office. Hays combined scouting and survey work for several years. There are numerous survey reports by Hays on file for 1838-1840. Even after his successful early ranger service, he continued work as a surveyor and was elected Bexar County Surveyor in August 1841. Not surprisingly, he returned to survey work after moving to California following the Mexican War.

4. Maverick, Mary A., *Memoirs of Mary A. Maverick* (San Antonio: Alamo Printing Co., 1921), edited by Rena Maverick Green, 29.

5. Lamar, *Papers*, V:409. The letter, dated February 15, 1840, is written to President Lamar by Cornelius Van Ness.

6. Frederick C. Chabot, *The Perote Prisoners, Being the Diary of James L. Truehart* (San Antonio: The Naylor Co., 1934), 11.

7. Maverick, *Memoirs*, 29-30.

8. Lamar, *Papers*, IV:Part I, 231-32.

9. Ibid., 232. February is given as the date, without any specific day of the month.

10. *Army Papers*, "Report of the Number of Volunteers & Drafted Militia for 1840."

11. Houston, *Writings*, II:425-26.

12. *Ordnance Papers*, Receipts of April 1,2, 1840, and June 13, 1840.

13. *Army Papers*, Felix Huston to the Speaker of the House, September 20, 1840.

14. Lamar, *Papers*, IV: Part I, 232-33. This and the following account were written by Hays as part of Lamar's proposed history. It is interesting to note Hays did not mention anything about service in 1837 with Deaf Smith, or about any of the 1836 activities mentioned by some writers.

15. Ibid., III:233. Lamar refers to Rafael Vásquez only as "a general," and newspaper accounts spelled the name Basques or Bosques.

16. Ibid. Without muster rolls or other specific documentation, there is no way of knowing exactly how long Hays served in 1840. Formed in February, the company was fighting at Laredo in May. The chase after Vásquez came later. Allowing an enlistment period of four to six months, Hays was out of the rangers when Plum Creek occurred in August.

17. Greer, *Hays*, 40.

18. Sowell, *Texas Indian Fighters*, 57-60.

19. This account is based on Adjutant General Hugh McLeod's report to President Lamar as printed in Brown, *Indian Wars and Pioneers*, 76-78, and the extensive story in the *Telegraph and Texas Register*, April 8, 1840.

20. This incident was reported in the *Telegraph and Texas Register*, April 22, 1840, as a follow-up to its earlier report on April 8.

21. Maverick, *Memoirs*, 34.

22. *Army Papers*, Cunningham to Clendenning, July 9, 1840. Reprinted in the *Journals of the House of Representatives of the Republic of Texas, Fifth Congress-First Session* (hereafter *Journals of the Fifth Congress*), Appendix, 151-53.

23. Jenkins, *Recollections*, 61.

24. Z.N. Morrell, *Flowers and Fruits from the Wilderness: or, Thirty-six Years in Texas and Two Winters in Honduras* (Boston: Gould and Lincoln, 1872), 128.

25. Donaly E. Brice, *The Great Comanche Raid* (Austin: Eakin Press, 1987). Brice has written an excellent account of this raid; his book lists each casualty by location and in most cases by name.

26. *Journals of the Fifth Congress*, Appendix, Felix Huston to Branch T. Archer, August 12, 1840, 141-43.

27. Jenkins, *Recollections*, 63-64.

28. Wilbarger, *Indian Depredations*, 31.

29. The Mexican involvement, examined in detail by Brice, *The Great Comanche Raid*, is outside the scope of this book.

30. *Journals of the Fifth Congress,* Appendix, Huston to Archer, September 28, 1840, 143-45.

31. Brice, *The Great Comanche Raid,* contains a list of all known participants.

32. Morrell, *Flowers,* 124-31.

33. *Telegraph and Texas Register,* September 3, 1840.

34. Ibid., November 18, 1840. Although not otherwise identified, this Captain Andrews was very likely Micah Andrews.

35. Moore's report was published in the *Telegraph and Texas Register,* November 14, 1840. There are also accounts in Jenkins, *Recollections,* 171-74, and Wilbarger, *Indian Depredations,* 184-85.

36. Houston, *Writings,* II:426.

37. *Telegraph and Texas Register,* October 7, 1840.

38. Jenkins, *Recollections,* 187-90, and Wilbarger, *Indian Depredations,* 374-75, contain accounts of this expedition.

39. *Telegraph and Texas Register,* December 18, 1840.

40. Maverick, *Memoirs,* 59.

41. *Army Papers,* Major George T. Howard to Branch T. Archer, December 16, 1840.

42. *Ibid.* Branch T. Archer to David G. Burnet, December 19, 1840.

43. *Army Papers,* December 25, 1840.

44. Gammel, *Laws,* II:475-76.

CHAPTER 5 — HAYS MAKES A NAME

1. Erath, *Memoirs,* 51. Erath called this the "Morehouse expedition," but other than this designation and his brief account nothing is known of it.

2. Ibid., 58.

3. Lamar, *Papers,* IV:I, 232-33.

4. *Muster and Pay Rolls,* Captain John T. Price, Company of Spies, Texas Militia, January 3-May 2, 1841; Antonio Pérez, Spy Company, January 20-May 20, 1841; Capt. John C. Hays, Company of Spies, January 10-May 10, 1841.

5. John Salmon Ford, *"Memoirs"* (typescript, Texas State Library), II:243-45.

6. *Muster and Pay Rolls,* Hays' Company of Spies, January 10-May 10, 1841.

7. Lamar, *Papers,* IV: I, 233-34.

8. *Muster and Pay Rolls,* Antonio Pérez' Spy Company, January 20-May 20, 1841.

9. *Army Papers,* Price to Archer, January 23, 1841.

10. Ibid., Gillam to Colonel Hugh McCloud, San Antonio, January 10, 1841.

11. Ibid., Price to Archer, January 23, 1841.

12. Ibid., from Dimmit dated January 9, 1841.

13. Ibid., Gillam to McCloud, January 10, 1841.

14. *Muster and Pay Rolls*, Hays' Spy Company, January-May 1841. Over the years the name Chevallie has been spelled in various ways. The version used here is based on his signature on three payrolls where he receipted for his money. The spelling and the handwriting are the same on all three documents.

15. Lamar, *Papers*, IV: I, 234.

16. Ibid., 234-35.

17. *Journals of the Sixth Congress of the Republic of Texas* (hereafter *Journals of the Sixth Congress*), III:411. This account is based on Hays' report, indorsed April 14, 1841.

18. *Telegraph and Texas Register*, June 16, 1841.

19. *Journals of the Sixth Congress*, III:409-10, Dolson to Branch T. Archer, April 2, 1841.

20. Ibid., 412, Eli Chandler to Branch T. Archer, Franklin, April 16, 1841.

21. Brown, *Indian Wars*, 84-85.

22. *Journals of the Sixth Congress*, III:413-14, Chandler to the Secretary of War, indorsed May 26, 1841.

23. Ibid., 414-16, M.B. Lewis to Branch T. Archer, indorsed June 2, 1841.

24. *Muster and Pay Rolls*, company of Captain John C. Hays, June 1-August 31, 1841.

25. Maverick, *Memoirs*, 55.

26. Webb, *Handbook*, II:279. George Wilkins Kendall, *Narrative of the Texan Santa Fe Expedition* (1844; reprint, New York: Harper and Brothers, 1856) is the classic account of this expedition.

27. Maverick, *Memoirs*, 59.

28. *Journals of the Sixth Congress*, III: 422, Hays to the Secretary of War, July 1, 1841.

29. Ibid., 423-24, Hays to Archer, August 13, 1841. This account is based on Hays' report.

30. *Muster and Pay Rolls*, John C. Hays' Company of Spies for the Protection of Bexar County, called into Service on the first of September 1841.

31. *Journals of the Sixth Congress*, III:424-25, Price to Archer, Victoria, July 2, 1841.

32. Ibid., 425-26, James W. Byrne to Branch T. Archer, and James Gourlay, Jr., to Branch T. Archer, Lamar, Refugio County, July 8, 1841.

33. *Telegraph and Texas Register*, July 14, 1841.

34. Ibid., August 18, 1841, reprinted from the *Austin Gazette*, as copied from the *Houston Morning Star.*

35. *Journals of the Sixth Congress*, III:419-21, Chandler to Archer, Franklin, June 19, 1841.

36. Ibid., 422-23, G.B. Erath to Branch T. Archer, Fort Bryant, August 12, 1841.

37. Ibid., 416-19, William N. Porter to Branch T. Archer, Bowie County, June 5, 1841.

38. Ibid., 419, Brigadier General James Smith to Mirabeau B. Lamar, Nacogdoches, June 13, 1841.

39. *Army Papers*, Bell to Archer, October 4, 1841.

40. *Muster and Pay Rolls*, Captain Joseph Sowell, Minute Men of Fannin County, July 17, 1841-September 20, 1841.

41. Ibid., Captain James H. Callahan, June-July, 1841, August-December, 1841.

42. Ibid., Captain John McDaniel, Refugio Minute Men, November-December, 1841, (paid for fifteen days) January 1-January 15, 1842.

CHAPTER 6 — INVASION

1. Gammel, *Laws*, II:74.

2. Brown, *History of Texas*, II:211-15, covers Vásquez' raid. He mentions that Antonio Coy was Jack Hays' servant, a disservice to a fine ranger. Nothing on any of the muster and payrolls containing Coy's name suggests he was anything other than a ranger. It hardly seems likely Hays would have dispatched a servant on a critical scouting mission. Jenkins, *Recollections*, 220, also covers this invasion, although he believed that it was McCulloch who brought word of the attack.

3. Brown, *History of Texas*, II:213.

4. Jenkins, *Recollections*, 220-21.

5. Ibid, 95-96. Jenkins was honest enough to note that losing a few pigs might not have been Seguín's reason for leaving Texas for Mexico.

6. Muster and Pay Rolls.

7. Davis, *Texana*, I:58.

8. Houston, *Writings*, II:509.

9. Ibid., II:509-10. Not all of the intricate maneuverings of Sam Houston can be outlined. It is enough to note he managed to prevent Ed Burleson from assuming command of any force formed to invade Mexico, even though Burleson was the overwhelming choice of most of the volunteers. For whatever reason, Somervell was his choice.

10. Ibid., II:510-11.

11. Ibid., III:34.

12. *Army Papers*. Chandler's form is dated April 9, 1842. He evidently was able to form a command, because Houston wrote him on May 13 congratulating him on being the first commander to submit returns. See also Houston, *Writings*, III: 49-50.

13. Houston, *Writings*, III:68-69.

14. Ibid., III:71-73.

15. Ibid., III:73.

16. *Journals of the Sixth Congress*, III:110.

17. Frederick C. Chabot, *Corpus Christi* (San Antonio, privately printed, 1942), 63-64. Chabot describes events from the Mexican viewpoint.

18. Ibid.

19. Ibid., 23-24.

20. A translation of Canales' report is printed in Chabot, *Corpus Christi*, 64-70.

21. *Journals of the House of Representatives of the Seventh Congress of the Republic of Texas* (hereafter *Journals of the Seventh Congress*), 14-15.

22. Report of the Secretary of War and Marine, November 12, 1842, printed in *Journals of the Seventh Congress*, 30. There is evidence, however, that Cameron's company was also still in service. Brown, *History of Texas*, 216, said Hays patrolled the region west of San Antonio while Cameron was responsible for the territory from Victoria to the Nueces. In an interesting note, Brown mentions Cameron's men were known as "cowboys" because they lived on wild cows, deer and other game.

23. Gammel, *Laws*, II:816.

24. *Journals of the Sixth Congress*, II:72.

25. Report of the Secretary of War and Marine, November 12, 1842, printed in *Journals of the Seventh Congress*, 30-31.

26. Ibid.

27. P. Hansborough Bell, Adjutant General of the Militia, to Branch T. Archer, October 4, 1842, printed in *Journals of the Sixth Congress*, III:434.

28. Houston, *Writings*, IV:144-45.

29. Ibid., IV:145-46.

30. *Journals of the Seventh Congress*, Appendix, 23-24. In his reports as printed in Nance, "Woll's Report," 524-25, General Adrian Woll has the date as August 29.

31. Sowell, *Texas Indian Fighters*, 58. As mentioned earlier, there are questions about Wallace's claims of serving with Hays. There are no muster rolls for 1842 to prove or disprove his statement, but he was very likely a member of Hays' detachment in 1842. Wallace was definitely in the fighting through the remainder of the year, and became a Mexican prisoner at Mier.

32. Ibid., 59-60.

33. Maverick, *Memoirs*, 66.

34. E.W. Winkler, ed., "The Bexar and Dawson Prisoners," TSHA, vol.13, no. 4, (1910), 294.

35. Ibid.

36. Nance, "Woll's Report," 37.

37. Ibid.

38. *Journals of the Seventh Congress*, Appendix, 18-19.

39. Nance, "Woll's Report," 535-38, lists the day-by-day marches of the Mexican column over prairie land, through dense woods, the numerous arroyo and river crossings. It was a considerable achievement and reflects great credit on the engineers with Woll.

40. Ibid., 529.

41. Nance, "Woll's Report," 295-96.

42. Hays to the Citizens of Texas, September 12, 1842, printed in *Journals of the Seventh Congress*, Appendix, 21-22. Hays may have overestimated Woll's force, because the Mexican commander said he left the Rio Grande with 957 effectives.

43. Hays to the Secretary of War, from Seguin, September 12, 1842, printed in *Journals of the Seventh Congress*, Appendix, 16.

44. Morrell, *Flowers*, 161.

45. Printed in *Journals of the Seventh Congress*, Appendix, 20-21.

46. Ibid., 19-20.

47. Morrell, *Flowers*, 163.

48. Ibid., 164.

49. *Telegraph and Texas Register, November 1, 1842. There is some confusion about how many men Caldwell led to Salado Creek. He mentioned 225 in his report, Journals of the Seventh Congress, Appendix, 16-18, but Morrell thought it was only 202 (Morrell, Flowers, 167).*

50. *Journals of the Seventh Congress*, Appendix, 22.

51. Morrell, *Flowers*, 164-65.

52. Ibid., 166.

53. Ibid., 167. These figures are undoubtedly high.

54. Caldwell's Report, *Journals of the Seventh Congress*, Appendix, 17. Again, his numbers reveal the excitement of combat. Woll stated he had about two hundred horsemen.

55. Nichols, *Horn*, 96; *Telegraph and Texas Register* November 1, 1842. It is necessary to examine the mention in the *Telegraph and Texas Register* of the Texas position as running east and west rather than north and south. Salado Creek runs generally north and south, but there are several sizable bends and turns in the stream where the creek changes direction and flows for a considerable distance to the west before again turning south. There is ample room to accomodate the five-hundred-yard Texas battle line on one of these east-west bends, which would have had the Mexican forces north of the creek, attacking to the south. This location would explain how Dawson's later arrival from the north and east would be in the rear of the Mexican position rather than from behind Caldwell's men, and also explains Nichols' statement about the creek's protecting the Texan rear. The abrupt direction change back to the south put Salado Creek on the Texans' west flank and in their rear, partially blocking any attack from the west by Mexican troops. Accounts of "southern" and "northern" ravines are puzzling, but there is enough slant from southeast to northwest of the generally east-west turn of the creek to explain this point. Wherever the position, Hays knew where Caldwell was waiting.

56. The exact location of the battleground is still debated. Morrell and Caldwell gave conflicting distances from town, eight and six miles respectively. The stream has many turns, with several fitting the general description of the site. There is, however, some agreement on a rather general location where old musket balls and cannon projectiles have been found.

57. Caldwell said he sent Hays into town around ten in the morning, which would allow Hays an hour to ride to San Antonio and return on the run.

58. Caldwell's Report has the name "Cordaway," but this is the infamous Vicente Cordova, back to continue his work of turning the Indians against the Texans. Among the volunteers from San Antonio in the Mexican Army was Antonio López, now a lieutenant colonel.

59. Morrell, *Flowers*, 169.

60. Nichols, *Horn*, 99.

61. Morrell, *Flowers*, 170.

62. Sowell, *Texas Indian Fighters*, 25. Nichols, *Horn*, tells this same story; Randall was a member of his detachment. John Henry Brown, however, who claimed to be an eye witness, credits John Lowe, another man in this detachment, with the death of Cordova. It was neither the first nor last time participants in a confused fight remembered events differently. Whoever fired the shot, Cordova was killed by someone defending the southern ravine.

63. Caldwell's Report.

64. Nichols, *Horn*, 102ff.

65. Caldwell's Report.

66. Maverick, *Memoirs*, 74.

67. Haven and Belden, *Colt Revolver*, 269-70. Walker was with Captain Jesse Billingsley's company, and this information of his scouting to find Caldwell is also in some editions of Reid, *Scouting Expeditions*.

68. Caldwell's Report.

69. Ibid.

70. Morrell, *Flowers*, 173.

71. Ibid., 170.

72. Green, *Journal*, 34.

73. Nance, "Woll's Report," 539-41.

74. Brown, *History of Texas*, II:228.

75. Morrell, *Flowers*, 175.

76. Ibid., 176-77.

77. Nichols, *Horn*, 112.

78. Morrell, *Flowers*, 177-78.

79. Nichols, *Horn*, 112.

80. Caldwell's Report.

81. Morrell, *Flowers*, 178. H.B. Morrell, the preacher's son, was finally released by the Mexicans on September 16, 1844. 82. Maverick, *Memoirs*, 76.

82. Maverick, *Memoirs*, 76.

83. Green, *Journal*, 36. Nichols also mentions there was talk the Vásquez invasion had been an attempt to disrupt the court hearings on confiscating lands belonging to Seguín and Pérez; learning the postponed court session would take place in September, he said the Woll invasion was planned to break up this session, which it did, but by accident.

84. E.W. Winkler, ed., "The Somervell Expedition to the Rio Grande, 1842, The Diary of Sterling Brown Hendricks," *SHQ* vol.23, no.2 (1919).

Unless otherwise stated, material in this account is based on Hendricks.

85. Houston, *Writings*, III:170-71. It is clear Houston never wanted an invasion or "ordered" one. An extract of a letter from Anson Jones to Isaac Van Zandt, February 16, 1843, indicates the official view at the time: "The late Campaign under Gen. Somervell was not projected or recommended by the President. It was merely *sanctioned* (italics in original) to satisfy popular clamour...." Reprinted in *SHQ* vol.23, no.2 (1919), 113.

86. Houston, *Writings*, III:185.

87. Green, *Journal*, 41.

88. Ibid., 44-46.

89. Winkler, "Diary of Sterling Brown Hendricks," 118; Green, *Journal*, 53-54.

90. Houston, *Writings*, III:197-99.

91. Green, *Journal*, 54. In his account of the campaign, Green glosses over his resignation, merely saying Hays and Bogart were in the advance and he accompanied them. His version agrees with Hendricks, although he does not always have events in the same sequence; for example, he actually resigned after the bog fiasco.

92. Ibid., 62-63. Green recalled this incident exactly as Hendricks remembered it.

93. Ibid., 65. He said Hays was the officer representing the Texans.

94. *Telegraph and Texas Register*, January 8, 1843. Memucan Hunt, in a report of the campaign, made a specific point of the condition of the men.

95. Green, *Journal*, 74.

96. Ibid.

97. *Journals of the Seventh Congress*, Appendix, 13-14. Somervell's report, written from Washington on the Brazos and dated February 1, 1843, is also reprinted in this journal, 70-74.

98. Ibid., 13-14.

99. Webb, *Handbook of Texas*, II:64-65.

100. Ibid., II:52.

101. *Telegraph and Texas Register* December 21. 1842.

102. "Report of the Secretary of War and Marine, 12 November 1842" printed in *Journals of the Seventh Congress*, Appendix, 33-35.

CHAPTER 7 — ONLY THE RANGERS

1. Gammel, *Laws*, III:846-48.

2. Ibid.

3. Houston, *Writings*, III:292-97.

4. *Telegraph and Texas Register*, May 17, 1843.

5. *Muster and Pay Rolls*, J.C. Hays, February-March, 1843.

6. Ibid., April, 1843.

7. M.C. Hamilton, Acting Secretary of War and Marine, to Col. Jacob Snively, February 16, 1843, as printed in H. Bailey Carroll, "Steward A. Miller and the Sniveley Expedition of 1843," *SHQ* vol.54, no.3 (1951), 264.

8. Ibid., 267.

9. Wilbarger, *Indian Depredations*, 51-58, has a condensed version of this expedition.

10. *Telegraph and Texas Register*, June 21, 1843.

11. Nichols, *Horn*, 122.

12. Ibid., 123.

13. Ibid., 124.

14. Ibid.

15. *Telegraph and Texas Register*, May 17, 1843.

16. Ibid.

17. Ibid.

18. Wilbarger, *Indian Depredations*, 42-49. Wilbarger includes an interesting narrative of one of the agents which graphically describes the conditions under which they lived while in the Comanche camp.

19. *Muster and Pay Rolls*, June-July 1843.

20. *Telegraph and Texas Register*, July 12, 1843.

21. Ibid., September 27, 1843.

22. Ibid., November 1, 1843.

23. Ibid., November 28, 1843.

24. *Army Papers*, Hays to G.W. Hill, November 12, 1843.

25. Houston, *Writings*, III:431.

26. *Quartermaster Papers*.

27. Ibid.

28. Ibid.

CHAPTER 8 — THE NEW COLTS

1. *Telegraph and Texas Register*, January 10, 1844.

2. Gammel, *Laws*, II:943-44. Hays, the only ranger commander to be so designated in a Texas Congressional Act, was sufficiently well known to receive this honor in 1844 and again in 1845.

3. *Muster and Pay Rolls*, Hays' Company, February-April 1844.

4. *Telegraph and Texas Register*, March 20, 1844.

5. Ibid.

6. John E. Parsons, *Sam Colt's Own Record of Transactions with Captain Walker and Eli Whitney, Jr.* (Hartford: The Connecticut Historical Society, 1949), 9-10.

7. Haven and Belden, *Colt Revolver*, 304.

8. *Journals of the House of Representatives of the Ninth Congress of the Republic of Texas*, 32-33.

9. *Houston Morning Star*, June 29, 1844.

10. Dorman H. Winfrey and James M. Day, *The Indian Papers of Texas and the Southwest, 1825-1916* (1959-61; reprint, Austin: Pemberton Press, 1966), II:72-73.

11. Maverick, *Memoirs*, 81-82.

12. Jenkins, *Recollections*, 145-46.

13. Sowell, *Texas Indian Fighters*, 132.

14. Anson Jones, *Memoranda and Offficial Correspondence Relating to the Republic of Texas, Its History and Annexation, 1836 to 1846* (1859; reprint, Chicago: Rio Grande Press, 1966), 374.

15. Sowell, *Texas Indian Fighters*, 127-28.

16. Ibid.

17. *Army Papers*, Hays to G.W. Hill, July 21, 1844.

18. Jenkins, *Recollections*, 194-98; Sowell, *Texas Indian Fighters*, 148-54. These versions agree on main details. Sowell's account by Thomas Galbreath is considerably longer and more dramatic.

19. Castro's diary, August 26, 1844, in Sowell, *Texas Indian Fighters*, 131-32.

20. *Quartermaster Papers*, October 22, 1844.

21. Ibid., December 1844.

22. *Muster and Pay Rolls*, Hays' Company, October-December 1844.

23. *Semanario Politico del Gobierno de Nuevo Leon*, March 20, 1844.

24. *Telegraph and Texas Register*, December 4, 1844.

25. Ibid., December 25, 1844.

26. Ford, *Memoirs*, II:323-25. Ford copied and included stories in the *Matagorda Dispatch* and the *San Augustine Redlander* for July 20, 1844.

27. Gammel, *Laws*, II:1049-50.

28. Wilbarger, *Indian Depredations*, 66, has a brief account of this event. On 290-95 he has a version prepared by John C. Duval for inclusion in a proposed book *Early Times in Texas* (1892; reprint, Dallas: Tardy Publishing Co., Inc., 1936). Duval's early account in Sowell is generally followed in his book; he stated the Comanches were in San Antonio to talk about another treaty, which is possible but does not explain why Kinney from Corpus Christi and riders from the Rio Grande happened to be in San Antonio. The handsome prizes and the organization of the event suggest considerable planning. In his version in Sowell, Duval called the Comanche rider Long Quest; when his book was first published in 1892 the Indian was given the more likely name Long Quirt. In later editions Duval embellished the tale and had Hays acting as director of the games. All versions have the contest between rangers and Comanches and Mexican riders.

29. Gammel, *Laws*, II:1124-26.

30. *Muster and Pay Rolls*, Hays' Company, February-May 1845.

31. *Telegraph and Texas Register*, April 30, 1845.

32. *Quartermaster Papers*, William Smith to the Republic of Texas, August 8, 1845.

33. Ibid., Wm Eliot to Republic of Texas, undated, marked "paid in full."

34 *Telegraph and Texas Register*, September 3, 1845; *Texas National Register*, September 4, 1845.

35. *Muster and Pay Rolls*, Hays' Company, August 12-September 28, 1845.

APPENDIX — BATTLES OR LEGENDS

1. Reid, *Scouting Expeditions*, 111-12.

2. Wilbarger, *Indian Depredations* 74-75; Sowell, *Texas Indian Fighters*, 334-35.

3. Caperton, "Hays", 29-31.

4. Sowell, *Texas Indian Fighters*, 317-19.

5. Ibid.

6. *Muster and Pay Rolls*, Jack Hays, 1843-44.

7. Sowell, *Texas Indian Fighters*, 20-21.

8. Ibid., 809-10. The extensive recollections of Taylor are now in the Archives Division of the Texas State Library.

9. Ford, *Memoirs*.

10. Sowell, *Texas Indian Fighters*, 319-22.

BIBLIOGRAPHY

Archives and Library Division,
Texas State Library, Austin, Texas:

Army Papers, Republic of Texas
Navy Papers, Republic of Texas
Ordnance Papers, Republic of Texas
Quartermaster Papers, Republic of Texas
Muster and Pay Rolls, Republic of Texas
Houston, Andrew Jackson. Papers.
Ford, John Salmon. "Memoirs." Typescript.

DOCUMENTARY SOURCES

*Journals of the Fourth Congress of the Republic of Texas, 1839-
    1840*. Volumes 2 and 3. Edited by Harriet Smither. Austin:
    Von Boeckmann-Jones Co., n.d.

*Journals of the House of Representatives of the Republic of Texas,
    Fifth Congress-First Session*. Austin: Cruger and Wing, Public
    Printers, 1841.

Journals of the Sixth Congress of the Republic of Texas. Volumes 2
    and 3. Edited by Harriet Smither. Austin: Capital Printing
    Co., Inc., 1944.

*Journals of the House of Representatives of the Seventh Congress
    of the Republic of Texas*. Washington, Tex.: Thomas Johnson,
    Public Printer, 1843.

*Journals of the House of Representatives of the Ninth Congress of
    the Republic of Texas*. Washington, Tex.: Miller & Cushney,
    Public Printers, 1845.

NEWSPAPERS

Dispatch, Matagorda, Texas.
Gazette, Austin, Texas.

Morning Star, Houston, Texas.

Picayune, New Orleans, Louisiana.

Redlander, San Augustine, Texas.

Semanario Politico del Gobierno de Nuevo Leon, Mexico

Telegraph and Texas Register, Houston, Texas.

Texas National Register, Washington-on-the-Brazos, Texas.

BOOKS, ARTICLES, MANUSCRIPTS

Barker, Eugene C. *The Life of Stephen F. Austin.* 1926. Reprint. Austin: University of Texas Press, 1985.

_____, "The Government of Austin's Colony, 1823-1831," *The Southwestern Historical Quarterly* vol.21, no.3 (1918).

_____, ed. "Journal of the Permanent Council," *The Quarterly of the Texas State Historical Association* vol.7 (1904).

Brice, Donaly E. *The Great Comanche Raid.* Austin: Eakin Press, 1987.

Brown, John Henry. *History of Texas, from 1685-1892.* St.Louis: L.E. Daniell, 1892.

_____. *Indian Wars and Pioneers of Texas.* 189-?. Reprint. Austin: State House Press, 1988.

Burnam, Jesse. "Reminiscences of Jesse Burnam," *The Quarterly of the Texas State Historical Association* vol.5, no.3 (1902).

Caperton, John. "Sketch of Colonel John C. Hays, Texas Ranger," subtitled "Sketch of Colonel John C. Hays, The Texas Rangers, Incidents in Texas and Mexico, ETC, from materials furnished by Col. Hays and Major John Caperton." Typescript annotated "copy of manuscript purchased from the University of California in 1922." The Center for American History, The University of Texas at Austin.

Carroll, H. Bailey. "Stewart A. Miller and the Snively Expedition of 1843," *The Southwestern Historical Quarterly* vol.54, no.3 (1951).

Chabot, Frederick C. *The Perote Prisoners, Being the Diary of James L. Truehart.* San Antonio: The Naylor Co., 1934.

_____. *Corpus Christi.* San Antonio: Privately printed, 1942.

Chriesman, Horatio. "Reminiscences of Horatio Chriesman," *The Quarterly of the Texas State Historical Association* vol.6 (1903).

Davis, Robert E., ed. *Texana.* Waco: Texian Press, 1963.

DeShields, James T. *Border Wars of Texas.* 1912. Reprint. Austin: State House Press, 1993.

Dillin, John G. *The Kentucky Rifle*. Washington, D.C.: National Rifle Association of America, 1924.

Duval, John C. *Early Times in Texas*. 1892. Reprint. Dallas: Tardy Publishing Co., Inc., 1936.

Erath, George Bernard. *The Memoirs of Major George B. Erath, 1813-1891*. As dictated to Lucy A. Erath. 1923. Reprint. Waco: The Heritage Society of Waco, 1956.

Fehrenbach, T.R. *Comanches*. New York: Alfred A. Knopf, 1974.

Ford, John Salmon. *Memoirs*. Typescript. Archives and Library Division, Texas State Library, Austin, Texas.

Gammel, Hans Peter Nielson, ed. *The Laws of Texas, 1822-1897*. 10 vols. Austin: The Gammel Book Company, 1898.

Garavaglia, Louis A. and Charles G. Worman. *Firearms of the American West*. Albuquerque: University of New Mexico Press, 1984.

Green, Thomas J. *Journal of the Texian Expedition Against Mier*. New York: Harper and Brothers, 1845.

Greer, James K. *Colonel Jack Hays, Texas Frontier Leader and California Builder*. New York: E.P. Dutton & Co., Inc., 1952.

Hanson, Charles E., Jr. *The Plains Rifle*. New York: Bramhall House, 1960.

Haven, Charles T. and Frank A. Belden. *A History of the Colt Revolver*. New York: Bonanza Books, 1940.

Hendricks, Sterling Brown. "The Somervell Expedition to the Rio Grande, 1842." Edited by E.W. Winkler. *The Southwestern Historical Quarterly* vol.23, no.2 (1919).

Hogan, William Ransom. *The Texas Republic: A Social and Economic History*. 1946. Reprint. Austin and London: University of Texas Press, 1969.

Houston, Sam. *The Writings of Sam Houston 1813-1863*. 8 vols. Edited by Amelia W. Williams and Eugene C. Barker. Austin: University of Texas Press, 1938-1943.

Jenkins, John Holland. *Recollections of Early Texas*. Edited by John H. Jenkins, III. Austin: University of Texas Press, 1958.

Jones, Anson. *Memoranda and Official Correspondence Relating to the Republic of Texas, Its History and Annexation, 1836 to 1846*. 1859. Reprint. Chicago: Rio Grande Press, 1966.

Kaufman, Henry J. *The Pennsylvania-Kentucky Rifle*. New York: Bonanza Books, 1960.

Kendall, George Wilkins. *Narrative of the Texan Santa Fe Expedition across the Great South Western Prairies*. 1844. Reprint. New York: Harper and Brothers, 1856.

Kuykendall, J.H. "Recollections of Capt. Gibson Kuykendall," *The Quarterly of the Texas State Historical Association* vol.7 (1904).

Kilgore, D.E. *A Ranger Legacy.* Austin; Madrona Press, 1973.

Lamar, Mirabeau Buonaparte. *The Papers of Mirabeau Buonaparte Lamar.* Edited by Charles Adams Gulick, Jr., *et al.* 6 vols. 1921-1927. Reprint. Austin & New York: The Pemberton Press, 1968.

Lee, Nelson. *Three Years Among the Comanches.* Albany: Baker Taylor, 1859.

Maverick, Mary A. *Memoirs of Mary A. Maverick.* Edited by Rena Maverick Green. San Antonio: Alamo Printing Co., 1921.

McCutchan, Joseph D. *Mier Expedition Diary.* Austin: University of Texas Press, 1978.

Morrell, Z.N. *Flowers and Fruits from the Wilderness: or, Thirty-Six Years in Texas and Two Winters in Honduras.* Boston: Gould and Lincoln, 1872.

Nance, Joseph Milton. "Brigadier General Adrian Woll's Report of His Expedition into Texas in 1842," *The Southwestern Historical Quarterly* vol.58, no.4 (1955).

Nichols, James. *Now You Hear My Horn.* Austin: University of Texas Press, 1967.

Parsons, John E. *Sam Colt's Own Record of Transactions with Captain Walker and Eli Whitney, Jr.* Hartford: The Connecticut Historical Society, 1949.

Reid, Samuel C., Jr. *The Scouting Expeditions of McCulloch's Texas Rangers.* 1847. Reprint. Austin: The Steck Company, 1935.

Smithwick, Noah. *The Evolution of a State, or Recollections of Old Texas Days.* 1900. Reprint. Austin: University of Texas Press, 1983.

Sowell, Andrew Jackson. *Texas Indian Fighters; Early Settlers and Indian Fighters of Southwest Texas.* 1900. Reprint. Austin: State House Press, 1986.

_____. *Rangers and Pioneers of Texas.* 1884. Reprint. Austin: State House Press, 1991.

Webb, Walter Prescott, editor-in-chief. *The Handbook of Texas.* 3 Vols. Austin: The Texas State Historical Association, 1952.

_____. *The Texas Rangers, A Century of Frontier Defense.* New York & Boston: Houghton Mifflin Company, 1935.

Wilbarger, J.W. *Indian Depredations in Texas.* 1889. Reprint. Austin: Eakin Press and State House Press, 1985.

Wilcox, S.S. "Laredo During the Texas Republic," *The Southwestern Historical Quarterly* vol.42, no.2 (1939).

Williams, J.W. *Old Texas Trails.* Edited by Kenneth F. Neighbors. Burnet: Eakin Press, 1979.

Winfrey, Dorman H. and James M. Day. *The Indian Papers of Texas and the Southwest, 1825 to 1916.* Vol.II. 1959-61. Reprint. Austin: Pemberton Press, 1966.

Winkler, E.W., ed. "The Bexar and Dawson Prisoners," *The Quarterly of the Texas State Historical Association* vol.13, no.4 (1910).

_____. "The Somervell Expedition to the Rio Grande, 1842, The Diary of Sterling Brown Hendricks," *The Southwestern Historical Quarterly* vol.23, no.2 (1919).

Yoakum, Henderson K. *History of Texas.* 2 Vols. New York: Redfield, 1855.

INDEX